Politics, Religion, and Rockets

Politics, Religion, and Rockets

ESSAYS IN

TWENTIETH-

CENTURY

AMERICAN

HISTORY

Paul A. Carter

The University of Arizona Press

Tucson

The University of Arizona Press
Copyright © 1991 by Paul A. Carter
All rights reserved
∞ This book is printed on acid-free, archival-quality paper.
Manufactured in the United States of America

96 95 94 93 92 91   6 5 4 3 2 1

Library of Congress Cataloging-in-Publication Data
Carter, Paul Allen, 1926–
    Politics, religion, and rockets : essays in twentieth-century American
history / Paul A. Carter.
        p.   cm.
    Includes index.
    ISBN 0-8165-1213-2 (acid free paper)
    1. United States—History—20th century.   2. United States—Church
history—20th century.   3. Church and state—United States—
History—20th century.
    E742.C37   1991   90-21111
    973.9—dc20   CIP

British Library Cataloguing in Publication data are available.

Most of the essays in this book appeared in an earlier form in *Change
and Continuity in Twentieth-Century America: The 1920's*, edited by John
Braeman, Robert H. Bremner, and David Brody (Columbus: Ohio State
University Press, 1968); *Space Voyages, 1591–1920: A Bibliography*, compiled
by Lynn S. Smith (Riverside: Library of the University of California, 1979);
The Uncertain World of Normalcy, edited by Paul A. Carter (New York: Pitman
Publishing Corp., 1971); and in *The American Scholar, American Studies,
Analog Science Fiction/Science Fact, Church History, The Columbia Forum, The
Journal of Popular Culture, The Pacific Northwest Quarterly, Theology Today*, and
The Wisconsin Magazine of History. They are reproduced here by permission.
The epigraph by Robert Carter is from an article in the *Tucson Citizen* of
December 2, 1986.

This Book Is for Robert Carter

I'm not saying that eternal peace is
probable, only that it's possible. It really
depends on whether we approach the
problem with hope or with despair.

ROBERT CARTER

CONTENTS

ACKNOWLEDGMENTS

*W*riters of books typically mention their spouses in their acknowledgments, usually at the end and with warm praise that actually amounts to no more than a pat on the head. Such a tribute would be most unfair to my wife, Julie Carter, whose critical input can be traced in all the essays I have written since we met. Since she also made a crucial editorial suggestion for two essays that had been written in my premarital years, that leaves only one—Chapter 8—for which I was entirely on my own. Had Julie been present for the composition of "The Negro and Methodist Union," I suspect that a certain graduate-student stuffiness in the writing style, and a couple of sweeping historical judgments, would have disappeared, to the manuscript's benefit. For her work on the remaining essays in this book, I offer her my heartfelt and quite inadequate thanks.

Mentors—Richard Hofstadter at Columbia and Robert Handy at Union Theological Seminary—made a difference in this work, as did professional colleagues. J. Leonard Bates generously shared with me some of his own library diggings for a biography of Tom Walsh upon which he was working, and these appear in Chapters 3 and 4; Sidney Mead, dean of American church historians, tangibly influenced Chapter 6; Arthur Mann read and critiqued Chapter 7. A whole joyous crew of history department members at Northern Illinois University had at Chapter 12 when I read a prior draft of it to their faculty colloquium; comment by Mary Furner in particular is warmly remembered.

By soliciting papers, the organizers of historical conventions helped bring several of these essays to life. Chapters 3 and 4 were read as one paper before the Organization of American Historians in 1961; Chapter 5 was presented to the Western History Association in 1972; Chapter 7 was read to the American Society of Church History in 1963; Chapter 10 originated at the American Historical Association's Annual Meeting in 1971. Comments at these sessions improved the eventual product. Of even more benefit, however, was the experience of reading to (or inflicting upon) captive student audiences early versions of Chapters 1 through 5 and 9.

Editors of academic journals commonly take the articles they accept "as is," with only minor copyediting changes to conform with their particular house styles. Exceptions include the tasteful editing and streamlining that improved the two *American Scholar* essays, and the really creative work Erik Wensberg at the *Columbia Forum* did with Chapter 2 before it saw print. The hardworking people in history departments who type professors' manuscripts—the word *secretaries* is all too inadequate to describe them—can also make an editorial difference. Wiladene Stickel improved my grammar in Chapter 12, and Nikki Matz, with a psychologically strategic hesitation just as the manuscript of Chapter 15 came to an end, spurred me to write some additional copy, to its benefit.

Professors, when not in their offices or classrooms, dwell in libraries, and the staffs of the following were unfailingly helpful: Northern Illinois University (Chapters 1, 5, 10, 12, and 14); the University of Montana (Chapters 2, 3, and 4); the College of Wooster, where I wrote Chapter 6 during a summer teaching term; Smith College (Chapter 7); several New York–area libraries (Columbia University, the Harlem branch of the New York Public Library, the Methodist archives in their building on Fifth Avenue, and other such archives at Drew University in Madison, New Jersey) for Chapter 8; the University of California, Berkeley (Chapter 9); the University of Arizona (Chapter 11). One library, at the University of California, Riverside, in effect commissioned Chapter 13 as an introduction to a bibliography of some of its holdings.

But history cannot be written only within the circles of library and school or it becomes *academic* in the bad sense of that word. Personal, nonprofessional encounters have shaped this work: the political talk of my elders in New England and Idaho for Part I; the often unchurchly ways of church people, old and young, for Part II; and the intense world of science fiction fandom for Part III. Without a visit to a longtime family friend, retired Methodist bishop Lewis O. Hartman at his home in Brookline, Massachusetts, Chapter 8 could not have been written (and since it was the first, conceivably none of the others that followed). Places as well as persons had a bearing upon this work. Chapter 2, for example, would not have taken the shape it did had I not been spending a summer in western Montana in 1972, a summer that coincided with the presidential nomination of George McGovern.

   The cartoon in chapter 5 of this book was drawn by my late father, Rev. Manfred A. Carter, to illustrate a church bulletin that was printed for a parish he served in New England during the 1930s. It represents a small sample of the manuscript materials, published and unpublished—poetry, essays, sermons, short stories, and other drawings—to be found in the Manfred Carter Collection at the George Arents Research Library, Syracuse University. I regret that he could not have lived to see this cartoon published in its present form.

The Apprenticeship
of a Historian

*S*ome vocations seem to have been pre-programmed. The person enters a parent's profession or a family business; or, perhaps, makes a choice (conscious or unconscious) against just such a fate. In contrast, some people's careers seem the product of sheer accident: the job happened to be open when one needed something to do. Or there may have been a casual remark by a respected role model which turned the person in a direction never previously thought of. Still others seem imperiously "called"—the original, literal meaning of *vocation*—to a particular line of work. How, looking back on it, one became a butcher, baker, or candlestick maker often seems a confusing blend of determinism and sheer drift. For the historian in particular, trained to be suspicious of easy assumptions about causation, the question of how he/she chose, or was chosen for, a life in history becomes murky indeed.

Personally, I did not plan beforehand to become a historian. My bent all through high school was toward the sciences. Not until a stiff, fast-paced Navy course in electronics showed me that mathematical thinking clearly did not come as naturally to me as reading did I begin to look in other directions. Yet there had been pre-adolescent encounters with various books—*The Story of Mankind*, by Hendrik Willem van Loon; *The*

Outline of History, by H. G. Wells; V. M. Hillyer's *A Child's History of the World*—which proved more decisive in the long run than, say, *The Stars for Sam*. Teachers also had something to do with this nurturing process; for example, the high school American history instructor who read to a class the passage from President James K. Polk's diary describing the decision to go to war with Mexico, a striking if elementary demonstration that back of all dull, memorizable textbooks lies something far more vivid and alive, which in graduate history programs one learns to call primary sources.

Parental and geographic influences had an inescapable impact, which schooling only reinforced. I grew up in a succession of Methodist parsonages in New England, a region almost oppressively conscious of its own history. Many of my family's senior members pursued elaborate inquiries into genealogy, tracing some of our genes back to the Puritan founders if not the Norman Conquest. In this and other ways the shadow of the past was inescapable. One town in which we lived celebrated its three hundredth anniversary during our time there—not much on a Roman or Chinese scale, but antiquated enough by American standards—and a direct descendant of one of the original settlers, having in fact the same name as his remote ancestor, still represented that town in the state legislature. However, just before my high school years began we moved to Idaho, a state then celebrating only its fiftieth year, and to a town of the same vintage, some of whose first inhabitants were still alert and active. This was (and is) a typically American contrast, between the short term and the long view, and no doubt the experience of that polarity has had some bearing on the way I "do" history.

The brand of churchmanship my minister father practiced in that town, molded by the Depression and the New Deal, was activist and liberal. As an influence upon me it was reinforced, not overthrown, by America's entrance into the struggle against fascism. I came of age during World War II, a time when a great many people were consciously *making* history. Although the cold war and other disillusionments were to follow, these never led me personally to the opposite view, that history is nothing but one damn thing after another. Moreover, underneath the social-action themes of liberal Methodism lay an assumption that denomination shared with other religious bodies—and shares, I should add, with many groups, like the Marxists, who reject the religion per se—the assumption that what happened in history is intrinsically important. One of the distinguishing marks of "Western" (that is, Judeo-Christian) religion as against "Eastern" religion is the former's rootedness in historical time when certain definite things happened: "out of the land of Egypt"; "suffered under Pontius Pilate," an actual, documentable Roman governor.

After graduating from high school, I went into the Navy. Shortly after I turned eighteen, there came a moment worth singling out in my personal process of becoming a historian. I was stationed in Gulfport, Mississippi, among scrub pines that grew out of yellow clay, studying AC/DC and electromagnetic theory. Classrooms and barracks were tin Quonset huts ventilated by huge electric fans; we shared the chow halls with cockroaches. Away from the base itself we were in the deepest of the Deep South, a region I found utterly strange; it sent few signals recognizable from either a New England or a Rocky Mountain West point of view. Evenings, while doing electronics homework in the base library, I sometimes interrupted puzzling over oscillator circuitry, or whatever, to pick up whatever else was lying around on the library tables (I have always been a browser). That is how I chanced to find Vernon Parrington's *Main Currents in American Thought*. Trying to make sense of the region where I then was, I opened the book to the section on John C. Calhoun and "Carolina imperialism"— a twenties liberal's interpretation of the history of the slave South. I was instantly hooked. Reading Parrington was, although I did not know it at the time, a decisive intellectual experience. In spite of the ocean of pro-con Parrington historiography that has since intervened, I am still reacting to that initial encounter.

Later, on a submarine tender anchored off Guam with little to do, I devoured the ship's reading fare, much of it in the form of paperback Armed Forces Editions that were produced inexpensively for distribution to service people overseas; somebody, whether in the military or in the New Deal government I do not know, showed some creative awareness of the uses of literacy. One work I found in that format and read for the first time was *The Education of Henry Adams*. Coupled with Parrington, and with the Marxism I had first encountered (in rudimentary, pamphlet form) just before sailing, this classic work suggested to me—quite contrary to Adams's own conclusion!—that history might make sense in some broad synoptic form, whatever skepticism I might feel toward the reputed details. That is an attitude toward history of which departments of history in the postwar period did not approve, and which, when they found it in their graduate students, they did their utmost to cure.

I also (brashly, with but a high school diploma) attempted to *teach* a history course to service personnel stationed on Guam, piecing out a rather routine Armed Forces Institute textbook in world history—which, in those days, meant merely western European history—with Will and Ariel Durant's colorful if simplistic popular histories of Greece and Rome. That experiment was mercifully interrupted, and in fact terminated, by a roaring Pacific typhoon. Soon afterward came my navy discharge and a resumption of civilian education.

College, for that generation's male members (and for the relatively few of its female members who had worn military uniforms), meant the GI Bill of Rights. For me personally, discharged late in the school admissions year and therefore with some limits on my options, it meant my father's alma mater, Wesleyan University in Middletown, Connecticut. By that time Wesleyan had sloughed off or outgrown its formal church connection. It was participating enthusiastically in the then much-discussed "rebirth of liberal education," which reflected the educational doctrine preached at the University of Chicago at that time by Robert M. Hutchins—a downplaying of the vocationalism that had lately been rampant in higher education (as it is again) and a reemphasis on the liberal arts. Even during wartime, while catering to the needs of future military officers, Wesleyan had established a required freshman course in the humanities, based on some of Hutchins's Great Books—the Bible, the *Communist Manifesto*, the works of Dante, Rabelais, Shakespeare. If the college had an ideology, it was that of Alfred North Whitehead's *Science and the Modern World*, another book which continues to influence my thinking. We veteran freshmen were also exposed to the just recently developed "source book" which some articulate young instructors at Columbia had designed for that school's freshman Introduction to Contemporary Civilization in the West—a course now known to Columbia undergraduates, irreverently, as Dead White Men. In such an atmosphere in 1946, however, becoming a history major seemed as natural as breathing.

Two pitfalls await the pursuer of that kind of education, apart from its implicit elitism and, until recently, the closed quality of its canon. One is the way the Great Books themselves come to be treated rather as Platonic Ideas, as Texts (one can almost hear the word capitalized) which float in the empyrean, expressing eternal values irrelevant to what goes on here below. At Wesleyan, strongly committed historians and historically minded people in other departments (philosophy, government, religion, comparative literature, art) vigorously combated this ethereal notion, insisting that the books we freshmen read be rooted in their historical contexts. Also, several of those teachers carried over enough from the heritage of 1930s-style intellectual radicalism to stress the bearing that all these classic tomes have on the here and now.

The other pitfall in this "humanities" approach to higher education, especially when implemented by people whose primary bent is literary, is that it can entrap the inquirer into a false forced choice: science *or* the humanities, not both, the entrapment described by C. P. Snow in his Reith Lectures on the Two Cultures. Despite certain genuflections toward the natural sciences—in that freshman humanities required course we read the physicist Erwin Schrödinger's *What is Life?*, and in an upper division elective course I was assigned Einstein and Infeld's *The Evolution of Physics*—Wesleyan was not entirely immune to this pro–liberal arts, anti–science bias. Some of the literati seemed to take Whitehead's devastating philosophic critique of the seventeenth-century roots of the modern scientific worldview as a judgment that one does not need to take science seriously, which was not Whitehead's intention at all.

Three members of the Wesleyan faculty had a preponderant influence over my work, although in a college that small (900 students) there is a sense in which everyone learns from everyone else. These were Carl Schorske (history), Sigmund Neumann (political theory), and Cornelius Krusé (philosophy). Under the last-named I did a senior honors thesis on Arnold Toynbee's philosophy of history. Evidently the spin the college and my own predilections were giving to my historical training was toward intellectual history, as differentiated from political or economic history. It became fashionable among militants later on to condemn intellectual history as a cop-out; as a retreat from political commitment into brooding over the Complexity of It All. I don't think that judgment would be fair to this particular group of mentors. Schorske, for example, served as faculty advisor to Wesleyan Students for [Henry] Wallace, the leftist presidential candidate in 1948, and Krusé had engaged in war refugee work with the Friends Service Committee. (Neumann was more conventional, but he qualified as one of the honorably exiled scholarly "class of '33" from Hitler's Germany.) Anyhow, in terms of the academic job market, "intellectual history" at the end of the forties was one of the places to be, and I have ever since listed myself as an intellectual historian on most résumés.

Occasionally, aware that the word *intellectual* is a bit pretentious, I have taught courses in this subject under some such camouflage as History of Thought or Social and Cultural History.

I may have been kept on the American side of the fence, rather than chasing after European philosophers, by S. H. Brockunier, locally nicknamed "the irrepressible democrat" for a book on Roger Williams he had written with that title. In his upper-division lecture course in American history, Brockunier took keen, sardonic delight in baiting fraternity boys with his Democratic party heresies. His syllabus was comprehensive and challenging; it included not only Richard Hofstadter's just-published *American Political Tradition* but also the black Marxist historian W.E.B. DuBois's not yet quite accepted *Black Reconstruction*. I was also influenced to opt for American rather than European intellectual history by the fact that a bridge had lately been thrown across to America from European intellectual life by the advent and lay public reception in America of German-derived critical theology—this was the heyday of Paul Tillich and Reinhold Niebuhr. In my senior year I read, and was bowled over by, Niebuhr's *The Nature and Destiny of Man*. I do not think as highly of Niebuhr now as I did then, but surely this exposure had something to do with the fact that when I went on to graduate study at Columbia University I also took courses across the street at Union Theological Seminary, where Niebuhr and Tillich reigned.

I chose Columbia in part from a sense of my own provincialism: it was in New York. I knew small-town New England and the small-town West, but aside from wartime sojourns in Chicago and San Francisco, I didn't really know much about Metroamerica. Once there, at times I felt that this choice had been a disastrous mistake. Small colleges pet and coddle their students, and obviously there was going to be none of *that* at Columbia. At Union, however, with its relatively small enrollment and its camaraderie (professors and students coming into the cafeteria for lunch while continuing a fierce classroom argument, for example), I found some compensation for Columbia's anonymity, with its 200-plus graduate students sitting in lecture courses, attentive to distinguished professors who knew none of them. The upshot, partly as a thought-out program of study and partly for sheer survival, was a major in American history from Columbia and a minor in Anglo-American church history from Union. My dissertation cosponsors were that wise ironist Richard Hofstadter, from the university, and the keen and affable Robert Handy, then a beginning instructor at the seminary (he subsequently served in several of Union's top administrative posts and still more recently wrote a fine book detailing the seminary's history).

Hofstadter's first book had been on *Social Darwinism in American Thought*, and graduate study at Columbia at that time surely was a struggle for existence and the survival of, if not the fittest, at least the most persistent. Of master's candidates in the graduate faculties, only 40 percent were finishing—an appalling waste of time, money, and human souls. Hofstadter's master's seminar that year (1950–51) had nine students enrolled; one left the university as early as October; two of us finished up that spring, and another the following December. The other five—the majority—our mentor never expected to see again. His class sessions were a constant effort (for him it must have been depressing and exasperating effort) to turn over student mental engines that just didn't want to fire. The contrast with the highly motivated, if overly pious, students in Handy's History of Religion in America course over at UTS was particularly painful. Nevertheless, as I later came to admit, Hofstadter in his low-key way gave us much. He introduced me, for example, to the exciting speculative work then being done at Columbia in sociology, a discipline which Wesleyan's people had rather snidely put down. Hofstadter's ad lib exposition in class of a pioneering essay on mass culture by Leo Lowenthal, "Biographies in Popular Magazines"—an excellent example, Hofstadter later wrote me, of "what a first-rate mind can do with tenth-rate materials"—has stayed with me; it has given a critical shape to my own consideration of popular culture, and in this book it has influenced both the essays on the twenties and those on science fiction.

It was in that master's seminar that I wrote what became the first-published of the articles comprising the present book. Written under the pedantic heading "The Debate Over the Status of the Negro in the Unification of American Methodism," a title accurately descriptive if long-winded, it was excerpted under the more reasonable rubric "The Negro and Methodist Union" and was accepted for the journal *Church History* before I took my doctoral orals. The research led me to the Schomburg Collection, that rich African-American history archive in the Harlem branch of the New York Public Library; to Methodist archives downtown on Fifth Avenue; to Drew Seminary, a Methodist institution nearby in New Jersey which held some indispensable southern (white) Methodist sources; and over to suburban Boston for an interview with a retired liberal Methodist bishop who had played a major part in the controversy I was describing. There was obviously a very personal element in all this, given my background— and, in a subtle way, it was a dissent from the party line I was receiving at Union.

One of the grand themes at Union Theological Seminary then, as in mainline WASP Protestantism generally in the 1950s, was what the theologians had given the jawbreaking name of the Ecumenical Movement; that is, the effort to work across lines of sectarian division toward church unity. Hofstadter expressed mild disagreement with the logic of that movement, citing James Madison's argument that the vigor Madison observed in American religion, in contrast to the moribund European state churches, might well derive in part from its sectarian dividedness; the competing sects kept each other on their toes. But Schism is a Sin, the High Church folk in the National Council of Churches insisted, and in Unity is Strength. Such also had been the reasoning among northern and southern Methodists, originally sundered in the antebellum slavery and secession crisis, when they finally got back together in 1939. In celebrating this ecumenical act, however, white church leaders glossed over, rationalized, or simply ignored the strenuous objections of black members of northern Methodism who believed they were being railroaded into a Jim Crow church. The story had not been told, at least not from that angle, and I told it. Even before the article excerpt appeared, a black Methodist official borrowed the thesis itself on interlibrary loan as ammunition for the continuing debate within the church.

During and after the activist 1960s, this kind of work by a history graduate student (or mentor) would have occasioned no surprise. But the early 1950s in many graduate history departments were years of Olympian austerity. In a required course called the Nature, Methods, and Types of History and Historiography, we were told (in a vehement lecture-diatribe against Arnold Toynbee) to confine ourselves to narrowly focused monographs; and in a plausible discourse on "Present-Mindedness Versus Historical-Mindedness" we were warned not to let the social and political concerns of the present intrude into our research and writing on the past, lest in our desire to score points we end by merely making propaganda. The latter argument has some merit; but it does not accord well with the social-critical tradition in American historical writing that goes back to

Charles Beard, whose essay "Written History as an Act of Faith" unabashedly advocated a faith that scholarship can, in its own way, make the world a little better.

Hofstadter himself, while respecting James Harvey Robinson's dictum that the present as it *is* flows out of the past as it *was*, nonetheless often tied his own monographs to a current sociopolitical agenda. A look at the publication dates of his major books and a consideration of what had gone on in American public life while they were being written makes this abundantly clear. He is glibly, and I think mistakenly, classed with the Consensus School of American historians that emerged in the 1950s, but he was far too ironic and skeptical to celebrate the American past uncritically in the way that school is reputed to have done. In fact, Hofstadter was not really a "school" person at all. Devoted to Columbia, within it he went his own private and reflective way.

Furthermore, a "school" of Hofstadter-trained graduate students simply does not exist—a comment I intend as high praise. I have known a number of them and have read the dissertations of others, as well as the festschrift some of them put together to honor his memory, and all I can find in common among them is a commitment to rational discourse, high-quality writing, and humane scholarship, which ought to be taken for granted in our line of work, but very often, sadly, is not. My own dissertation experience was quite typical in its schoollessness. Hofstadter—unlike my cosponsor Handy, who was an ordained Baptist minister—was a freethinker or, as we say nowadays, a secular humanist ("I'm a pragmatist because pragmatism lets me make moral judgments without invoking spooks"). He was very far in temperament from the intense religiosity that suffused UTS. But he let me have my way with my chosen topic, the Protestant social gospel in America between the two world wars. The disadvantage of working with Hofstadter as a mentor was that he could be *too* permissive; he let his students flounder until they had a manuscript draft to show him. Meanwhile they suffered alone in the library as only a graduate student can. But this was more than offset by the compensating advantage that there was never, toward Hofstadter's students, the authoritarian decree of "Jones, you are going to work on *this*, and it will be a footnote in my next book."

My dissertation came out in book form in 1956. Other than a book review or two, I wrote nothing further for publication for five years. However, I do not count that half-decade as a period of idleness. Spent at the University of Montana, quite at the other pole from Metroamerica, it was a time of utmost importance for me personally. When two academic scholars meet and each says to the other "What are you working on?" they always mean a research and writing project. But there are other things one can be working on, as Henry David Thoreau noted when he referred to himself as an "inspector of snowstorms." One can be absorbing, germinating, sorting out. After gypsying through four campuses in two years, I had an uninterrupted spell of teaching at one place—*merely* teaching, some conscientious publication-oriented colleagues might say. When I did return to writing, it became possible to put together the production ethos of graduate school with the hands-on-the-blackboard experience of the classroom and come to some conclusions about the everlasting, wearily repetitive, argument in academia about teaching versus research. Personally, I have found this a false conflict; scholarship keeps one fresh and current in one's teaching, and students keep one's scholarship from turning dusty.

What brought me back to the typewriter was an invitation in 1961 to deliver a paper on the presidential campaign of 1928. This invitation coincided with the early presidency of John Kennedy, whose election the previous fall had confounded previous expert judgments about *always* and *never* as applied to politics and Catholicism in America. (Earlier in that election year I had offered a course at Montana on "Catholic-Protestant Tensions in American History," an illustration of the crossover between teaching and research which since then has characterized all my work.) For a locally researchable theme, I followed the presidential candidacy, prior to the 1928 Democratic national convention, of Montana's Senator Thomas J. Walsh. That candidacy was an attempt to de-coalesce the cliches that clustered around Al Smith; Walsh was a Catholic, like Smith, but "dry," representative of a thinly populated western state, and a crusader against the political corruption to which many believed Smith was beholden. That line of reasoning plunged me into the historiography of Al Smith's campaign, and the paper I read before the Mississippi Valley Historical Association (now known more tepidly as the Organization of American Historians) became an element in that debate. Afterward I split the paper, which was too long for publication in one journal, into two articles. They were published as you find them here; one on the historiography, the other on Walsh.

But the campaign of 1928 came as the political and social climax of an entire American decade. When thinking about the broader implications of that campaign, I found myself back in my parents' time, the allegedly roaring twenties, and the deeper I delved, the more complex and interesting the decade became. My father and mother had spent their college years in the first half of that ten-year span. But for them the twenties definitely did not roar. When I later found and read conventional accounts of the period, they simply did not square with the experience of the twenties about which I had been told firsthand. My mother was a strikingly attractive, high-spirited woman, as photographs from that era attest, but she was no *flapper* as that term is usually employed. Her idea of fun was a church social, and for vacations she and my father inexpensively went camping. He, similarly, never owned a raccoon coat in college, although at the bottom of the Depression he bought one at a secondhand store. And although he was in college at the time when *This Side of Paradise* (that supposedly archetypal novel by, for, and about the college student) was published, he never—then, or later in life—got around to reading it.

So, I suppose, one force which has influenced the way I write history has been my skepticism toward the reported record. What "they say" happened in history cannot be squared with what one feels *did* happen, and so one goes in quest of the actual happening. The first of the three groups of essays in this book reflects that quest. More specifically, it delves into the political history of the twenties, which even today is heavily marked by judgments of the "everybody knows" variety—what "they say." The second group, too, takes exception at a number of points to what, when I began thinking about and writing history, "everybody knew" about religion in America; and the third takes issue with what "everybody knows" about science fiction.

In addition to the essays on the twenties which appear here, I eventually wrote two books on the subject, and I also edited a collection of magazine articles from the twenties by people like John Dewey, Bernard De Voto, and Lewis Mumford (its introduction is included as chapter 1 in this collection). Like other laborers in this vineyard, I was discovering that the twenties constitute the first period in U.S. history which strikes us as unmistakably *modern*. We respond to that era's music, its media, its stresses in quite a different way from the way we react to the steam-powered, hoop-skirted, tobacco-spitting culture of America's nineteenth century. Internationally also, the age of Queen Victoria seems much farther from us than the times of her great-grandson Edward, Prince of Wales. The twenties were lit by electricity, not gas.

Yet when we get more deeply into that decade's anxieties and aspirations, we find that people were playing nostalgia games, were looking for a way back to Normalcy. Nowhere were issues of the old versus the new more sharply drawn in the twenties than in the contrast between Herbert Hoover and Al Smith in 1928. But this nostalgia has echoes, too, in later decades, which is reflected even in George McGovern's "radical" presidential campaign in 1972 (as shown in one of these essays). Conversely, much that at first seems exotic or aberrant in the culture of Normalcy really was, in the context of its history and setting, normal. A case in point is Prohibition, the subject of the last essay in the first section: a far more typically American political experience than the bizarre caper generally portrayed in accounts of the "dry decade."

Prohibition, modernization, and the Al Smith campaign also make a transition to the second of this book's themes: the perennial role of religion in America's cultural and political life. Here again the reader will find an interplay between the short term and the long view. All the articles in this group except the essay on black Methodism were first published during or shortly after the sixties and bear the impress of that hopeful, terrible decade. If an article begins with George Washington or the Bible, its context is the rightward tilt of civic religion since the sixties or the Death of God flurry of that same era. Much of my own professional time during the sixties was spent at Northern Illinois University among keen, humane, knowledgeable, and dedicated Marxists, and any historical research and writing in such a setting demanded respect for Karl Marx's dictum that "All criticism begins with the criticism of religion."

Yet the sixties were not fully explanatory even of themselves. The phrase "Death of God" was coined by Friedrich Nietzsche, not by the sixties people, and Americans had already had at least two great wrestling matches with that dark challenge, once in the Gilded Age (corresponding in Europe to Nietzsche's time) and again in the twenties. The essay on fundamentalism in this volume ties these wider, earlier, and later religious issues back to one of the central controversies of the twenties, thus linking the second group of articles back to the first. Incidentally, the essay on fundamentalism was, I believe, the first historical essay by a nonfundamentalist that did not treat the movement as moribund. Many of us have learned better, to our discomfort, since then.

Fundamentalism—a belief in the absolute and literal truth of the Bible—inevitably leads the inquirer into the classic confrontation between religious and scientific ideas, as set forth in this book in the essay "Science and the Death of God." But a discussion of science as a public phenomenon which must be reckoned with by nonscientists raises questions in addition to science's clash with religion. The amazing reception the American public accorded Albert Einstein—the archetypal, incomprehensible absentminded professor—as a popular idol in large part *because* his discourse ran far beyond that public's grasp, contains a clue to the relationship between science and popular culture, and in particular to the issue of how science gets transmitted into that culture, an issue which continues to trouble us today.

A more informal channel for such transmission consisted of the science fiction magazines, the first of which began publication in America in 1926 (another twenties witness to modernity). The magazines' editors, writers, and readers, despite frequent and obvious lapses, took their work of scientific and technological extrapolation very seriously. The final group of essays examines that commitment in some detail, ending with a speculative piece whose takeoff point is a suggestion Isaac Asimov made in 1939 that the most serious obstacle to putting a person on the moon might be not scientific or technical but political and social: an objection to space travel based on religious fundamentalism, thus returning to the themes of Parts I and II of this work. Once again, as in my suggestion later in this book that Shakespeare's *Tempest* can be understood thematically as science fiction, we find a dialectical interplay between the short and the long view.

It would not have been possible, however, to publish articles such as these in conventional academic media until research and scholarship on science fiction became an activity the scholarly establishment deemed acceptable. That did not happen until the *Apollo 11* moon walk in 1969, following which science fiction, as I have written elsewhere, suffered a fall into respectability. Science fiction had, however, been a "closet" interest of mine for many years. After my turn from the study of science to that of history, science fiction became, in a sense, my hostage to the other of the Two Cultures. I wrote and published short stories in the genre while I was also writing on Prohibition, fundamentalism, and black Methodists. And there *is* a connection; as my philosophy mentor Cornelius Krusé often remarked, "All things are related to all other things." Science fiction—sometimes crudely, sometimes with epic grandeur—asks some of the staggering questions which fundamentalists and modernists, scientists and laypeople, Marxists and conservatives also ask: What is man, that Thou art mindful of him? and Is anybody out there? and, Where are we all going?

The more mundane process of confining such sweeping concerns within a brief monographic compass leaves us still with very disparate parts of a perhaps implicit whole. Partly this results from the process of production. Articles, unless written as serial installments of an eventual book, are written ad hoc, in response to a program chairman's request for a paper on a particular theme (five of these articles were written that way) or because the writer finds conveniently nearby a library rich in sources on a particular topic (four of these articles could not have been written otherwise). Simply listing these items on a contents page in their chronological order of composition would therefore not have been very enlightening.

In thinking about such a contents page, I was struck by how much unity of theme and outlook there actually is in these essays. Try mixing-and-matching them: *Politics*: Hoover, Smith, Walsh, McGovern, William Jennings Bryan, "wets" and "drys," imagined Supreme Court justices; *Religion*: the same cast of political characters, plus black and white Methodists and George Washington; *Science*: the actors in the fundamentalist-modernist conflict, plus Albert Einstein and the rocket speculators; *Conservatism vs. liberalism*: all of the above. There is a unity of theme here partly because, as one of my editors has pointed out, these essays are all the product of one person's work.

But that editorial insight raises the specter of societal or subjective relativism, which throughout the twentieth century has inhibited so much intellectual work. In history it is expressed in the title of a famous, or notorious, essay by Carl Becker: "Everyman His Own Historian." All historians, this thesis asserts, are creatures of their own time, place, and circumstance, and cannot transcend them. The fact that Becker's title would now have to be amended to remove *man* and *his* gives the thesis additional persuasive force. The shifting ground upon which these essays rest became apparent when I started going through them, taking account of changing time and circumstance by copyediting out the presentist expressions (changing present perfect verb tenses to past, striking *recent* from something which no longer is, and the like), and updating the usage—changing *Negro* to *black*, eliminating *man* as a generic term, and so on. I have not changed judgment calls, however, or updated the documentation, which may be found in detail in the notes published with the original journal articles. An essay is something one commits to the world of letters, and once out there it has to fend for itself, however much one might change it if writing it today. (This is particularly true of a piece which has accumulated a little subsequent historiography of its own, as several of these essays have.) *Pecca fortiter*, Luther said, "Sin bravely"—and take the consequences. Perhaps somewhere, beyond all temporal conditionings, psychological rationalizations, and bourgeois false consciousness, such essays as these connect with something one may properly call historical reality.

In 1962 the American historian Arthur Link, a major biographer of Woodrow Wilson, proposed that such a connection could best be made by translating what Becker had put forth purely in secular terms quite frankly into out-and-out theology. One falls into the mini-hell of solipsism, in which everyone is his or her own historian, Link argued, "because the ego in its unredeemed or natural state is not able to see history apart from itself." To writers and readers versed in traditional religious discourse, as Link evidently was, Becker's thesis was not news. The coerciveness of the human ego, setting itself imperiously at the center of its experience and interpreting the world from that imagined center, is indeed one of the classic definitions of original sin. St. Augustine in his autobiographical musings patently was haunted by a sense that in his own time, place, and circumstance—prior to his conversion—he had been, if not his own historian, then certainly his own philosopher (and upwardly mobile young professional). His studies in rhetoric during his late-teen years, he admitted, led him to "books of eloquence, wherein I desired to be eminent out of a damnable and vain glorious end, a joy in human vanity" (*Confessions*, Book III, IV:7, Pusey translation). Even if the self were able of its own volition to break out of that self-referential circle, the same orthodox tradition continues, such knowledge as the unassisted human intellect might acquire would of necessity be wretchedly fragmentary and incomplete. "For we know in part, and we prophesy in part," wrote Paul the Apostle, "but when that which is perfect is come, then that which is in part shall be done away."

It followed logically, for Paul and Augustine, that the one sure way to intellectual wholeness is through religious conversion—a conclusion that has commended itself to many, and by many others has been indignantly rejected. Alas, the problem, if approached in this way, often is only displaced, not solved. Instead of Everyman his own historian we have every sect *its* own historian; and that history—which, indeed, it may forcefully impose upon its own members as doctrine not to be questioned—is likely to be judged by an outsider as no more than an agreed-upon set of social lies. One pointed answer to Paul and Augustine is the one attributed to Galileo, who, when told by the Inquisition that he must affirm against his own reason that the earth sits immovably at the center of the universe, is said to have replied under his breath, "Nevertheless, it moves."

Galileo's answer can be taken as a reply not only to the church but to Becker as well. Were history a science, we could transcend both the subjectivism of the private scholar and the dogmatism of the public authority—for churches, of course, are not alone in enforcing that kind of dogmatic unanimity—by appealing to what Lester Ward once called "the dry light of science," a dispassionate, objective examination of the facts. That is what historians a century ago thought they were on the verge of accomplishing. Becker would have replied that it cannot be done; one cannot replicate *all* the facts, and the moment one decides that some facts are more important than others—for example, that what kings do is more important than how homeless people live—it becomes necessary to ask, From whose point of view?

Moreover, the facts—even if their relative importance is agreed upon—have to be arranged, and different historians arrange them differently. Two biographers of Abraham Lincoln, Lord Charnwood and Albert P. Beveridge, using the same data, managed to come up with two different Lincolns. As Allan Nevins, himself a major chronicler of Lincoln's political career, observed: "The same facts can be arranged in an order tending to prove that Lincoln in 1854–56 was more statesmanlike than [Stephen A.] Douglas (as Lord Charnwood arranges them), or in an order indicating that Douglas was more the statesman (as Beveridge arranges them)." Nevins concluded: "Facts cannot be selected without some personal conviction as to what is the truth . . . and this conviction is a bias." We seem to have arrived back where we started.

One of my undergraduate teachers, a wise and mellow young man, actually began a course in European history since 1815 by telling the class that the only sensible approach he could take to history was through *fic-*

tionalism—Hans Vaihinger's bargain-basement version of Kant, which sees the world only as a phenomenological shimmer of "as if." To many historians after the fifties, at least, such a metaphysically self-denying stance would have been profoundly unsatisfying. One breakout from subjective relativism or post-Kantian phenomenology is implicit in a letter Friedrich Engels, Marx's great disciple, wrote in 1890: "We make our own history, but under certain definite conditions." It is not surprising that in the sixties a good many American historians—not to mention philosophers, literary critics, political scientists, and even a few (mostly untenured) economists—got a handhold on reality by embracing Marxism.

As the sixties drooped into the seventies, many of these Marxist conversions did not stick. However, that (in some quarters) radical decade had one beneficial side-effect: it made a number of non-Marxists less condescending toward, or less afraid of, Marxism as an intellectual option. The cheap-shot anti-Marxist ploys of the fifties were set aside; other kinds of scholars became aware that Marx did *not* say that every man has his price or acts mechanically in accord with his economic class interest. Marxism, as a clearheaded diagnosis of the plight of the world's poor, found acceptance among people who did not concur in its metaphysical foundations or its embodiment in party programs. Certain stubborn noneconomic realities— racism, sexism—resisted translation into Marxist terms without becoming stretched away from Marxism altogether. But the academy is unlikely ever to return to the condescension of the worst cold war years, when some academicians actually argued that McCarthyism or its equivalent was not really necessary in order to purge college faculties of Marxists; their professional colleagues, left to themselves, in effect would accomplish that same goal from their knowledge that a Marxist is *by definition* intellectually incompetent to form a sound professional judgment.

We have reverted, rather, to the wise position taken by Max Weber, who argued that a law faculty (even in authoritarian Wilhelmian Germany) would be justified in admitting an anarchist, for example, to its membership for intellectual enrichment, since the anarchist would bring to its collective discourse a radically different conception of what one means by *law*. Marxism in short has earned a place in the plurality of scholarship, and some Marxists of my acquaintance, while continuing to picket, demonstrate, and write letters of protest (alongside non-Marxist colleagues), seem content, in practice and for the time being, with this relationship. In the classroom, I have found that some of the conclusions of the sixties "new left" historians—the reinterpretation of the history of American foreign policy by William Appleman Williams and his school, for example—provide a healthy corrective to the complacent, simpleminded business-knows-best outlook some of my students have brought into those classrooms during the sloganeering Reagan-Bush years.

A sidebar to this refurbished Marxism has been the deconstruction- ism of Jacques Derrida, which has lately been in vogue among literary critics, historians, and even a philosopher or two. Philosophical skepticism and political radicalism have from time to time been uneasy allies; we do have to get rid of false consciousness, so perhaps we can deconstruct it. But in some important respects this is only Beckerism in a new guise. To assert, as did one adherent of this school in 1986, that "historical writing is about historical writing, which is about historical writing," that written history "has no center beyond itself," is to give up the game altogether. Is that all we can do—chase texts from here to eternity?

Perhaps that chase can be transcended, other voguish historical col- leagues assert, by applying to historical study the quantitative methods made possible by the computer revolution; we may finally be able to do scientific history, as historians believed they could a hundred years ago, by employing in our research not ordinary, garden-variety empiricism—the kind all historians use, more or less—but what the more eager among these quantitative historians are pleased to call *hard* empiricism. We have learned a good deal from quantification; new and exciting modes of social history would not have been possible without it. But a computer program is only as good as its programmer; we run the risk here of Beckerian subjectivism disguised as numerical factuality.

"We must know the truth; and we must avoid error," said William James in 1896, but "these are two materially different laws," and we can- not fully obey both at the same time. All of us must choose, he argued, either to "keep your mind in suspense forever, rather than by closing it on insufficient evidence incur the awful risk of believing lies," or to "be ready to be duped many times in your investigation rather than postpone indefi- nitely the chance of guessing true." Professors, being cautious souls, tend to prefer the first option; James vigorously went with the second. In defense against the Everyman thesis he invoked his broader philosophy of pragma- tism: the truth of a proposition can be known from its consequences. If we discipline that method by socializing it, as did James's younger colleague in pragmatism John Dewey, and if we add the scientific researcher's caution that no guess at the truth should be accepted without independent verification by other investigators, we will arrive at a viable way of doing history without simply floating freely in the transiency of time, place, and circumstance. The umpire calls 'em as he sees 'em, but there are other umpires on that playing field, and each sees the way the ball was played from a different angle. But the ball *did*, in fact, land fair or foul. A belief that it really did is intrinsic to my personal study of history. I may think differently on this matter a year or a decade hence; that is why I can still present my work, thirty-six years out of graduate school, as only the product of an apprenticeship in history.

PART ONE

Perspectives
on Jazz-Age
Democracy

CHAPTER ONE

The Uncertain World of Normalcy

An Introduction

*F*rom the physical and social wreckage of the past certain historical fragments have been retrieved. The monumental statuary at Abu Simbel was sawn into blocks and therefore saved from the rising waters of the Nile. London Bridge was taken down and rebuilt, stone by stone, in the desert of Arizona. Public-spirited citizens of Manhattan kept the remorseless redevelopers from tearing down Carnegie Hall. And a resident of Vancouver, British Columbia, purchased from the National Wrecking Company of Chicago the brick wall in front of which, on Saint Valentine's Day of 1929, seven men had stood and been shot. It may say more about the temper of the year the purchase was made (1968) than it does about that of 1929 that a food-company executive should have bought so grisly and expensive a relic for reconstruction in his den. But his act was a forcible reminder that the twenties, once so near to us psychically that a book about them became a best-seller under the title *Only Yesterday*, had become "antiquity." Between the parents who founded their families under the cloud of Hiroshima and their children who struggled into selfhood in the shadow of Vietnam stretched a much-discussed "generation

An earlier form of this essay appeared in *The Uncertain World of Normalcy: The 1920s* (New York: Jerome S. Ozer/Pitman Publishing Corp., 1971), 1–9.

gap," but still further beyond that gulf stood the grandparents, whose living experience had become shrouded in legend. The typical undergraduate of the sixties, upon hearing a professor lecture on "the Lost Generation," does not seem to have gone home afterward and asked, "But, Grandma, did he mean *you?*"

It was easy to forget, moreover, that those grandparents had had to hurdle a generation gap of their own. "The mothers and fathers and uncles and aunts of the youth of both sexes between twenty and thirty" who in the year 1915 were launching their own businesses and professional careers, Randolph Bourne wrote, were unworthy of their children's loyalty. Complacent, selfish, and hypocritical, the older generation, he said, has "grown weary of thinking. . . . It tends more and more to treat human beings as moving masses of matter instead of as personalities. . . . The older generation has stamped, through all its agencies of family, church, and school, upon the younger generation, just those seductive ideals which would preserve its position. . . . Its influence is profoundly pernicious." Even as Bourne wrote these words, the seductive ideals of the older generation were hurling the young at each other's throats by the millions, in the shell-churned muck that the green fields of France, by the grace of modern technology, had become. Henry F. May, in his book *The End of American Innocence*, is quite right to have pointed out that disillusionment such as Bourne expressed antedated the First World War and therefore that the war did not "cause" the rebelliousness associated with the twenties; but for many participants in that rebellion the war was what clinched it. The older generation had forfeited any claim to moral authority because its own ideals—or ingrained hatreds and systematic stupidities rationalized as ideals—had brought on the war and then had trapped the younger generation into paying the price of their elders' folly.

Young men who had been through the maelstrom themselves were understandably a bit self-righteous on this point. As a volunteer ambulance driver at the front, twenty-one-year-old John Dos Passos thought himself and his friends "frightfully decent—all young men are frightfully decent. If we only governed the world instead of the swagbellied old fogies that do . . . Down with the middle-aged!" Four years later on the night train up to Tiflis from Batum in the USSR he heard enthusiastic young Bolsheviks talk excitedly of the brave new world they were building: "food and schools, peace and freedom for all, except for the damn *burzoi* that were

4

causing them so much trouble"—and, Dos Passos reflected afterward, "In the summer of 1921 it would have been hard to find a war veteran who wouldn't have endorsed that program."

They didn't all come out of the war wanting to govern the world. Some of them chose to stand aside and treat it as a bad joke, or to turn their backs on it in quest of some private Grail—excellence in writing, or courage in the bull ring, or perfection in sex. Nor did all of them blame the troubles of the time on the middle-aged; many joined the American Legion and cheered Colonel Theodore Roosevelt, Jr., when he cried, "You will always find us ready to stand for the ideals of this country handed down by our fathers. . . . Bolshevists, the I.W.W., and red flag Socialists I see as criminals, to be treated as such." (In any case, revolutionary ideals do not always derive from a "generation gap"; disagreeing with Bourne, the young insurgent might rather have felt that his radicalism confirmed his basic family loyalties, in the spirit expressed in 1929 by an American champion of Soviet Communism, Mike Gold: "Mother! Momma! . . . I must remain faithful to the poor because I can't be faithless to you.") And there were quiet backwaters where the upheavals of the time seem scarcely to have raised a ripple. Rosemary Park, in later years vice-chancellor of UCLA, once told a convocation audience that when she entered college in 1924, "a burning issue was whether one complied with a college regulation and wore a hat in Harvard Square."

> As far as we knew, we could discuss anything we liked on campus. The university was a free market of ideas, but there were no very profound ones about. Young instructors told us they had been reprimanded for referring to a Viennese psychiatrist, Sigmund Freud, and in our history classes or in art and literature, modern as an historical term stopped at 1850. . . . The University . . . was rightly removed from the vulgarities and disputes of the outer world, and its task was to develop the standards by which we came to understand and to evaluate what was beyond—it was a good and quiet university.

College, of course, embraced a far smaller proportion of the student-aged population then than it would later. The great majority of Americans in the twenties had never lived in the kind of cloister Miss Park described, and their firsthand encounters with the vulgarities and disputes of the outer world *might* have bred in them a greater realism than was manifested by the inmates of the ivied halls, but the sweeping dogmatisms, sometimes

5

radical, usually conservative, with which "self-made men" were wont to meet the challenges of the day make me doubt this. It would seem that "innocence"—in the meaning Henry May has attached to the term—far from having altogether ended in the First World War, had an extraordinary persistence into the twenties. We find it all the way across the social and political spectrum, from Warren Harding declaring that the "Spirit of '76" was counterrevolutionary ("If revolution insists upon overturning established order let other peoples make the tragic experiment. There is no place for it in America.") to Michael Gold declaring that another people's experiment in revolutionary overturn had created in the Soviet Union a land where man's inhumanity to man was unknown.

Echoes of that innocent spirit ring through the period's media. Even so disillusioning an experience as war itself could be sentimentalized; witness the first Academy Award-winning motion picture ever made, *Wings* (1928), in which well-groomed young men go off in their Spad biplanes "on the high seas of heaven" (as one of that silent film's titles put it) in pursuit of the wolfishly grinning Count von Kellermann and his Flying Circus. Sometimes, such is the documentary force of cinema, the monstrousness of the war did break through; I found the close-ups of tanks clattering over the trenches still genuinely terrifying. The picture also captured the ecstasy human beings felt in being airborne, at a time when powered flight was an experience still relatively fresh and new. But the First World War as portrayed by Richard Arlen, Buddy Rogers, Clara Bow, and even the six doom-haunted minutes onscreen of a youthful Gary Cooper, was hardly the war experienced by e. e. cummings and John Dos Passos and Ernest Hemingway, nor was it the war visually captured in such films of the thirties as *All Quiet on the Western Front* and *Grand Illusion*.

It would be all too easy for a modern person to condescend to such testimonies from the twenties. But innocence can also engender keenness of vision, like that of the small child who—naïvely unaware of his elders' complicated reasons for believing otherwise—insisted that the emperor really had no clothes. Ingenuous and ill-informed the writers of the twenties sometimes were, but at their best they could be embarrassingly observant; and they were in the habit of asking questions in a way that forced the respondent to commit him or herself to a *yes* or *no* rather than to take refuge in one of the seven types of ambiguity. The so-called Lost Generation seemed almost perversely aware that the phrase "There are no easy answers" can itself be the easiest of answers.

As a result, they lived in a sharply polarized universe of ideas. Political controversialists of a later day, for example, except for a handful on the far right and the nihilist left, might have begun by affirming that democracy was a "good thing" and then disagreed passionately as to how it was to be achieved; but in the twenties the controversy extended to the democratic principle itself. If some Americans followed John Dewey and the progressive educators in their earnest conviction that learning could be a democratic and universal enterprise, others concluded from the psychologists' tests of "innate" mental ability just then coming into vogue that some people are inherently uneducable and therefore that egalitarian democracy is a fraud.

Polarities of this extreme kind meet the investigator of the twenties at every turn. The name of William Jennings Bryan, for example, was still a household word for millions of Americans in the twenties, but the name of Albert Einstein had almost equal incantatory power. The jaunty hymns to sex in the springtime by e. e. cummings and the dark broodings about wounded hawks by Robinson Jeffers were equally authentic poetic expressions of the age. Both the expatriate and the Rotarian, both the founders of the American Legion and the founders of the Communist party, both the member of the American Civil Liberties Union and the member of the Ku Klux Klan were *typical* of the spirit of those years. Small wonder that the student and teacher of American history have so often met in the lecture on the twenties their classroom Waterloo!

If we turn to foreign commentators upon the American scene in the twenties we find their witness as divided as our own. Isoroku Yamamoto, the man who planned the attack on Pearl Harbor, was in the United States from 1925 to 1927 as Japanese naval attaché. Still earlier as a Harvard student he had hitchhiked from Boston down to Mexico. On the basis of his experiences here, he later warned the students of his old Middle School in Japan: "It is a mistake to regard the Americans as luxury-loving and weak. I can tell you Americans are full of the spirit of justice, fight and adventure. . . . Lindbergh's solo crossing of the Atlantic is the sort of valiant act which is normal for them"—a different assessment indeed from that of many other judges, both foreign and domestic, of the American national character. To the dismay of the busy note taker, the twenties perversely defy generalization.

Were the twenties in America—or in Japan, or in France, or in Weimar Germany, or in Mussolini's Italy, or in Ramsay MacDonald's Brit-

7

ain, for we are dealing here with an international experience—a revolutionary epoch devoted to smashing old idols and clearing away the rubble so that people could build anew? If so, the revolution was somehow heralded in Japan by state Shinto and in the United States by Republican landslides. Or were the twenties instead an age of repression, marked by fear, conformism, and downright stuffiness? One then recalls the motto of *The New Yorker*, founded in 1925: "Not for the old lady from Dubuque," a strong reminder that much could be said and done in 1925 that could not have been said and done, or even imagined, in 1875.

Said and done, yes, our note taker may concede; but in what spirit? Did men and women act and work and love in the twenties under a pall of despair—able at times to enjoy the spectacle with H. L. Mencken, collecting his specimens of Americana for the *American Mercury*, or Anita Loos, collecting specimens of another sort in her best-selling *Gentlemen Prefer Blondes*, but aware nonetheless that the world they had known before 1914 had come to an end? Newspaper critic and reporter Lewis Gannett did not remember it that way; in 1940, recalling the good times he had had in the twenties working for *The Nation*, he wrote: "It is almost impossible to believe today that a world could ever have seemed so full of hope." Nor did John Dos Passos remember his New York nights in the twenties with regret. "There is a time in a man's life when every evening is a prelude," he wrote in his memoir *The Best Times* (1966). "Toward five o'clock the air begins to tingle. It's tonight if you drink enough, talk enough, walk far enough, that the train of magical events will begin."

Was, then, the Jazz Age a joyous, optimistic era when people believed the world was their oyster and the sky the limit? At once one thinks of *The Waste Land*, of the vogue for Oswald Spengler, and of "all the sad young men"—or, at another level in the literary establishment, of H. P. Lovecraft, who opened one of the horror stories he wrote during the twenties with a paragraph that outdid Joseph Wood Krutch at his most rueful:

> The most merciful thing in all the world, I think, is the inability of the human mind to correlate all its contents. We live on a placid island of ignorance in the midst of black seas of infinity, and it was not meant that we should voyage far. The sciences, each straining in its own direction, have hitherto harmed us little; but some day the piecing together of dissociated knowledge will open up such terrifying vistas of reality, and of our frightful position therein, that we shall either go mad from the revelation or flee from the deadly light into the peace and safety of a new dark age.

But the apocalyptic grimness of a reflection like this is, in the recollections of people who lived through the twenties, set against moments of rollicksome humor. "I am glad that, however serious, we are never solemn in these essays," Harold Stearns wrote in the preface to *Civilization in the United States* (1922). "It would be a humourless person indeed who could not read many of them, even when the thrusts are at himself, with that laughter which Rabelais tells us is proper to the man." On what they considered the proper occasion, critical-minded Americans in the Jazz Age could be deadly serious. When Heywood Broun, the crusading columnist for the *New York World*, learned that the last appeal for clemency for Sacco and Vanzetti had been rejected, he immediately sat down at the typewriter and rolled off a column of smoking-hot prose that shortly thereafter cost him his job. But Broun was also a member in good standing of the Thanatopsis Literary and Inside Straight Poker Club, and if he cried out in anger over Sacco and Vanzetti, he also cried out with delight over Babe Ruth. In fact, when the Harold Stearns volume appeared, Broun gave it an adverse review, precisely because he felt that the contributors to *Civilization in the United States* had slid downhill from seriousness into solemnity. "Lost" though the generation of the twenties sometimes called themselves, the tone of their protests seems by comparison far less grim than that of some of their spiritual descendants.

Still, to anyone who has lived through the quarrels of more recent decades, the cries of those who were young—and not so young—in the twenties can sound hauntingly familiar. Even so dated, so over-and-done-with a controversy of the twenties as Prohibition turns out upon examination to have a surprisingly modern sound. The moral fury aroused over the Eighteenth Amendment, pro and con, so incomprehensible to a later generation, may have become more intelligible to us since the invention of LSD. We too have discovered that people can get excited about the connection between morality and chemistry. Moreover, the Prohibition issue was connected with larger questions of social control. "Enforcement of law and obedience to law," said Calvin Coolidge apropos of the Volstead Act, "are not matters of choice in this republic," a *leitmotiv* that was destined to be heard again.

It is easy enough to find evidence to substantiate the argument that the twenties contained in embryo the portents of our own age. The literary world of the twenties, for example, showed the same sharp divergences that one found in politics, religion, or education, ranging as it did from the radical stylistic innovations of Dos Passos and Hemingway to the old-fashioned craftsmanship of Willa Cather and Edith Wharton; but it was precisely "the complexity and depth of Jazz Age fiction," Frederick J. Hoffman concluded in a posthumously published essay, that had given to subsequent generations "the attitudes toward modern reality that it is now possible for us to take." This view of the postwar decade has been vigorously contested, most notably by Bernard De Voto in *The Literary Fallacy*. Nevertheless, and especially beyond the boundaries of formal literature, it is quite possible that in proclaiming the twenties to have been "the true sign of beginnings in our own century," Hoffman was right.

One reason why *Middletown*, published in 1929, would later come back into vogue as collateral reading in college classrooms may have been that Robert and Helen Lynd reported in their book not only what a medium-sized midwestern city was like in the twenties but also what American society as a whole was likely to become. The automobile already exercised its tyranny over the family budget ("I'll go without food before I'll see us give up the car," declared one working-class wife in Middletown); the "realtor," that demiurge of the suburbs, was already plying his trade; and even though television was not yet on the scene, the recreational pursuits of Middletownians were already "largely passive, i.e., looking at or listening to something or talking or playing cards or riding in an auto; the leisure of virtually all women and most men over thirty is mostly spent sitting down." As for young people, what the Lynds found out about Middletown's schools—where teachers, paid about as well as retail clerks, taught a miscellany of unrelated information quite irrelevant to "life as Middletown adults live it"—suggests that in 1929 it was already possible in American cities for young people to grow up absurd. Here in 1929 was a culture which clearly foreshadowed the oncoming consumer society.

"We have had the alternative of humanizing the industrial city or dehumanizing the population," wrote Lewis Mumford as a contributor to Harold Stearns's compendium on *Civilization in the United States*; "so far we have dehumanized the population." Four decades later Mumford continued his argument unbroken as he told a worried Senate committee: "Unless human needs and human interactions and human responses are the first consideration, the city, in any valid sense, cannot be said to exist." In the same fashion, forty-five years after the publication of *Civilization in the United States*, contributors to the *Partisan Review* symposium "What's

Happening to America?" were able to pick up the chorus without missing a beat. Our industrial cities were still inhuman, our adult population was still hopelessly implicated in the "system," and whatever grounds there were for hope in the future still lay, if anywhere, in the activities of the young.

But had it not always been so? A century ago the Boston Brahmin John Fiske was already writing that the chief difference between ancient Athens and modern America was our speed and nervous tension, and much in the national character that we are inclined to think of as new or unique in the twentieth century ("other-directedness," for example) can be found in abundance in works on America published as long ago as the Age of Jackson—in the writings of Cooper, Tocqueville, and Harriet Martineau. Moreover, one must constantly be on the alert for those traits of the twenties which did not simply foreshadow what was to come. Otherwise we constrain men and women who were alive in their own day, with their own sense of immediacy and purpose, to make themselves intelligible on our terms rather than theirs.

The last of many ironies in the twenties was the way they ended, as Clio rang down the curtain on the decade with a great Crash. We know, of course, that Coolidge prosperity was not all it seemed to be; any tenant farmer or black American could have testified to that. And we know that the spirit of the times would inevitably have changed, with or without a depression; for example, there is evidence that by the end of 1928 Mencken's *American Mercury* had already lost much of its characteristic elan. Nevertheless, writes John Kenneth Galbraith, "Some years, like some poets and politicians and some lovely women, are singled out for fame far beyond the common lot, and 1929 was clearly such a year. Like 1066, 1776, and 1914, it is a year that everyone remembers." For twenty years afterward, as J. P. Marquand had the central character observe in his novel *Point of No Return* (1949), otherwise reasonable people kept on discussing the details of the stock-market disaster, "apparently for the same reason that old ladies enjoyed describing surgical operations and sessions with their dentists. There was a snob value in boasting of old pain." And the result was inevitable. The conflicts and anxieties of the years preceding the Crash were either repudiated, in the style of the tough young leftists of the thirties, or they were blotted out in nostalgia. The turning point 1914, before which the world was assumed to have been relaxed, peaceful, and secure, was moved up to 1929.

Were the twenties, then, historically not an exceptional period after all? Frederick Lewis Allen lived to confess in 1946 that he had illustrated some of the trends of the twenties with "rather extreme, though authentic, examples of odd and excited behavior" in his classic *Only Yesterday*, noting that "one could gather just such preposterous examples of American behavior today." Professor David Burner more recently suggested that most of the wildness we associate with the period can be localized in the single year 1919; once the special hysterias arising directly from the First World War had spent themselves, the bitter social polarities found in this country during the last days of the Wilson administration gave place to a "deep-rooted consensus that easily outlasted the conflict of the postwar months" in a "victory for the middle elements in American life." In short, then, the *zeitgeist* was exactly what Warren Harding said it was: Normalcy.

Who has the right of it here? Will the conflicts of the twenties smooth down into consensus over the long perspective of history, as Professor Burner seems to imply? Will they appear in retrospect to have been signposts on a scenic but exasperating detour from the main high road of our history? Or will they be diagnosed eventually as the birth pangs of a new historical epoch, perhaps even of a planetwide new social order?

CHAPTER TWO

Just Off Main Street

Towns and Roads, Three Novelists, and George McGovern

*T*he year 1920 was a good one for government investigators. Some of them swooped down upon suspected "Reds," netting a grand haul of four thousand in a coordinated coast-to-coast raid one wild January night. Others tramped through the mountains sniffing out illicit stills, or walked the city streets to knock on the doors of outlaw saloons. Presumably still others scrutinized the taxable incomes of the suddenly affluent, like young Francis Scott Key Fitzgerald, who had just cranked out an instant best-seller, *This Side of Paradise*, after an Alabama belle declined to marry him until he had proved his earning power.

Even the hardworking inquirers who only compiled statistics had a banner year. Those employed by the Bureau of the Census for the decennial counting of the American people discovered that in 1920, for the first time in the Republic's history, more than 50 percent of the American population was definably urban. Half-truths in history probably outnumber the outright whoppers. This particular statistic has been interpreted ever since as marking a great watershed in American history, as the moment when the long opposition between the country bumpkin and the city slicker

An earlier form of this essay appeared in *The Columbia Forum*, n.s., 2 (Spring 1973): 10–16, and later in *Another Part of the Twenties* (New York: Columbia University Press, 1977).

entered its final phase. Thomas Jefferson's agrarian faith that those who labor in the earth are the chosen people of God had apparently lost out to Alexander Hamilton's vision of the rich, the wellborn, and the able presiding over an industrial America. The "roar" of the Roaring Twenties seemed to be the roar of urban traffic and industry. According to a music critic writing in 1929, even the preindustrial human rhythms of jazz had become "caught up in the incessant movement of the machine, pounding not only in our ears but also continuously in our consciousness . . . with its unrelieved tension." Except for a few nostalgic rallyings—the Scopes trial in Dayton, Tennessee, or the defeat of Al Smith—the rural America of the Founding Fathers is supposed to have lost its hold on the American imagination after 1920.

The half-truth in the 1920 statistic lay in the census-takers' definition of urban people as those inhabiting towns of more than 2,500 people. By an act of mathematical magic resembling Whitehead's fallacy of misplaced concreteness, a community of only 2,499 souls became a benighted village, while 2,501 residents made a cosmopolis. Such figures make the urban hegemony look less convincing. And in fact, gazing away from Manhattan's Great White Way any night during the decade following 1920, one could have seen wide, dark stretches of the continent where the roar of the twenties was muted indeed, where life was lived by a rhythm in which there was not the faintest echo of jazz.

The novelist, poet, and editor August Derleth—ten years old in 1919, twenty years old as the Jazz Age ended—remembered "hearing the howl of wolves in childhood." His experience of the twenties had been a world which marked the seasons not by greeting cards displayed in store windows but by the coming and going of plants and birds; a world of farming and gossip and fishing, of men conversing in harness shops, of dam building on rain-freshened brooks, of wild crab apples and woodchucks and harvest moons—all within shopping distance of Madison, Wisconsin. (Robert Frost, in the twenties and long afterward, wrote of such a world, but he had entered from the outside; Frost's readers were forever being surprised to learn that the "Yankee" poet with the northern New England accent had in fact been born in racy San Francisco.) Of course, urbanism and its burdens are relative. Even in August Derleth's Sac Prairie, whose population hovered just at the Census Bureau's mystical 2,500, there were those who felt the need of "going into the country for the summer . . . to get away from Sac Prairie."

Writers, and their most sympathetic protagonists, are commonly supposed to have fled such places in the twenties as fast as wheels or feet would carry them. But when the denizens of Sac Prairie ventured deep into urban America they seem only to have become desperately homesick. In a novella titled *Any Day Now*, published in 1938 but opening in the year 1916, Derleth took one of his characters to Chicago, where she lay awake at night listening to

> the thousand secret sounds of the city, the strange mysterious voices from the great, never-sleeping heart of this alien place, the sullen murmurs of a nocturnal life beyond her knowledge . . . nothing comforting and familiar, like the river's sound at sandbars, or cows lowing in night pastures, or cries of birds and furred creatures in the bottoms south of Sac Prairie.

Not that time stops in Sac Prairie, a real town Derleth sketched in fiction: "The German population filtered slowly away, to German cities [Milwaukee, Chicago, St. Louis] from the German villages along the Wisconsin." In the midwinter of 1917, Renna, the heroine of *Any Day Now*, as she reads of professors and students at the University of Wisconsin burning in effigy their own great antiwar Senator Robert LaFollette, begins "to be conscious of change, of something different in the air, some psychic thing, intangible and foreign: the hushed madness of the world around her." Presently World War I calls away the sons of Sac Prairie and Chicago and Brooklyn, and impersonally blows some of them apart in France. The lover Renna has rejected comes through the war unscathed only to kill himself back home in an automobile joy ride. Yet all of this is told offstage. The outer world is a *deus ex machina*, and although it causes people to age before their time, and to be hurt and die, such things had been happening to their forebears in that place for many generations.

If the figure 2,500 divided the rural from the urban in the twenties, multiplying it by ten should bring us well over to the indubitable city side. In fact, it gives the approximate population during the twenties of Waukegan, Illinois. According to Ray Bradbury, exactly 26,349 people resided there in the summer of 1928, a season he celebrated in his semifantastic, semiautobiographical novel *Dandelion Wine*. (Bradbury had actually turned eight years old in Waukegan that summer, but by an exercise of author's license his alter ego, Douglas Spaulding, is twelve—the timeless, archetypal boy-age, the age of Tarkington's Penrod.)

Bradbury's present-day readers, if they think of Waukegan at all, may remember the racking racial tensions there in the 1960s, complicated by the repressive tactics of the city's avowedly racist mayor; in the 1940s Waukegan was always good for a laugh as the home town of the radio comedian Jack Benny. In the twenties no racial tensions were noticed, and Benny was an unknown young man on the vaudeville circuit. But in the twenties Waukegan had also long since been locked into the structure of Chicago's North Shore suburbia, attached to the lake metropolis by interurban trolley. It was no Sac Prairie. And yet, incredibly, that is the way Bradbury seemed to have remembered it—as "this little town deep far away from everything, kept to itself by a river and a forest and a meadow and a lake." This streetcar subdivision forty miles north of Chicago became Green Town, Illinois.

A book like *Dandelion Wine* is a powerful tribute to the selectivity of memory and ought to caution us about relying on any fiction for history or biography. In the course of that remembered summer, Grandfather makes several batches of dandelion wine, but there is never a mention of Prohibition. Nearby Fort Sheridan, whence Grover Cleveland had summoned troops in 1894 to smash the Pullman Strike, is simply absent, as is the Great Lakes Naval Training Center; so is the city's own harbor on Lake Michigan, with its grimy coal docks. One would not know Waukegan was linked to the Chicago-Milwaukee industrial complex in any way. Bradbury's Green Town is all tree-shaded streets, Victorian frame houses, and ice-cream parlors, surrounded by a green ocean of presumably unpolluted prairie:

> The thin lapping of the great continental sea of grass and flower, starting out in lonely farm country, moved inward with the thrust of seasons. Each night the wilderness, the meadows, the far country flowed down-creek through ravine and welled up in town with a smell of grass and water. . . . It was this, then, the mystery of man seizing from the land and the land seizing back, year after year, that drew Douglas, knowing the towns never really won. . . . Any moment the town would capsize, go down and leave not a stir in the clover and weeds.

A generation steeped in ecology has taught us more than the mystery of man seizing from the land, but few and far between have been the instances of the land seizing back. It was, of course, an older Ray Bradbury who wrote of his boyhood that way, and between the boyhood and the writing a busy span of history stretched, one which included the atomic bomb. Since 1945, Bradbury's judgment that one's town might capsize at any moment—a victim not so much of untamed nature as of untamed technology—has appeared to many as less a poetic conceit than a rational possibility. But no hint of this later knowledge was allowed to enter his vision of 1928 in Green Town, Illinois.

More surprising, especially considering that when he did turn twelve years old Bradbury emigrated to Arizona, and two years thereafter to Los Angeles—a town that has erected roads and cars into its state religion—the automobile receives only scant mention in *Dandelion Wine*. The only car to figure importantly in the story is a deliberately symbolic "period piece," even for the twenties: a green electric runabout driven by two old maids at a top speed of "fifteen slow and pleasurable miles an hour."

Yet Bradbury's fictional Green Town is contemporaneous with Robert and Helen Lynd's real-life Middletown (Muncie, Indiana) and is located in the same midwestern flatland, and the painstaking sociologists who described Middletown in 1929 made it quite clear that the automobile was transforming the inhabitants' entire way of life. It was in the 1890s, not the 1920s, that Middletownians had sat on porch swings on summer evenings; in the Jazz Age they spent their evenings and Sunday afternoons in their cars. "Be off with smiles down the nearest road," cried a *Saturday Evening Post* double-spread car ad, "free, loose, and happy—bound for green wonderlands." The Lynds sarcastically pointed out that "the nearest lakes or hills are one hundred miles from Middletown in either direction and . . . an afternoon's motoring brings only mile upon mile of level stretches like Middletown itself." Were Muncie and Waukegan so very different from each other in the twenties? Was Green Town immune from the relentless modern pressures so trenchantly described in the Lynds' chapters titled "The Long Arm of the Job" and "Why Do They Work So Hard"?

Bradbury, interviewed on television the day after the first Apollo moon shot—an exploit he admired—confessed that he had never learned to drive a car. That a graduate of a Los Angeles high school could so escape the ruthlessly conformist pressures of Southern California is a tribute either to the staying power of American individualism or to the even stronger molding force of a town in the Midwest. No doubt the suppression of the automobile from his Waukegan remembrance bespeaks a personality trait of his own. Yet is it also possible that a boy growing up in what we have usually thought of as a rapidly urbanizing America in the twenties *typically* remembered his early surroundings as a Green Town? Perhaps a growing boy, perceiving as a trackless desert or jungle the vacant lot his father saw only as a piece of undeveloped property, lived in a mental world altogether foreign to the one that journalists and historians have set down and dignified as "history."

Those elders he recalls on their porch swings in the summer of 1928 may in fact have been talking of Al Smith and Al Capone, of war debts and "flaming youth," of Prohibition and the stock market and Henry Ford. But in Bradbury's remembrance, all such content of their talk disappeared, leaving only its sensory and ritual qualities. Perhaps such an account is not poetic embroidery but accurate reporting of how it all sounded to a Douglas Spaulding at the age of eight, or twelve:

> Douglas sprawled back on the dry porch planks, completely contented and reassured by these voices, which would speak on through eternity, flow in a stream of murmurings over his body, over his closed eyelids, into his drowsy ears, for all time.

Through hindsight we know that it was not to be for all time. The Depression would strike Waukegan as it struck the rest of America, and young Bradbury and his family would find themselves on the open road in quest not of joy rides but of economic survival, as they rolled southwestward in a beat-up old car and "blew tires and flung fan belts like lost garters down Highway 66."

Main Street, the leading fiction best-seller of 1920, has seemed to many of its readers a savage indictment of small-town America, and Sinclair Lewis's Gopher Prairie, Minnesota, must certainly be called a less benign microcosmos than either August Derleth's Sac Prairie or Bradbury's Green Town. Yet Sinclair Lewis told August Derleth in November 1937 that if there had ever been a "revolt against the village" by America's regional writers, as the critic Carl Van Doren had asserted and about which most literary scholarship since has concurred, Lewis himself had not been part of it: "The trouble with critics," he declared, "is that they like to create a horse and ride it to death."

"Then you didn't feel you were rebelling against the village?" Derleth asked. "Nothing of it," said Lewis. "I dislike some things about village life. I disliked some things about city life, too. I got out of Sauk Center [the original Gopher Prairie] because there weren't any opportunities for me there. Carl [Van Doren] said I couldn't stand the dull people. Well, . . . I loved those people—Carol Kennicott and Sam and Champ and Will Kennicott and Bea. I put into my books what I saw and what I felt. I didn't think it was rebellious then. I don't think it is now, either."

Seventeen years had elapsed since the publication of *Main Street* when he said this. Perhaps Lewis was only doing what countless others have done, romanticizing a reality it is too late to change. The hard historical fact is that he had had to leave Sauk Center, and died in far-off Rome. Or perhaps Lewis was that most typical American, the romantic disguised as a realist, as Vernon Parrington said he was. Certainly in some of his earlier writings the Romantic came unabashedly to the fore.

In 1918 Lewis wrote a serial for the *Saturday Evening Post* that when published in hard covers the following year was titled *Free Air*. Its hero hails from the hamlet of Schoenstrom ("Neither the village itself nor the nearby *Strom*," Lewis wrote, "is really *schoen*."), but village life is not what this novel is about. At heart it is a celebration of the automobile, and most of it takes place on a motor tour from the Twin Cities to Washington State. The "free air" of the title refers not only to the signs that used to appear over the air pumps of American gas stations but also to psychic freedom—and, Lewis hints, the political or social liberation—that was to be experienced on the open road.

The story's plot has been dismissed as soap opera: will high-born Claire Boltwood of Brooklyn Heights spurn her fashionable, snobbish friends to marry Milt Daggett, the hardworking garage owner–mechanic from Schoenstrom, Minnesota? The theme is as ancient as social rank itself. What is unique and touching here is Lewis's notion that the "free air" of the highway his characters travel is the transforming social instrument through which Claire's "adventure into democracy"—and at the same time Milt's growth out of provincialism—can be accomplished. Milt Daggett's road is like Huck Finn's river, its placid, natural freedom contrasted with the corruptions of civilization to be found on its banks. Back of Claire's pilgrimage is East Coast high society, and at its end is the even sillier social pretensions of wealthy Seattlites, who "believed that their West was desirable in proportion as it became like the East; and that they, though

Westerners, were as superior to workmen with hard hands as was Brooklyn Heights itself." Renouncing the polar East and West, an emancipated Claire tells off her class-conscious relatives, and she and Milt elope.

Plot aside, the theme of redemption-by-highway is not calculated to speak to the contemporary American locked into the urban-suburban commuter stream. If Claire has discovered that "these Minnesota country roads had no respect for her polite experience on Long Island parkways," the contemporary reader may well reflect that driving on Long Island parkways is now a good deal less polite than driving on country roads. But we are in 1916. Only a few years earlier, Henry B. Joy, president of the Packard Motor Car Company, had asked the Packard distributor in Omaha for directions to the road west and been told, "There isn't any."

"Then how do I go?" Joy reportedly asked.

"Follow me and I'll show you." They drove westward to a barbedwire fence, at which the executive was told: "Just take down the fence and drive on and when you come to the next fence, take that down and go on again." According to Henry Joy, "A little farther and there were no fences, no fields, nothing but two ruts across the prairie." A short distance beyond, however, he found "plenty of ruts, deep, grass-grown ones, marked by rotted bits of broken wagons."

For Lewis's early automobilists it was still possible on an American road to pass an occasional prairie schooner. As recently as 1880, five years before Sinclair Lewis was born, the exclusive responsibility for providing rural roads had rested with local governments, and the chief means of financing road construction had been the medieval *corvée*; freedom-loving Americans preferred to call it "working out the road tax."

In practice, these daily stints seem usually to have been leisurely, sociable affairs. Men gathered with their teams, scrapers, and plows, casually scratched at the road, sat on the fence (according to one observer) "smoking clay pipes and swapping stale stories"—and by the next rain, as often as not, the product of their handiwork was again impassable. If an occasional over-eager local supervisor secured a well-graded and drained stretch of highway, his achievement reached only as far as his political jurisdiction—some three or four miles. In 1912, according to one account, America's highway system consisted of "two million miles of unrelated, unconnected roads, broken into thousands of star-like independent groups, each railroad station or market town the center of a star."

By the time Sinclair Lewis wrote *Free Air*, this system—if that be the right word for it—was undergoing rapid and radical transformation. The Progressive Era had seen the rise of the Good Roads Movement—a motley alliance of bicycle manufacturers, railroad interests, automobilists (the progenitors of the present AAA), professional highway engineers, and the National Grange—which effectively propagandized for highway improvement. The presence in the Good Roads Movement of the Grange, once a radical farmers' organization, is a little sad. Rural leaders apparently did not believe that better highways would accelerate the drain of the farm population away to the cities and so threaten their way of life. "Year after year the human tide flows from the country to the city," declaimed Senator John Bankhead of Alabama in a rolling burst of southern oratory.

> Do not let us have great mobs of the unemployed, combining the scum of Europe with the misled boys from our American farms, so long as there are millions of acres of land waiting to be tilled and homes waiting to be built. Good roads will make farm life attractive; they will bring the isolated dweller closer to his neighbor, and I feel confident they will check the movement of our rural population to the great cities.

Nineteen-sixteen, the year in which the action in *Free Air* is supposedly taking place, also saw the passage of the Federal Road Aid Act. By 1917 all the states had full-fledged highway departments, and in 1921 an additional Federal Highway Act was passed. Although national management of highways was still extremely limited in scope, here was a powerful new force for administrative centralization and control.

What Senator Bankhead had expected to pour out along this growing national network were settlers, sharing the moral rejuvenation many Americans believed had invigorated the original pioneers; what came instead was tourism. "A stream of tourists bowls or bumps along all the open trails from Maine to California," wrote Anne O'Hare McCormick in *The New York Times* for August 13, 1922. "Camp fires and tent villages mark its daily course. It draws Main Street across a continent and changes a sparsely settled countryside into a vast and populous suburbia"—not, perhaps, what the idealists of *Free Air* had in mind. After the Great Crash there came a different wave, for whom camping out was not a lark but a tragic necessity; it culminated in the "Okies," pushing their dilapidated cars from the Dust Bowl toward California's promised land. In fiction, Sinclair Lewis rounded out the decade of the twenties by creating the pathetic Sam

Dodsworth, who retires from manufacturing automobiles just in time to see his marriage destroyed.

But of these grim modern futures Claire Boltwood and Milt Daggett are oblivious. When they drive out on the road away from Gopher Prairie, although it takes them eventually to Seattle, in another sense it has not taken them very far: Lewis's native village goes with them. The rural milieu of *Main Street* extends out along that road and is heightened into transcendence by its passage:

> Never a tawny-beached ocean has the sweetness of the prairie slew. Rippling and blue, with long grass up to its edge, a spot of dancing light set in the miles of rustling wheat, it retains even in July, on an afternoon of glare and brazen locusts, the freshness of a spring morning. . . . For two days of sunshine and drying mud she followed a road flung straight across flat wheatlands, then curving among low hills. Often there were no fences; she was so intimately in among the grain that the fenders of the car brushed wheat stalks, and she became no stranger, but a part of all this vast-horizoned land. . . . Claire had discovered America, and she felt stronger, and all her days were colored with the sun.

"There never was anything to this revolt against the village business," snapped the aged Edgar Lee Masters when August Derleth put the question to him in 1940. "We didn't do any such thing. Maybe Lewis backed away from something that hurt him, but he wasn't rebelling against the American small town any more than I was, and my guess is he'd have stayed there if the people had accepted him as he was." But of course, they had not. Perhaps the experience of such men was not so much a revolt against the village as a rejection by the village. Not only literary men underwent this experience; George McGovern in the summer of 1972 could testify to a similar home-town reaction. "When I came back to Mitchell after graduate school, I found that my progressive ideas had outpaced the conservative views of my town, of people who had always before dealt with me as a nonpolitical person. That has been a source of unease with me ever since. I feel part of the town doesn't like me anymore."

Sigmund Freud claimed that by the time a person is six years old his general character is formed. If Freud was right, then McGovern—impossible as it might have seemed to some of the youths who followed him in the Age of Aquarius—was also a product of the twenties. In 1928, the year Ray Bradbury celebrated as the vintage season for dandelion wine in Waukegan, the six-year-old future senator moved with his parents from Avon, South

Dakota, the almost invisible hamlet where he had been born, to Mitchell, South Dakota. Mitchell's population was upwards of eight thousand, well above the abstract line the Census Bureau defined as urban but not far from the five thousand Sinclair Lewis had allotted to Gopher Prairie. And yet, though in the year he won the Democratic presidential nomination, he felt that part of Mitchell didn't like him anymore, quite obviously McGovern's relationship to the town was not exactly one of estrangement:

> I still love to go back to Mitchell and wander up and down those streets. It just kind of reassures me again that there is a place that I know thoroughly, where the roots are deep.
>
> There are the big old cottonwood trees, the big American elms, the little roadways in and out of town that have always been there—without much work ever done on them. . . . Everything had a place, a specific definition.
>
> I think that it makes it easier to find one's place in the world. When people talk about the small-town sense of community, the role of the family, relationship with the neighbors, fellowship of the church, school spirit—I had all those things, and they meant a great deal to me in providing guidelines, a foundation, a personal security.

History as it is made is always more untidy than what gets written down. Were a political analyst to look for the influences of the twenties upon the politics of the early seventies, surely he would have looked almost anywhere except in South Dakota. Imagine what H. L. Mencken, with his contempt for the rural "booboisie," might have made of some of McGovern's cornier lines. Imagine the panic of an embattled science professor, testifying in favor of evolution at the Scopes trial, at the thought of a fundamentalist Methodist minister's son as a candidate for the presidency; one who, moreover, voiced political opinions with much of the preacher's tone of ethical certainty. Imagine, on the other hand, the views of the stiff-backed Andrew Mellon, Harding's and Coolidge's millionaire secretary of the treasury, at McGovern's plans for tax reform.

George McGovern clearly did not think of his rural upbringing in the 1920s as something he had had to cast aside in order to go into the "new politics" of the 1970s; he had never had to be radicalized. His mature political radicalism and his severely traditional upbringing seemed to him a coherent whole:

> I do consider myself a radical in the sense that I am willing to go beyond the conventional view. I think fundamental change is what's needed, so in that sense I don't mind people calling me a radical. I've so often wondered

whether those plains where I grew up don't invite you to the conclusion that you can move easily in any direction you want to go—a mood quieting and yet restive at the same time.

Towns small enough to breed personal identity out of close and continuous face-to-face relationships but at the same time the possibility, the challenge, of testing that identity by going away: the dialectic is as old as the Republic. Rural America was never quite peasant America, and much of the liberal urban intellectual's alarm over "inherent rural conservatism," both in the twenties and afterward, was wide of the mark. Speaking of large national and international goals a few days before the 1972 Democratic National Convention, McGovern concluded: "In a sense, I guess these are small-town values-neighborliness, responsibility for others—extensions of what I was always taught to believe."

There is rich historical irony in the fact that a man with such a background developed a charismatic appeal to just those elements of the population for whom such supportive relationships had become least possible: the floating students, intense in their four-year friendships but transient, facing vocational choices ranging from desperate to absurd; the migrant workers and ghetto dwellers, deprived by their lethal environments of normal community or family ties; the liberal professionals with their primary loyalties not to a place but to a guild, accustomed to forming and coolly breaking relationships with each move up the institutional ladder. Whatever moved the insurgent forces that suddenly coalesced behind McGovern's leadership in a few scant months in 1972, surely it was not "identification"—at least not as Main Street Americans had identified with Harry Truman or as college professors had identified with Adlai Stevenson. The upstart young politicians who ousted the old professionals for a season called what they were doing the "new" politics, but in the process they found themselves in step with something very old. If, as Henry May wrote, there was an "end of American innocence" even before the twenties, some Americans seem never to have gotten the message.

CHAPTER THREE

The Campaign of 1928

A Study in Political Folklore

*A*t an early stage in the presidential campaign of 1960, Denis Brogan, interpreting that campaign from a foreign perspective, wrote: "American politicians live to an extraordinary degree by historical shorthand, by the memory of the past . . . episodes that 'prove' that this *must* happen or that this *cannot* happen. And high on the list of such political rules of thumb is the belief that 'Al' Smith was defeated in 1928 because he was a Catholic."

Up until election night of 1960, and indeed in some worried minds up until the meeting of the electoral college in December, the conclusion commonly drawn from this rule of thumb was that any Catholic American who sought the presidency could expect the same fate as Smith. But even before the nomination and election of John F. Kennedy as the first Catholic president of the United States, the rule of thumb had begun to be challenged. Richard Hofstadter, for example, said in an article published early in 1960: "There was not a Democrat alive, Protestant or Catholic, who could have beaten Hoover in 1928." John D. Hicks in a review in 1958 declared: "Had Smith been nominated in 1932, he would almost certainly

An earlier form of this essay appeared in the *Wisconsin Magazine of History* 46 (Summer 1963): 263–72.

have won." And in 1952 Samuel Lubell, in an arresting sentence which did much to reshape the historiography of the 1920s, maintained that the 1928 election demonstrated, not the fatal weakness of a Catholic candidate for the presidency, but precisely the reverse: "Before the Roosevelt Revolution there was an Al Smith revolution."

Yet political folklore dies hard. As late as 1956, the year in which the first American Catholic to occupy the White House began his spectacular drive to power, Edmund A. Moore examined the 1928 presidential campaign and warned that the supposed "unwritten law" against Catholic presidents might still be in effect; therefore, politicians who were Catholics would be better advised to aim at the relatively modest office of the vice-presidency as a more realistic personal and political goal. Two years later, in the denouement of his lucid and moving biography of Al Smith, Oscar Handlin wrote that at the time of Smith's death, "no Catholic . . . could aspire to be President, whatever other avenues of advance might be open."

"Can a Catholic be President?" As early as 1924, at least one American Catholic, Martin Conboy, put the question in such a way as to imply the answer, Yes. In that era, when Alfred E. Smith was governor of the nation's most populous state, there had already been a number of Catholic governors and senators and two chief justices of the United States. "Short of the presidency, Catholics have held every position of importance within the gift of their fellow citizens"—therefore, Conboy reasoned, why not the presidency? The closing of the question in the affirmative as of 1960 invites at least a reexamination of the question as of 1924 and especially as of 1928.

One of the discoveries of the 1960 election was that when Americans asked themselves whether a Catholic could be president of the United States, it was necessary to specify the kind of Catholic. During 1959 and 1960, the thought of John F. Kennedy as a prospective president prompted all kinds of misgivings, both among liberals and conservatives, which had nothing whatever to do with religion. Mutatis mutandis the same may be presumed of Al Smith in his day—although the misgivings roused by the man from Fulton Street would have been of a different sort from those roused by the man from Hyannis Port. One of President Kennedy's preelection critics, Douglass Cater, for example, summed up his impression of the candidate in the title of an article: "The Cool Eye of John F. Kennedy." It is difficult to imagine anyone making precisely that assessment of Smith. Stock campaign jokes of 1960 about the Democratic candidate's Harvard accent and his father's millions—related, no doubt, to the "country squire" stereotype of Franklin Roosevelt which was then still popular among aging Republicans—were a far cry indeed from the Al Smith portrayed in some of the more savage political cartoons of 1928: a bibulous, ungrammatical roughneck.

Professor Moore in his study of the 1928 campaign has shown that the anti-Smith feeling contained a considerable element of sheer social snobbery, connected perhaps with the traditional middle-class Republican image of the Opposition as shiftless good-for-nothings—an image classically set forth in 1896 in William Allen White's widely circulated editorial "What's the Matter with Kansas?" "Can you imagine Al Smith in the White House?" the Republican national committeewoman for Texas asked a WCTU meeting in Houston, visualizing for them a President Smith committing gaucheries of grammar and etiquette, and more to the point for that audience, "Can you imagine *Mrs.* Smith in the White House?" Those last words would have rather a different ring had they been said about the former Jacqueline Bouvier!

While Moore's point on the effect of snobbery in the 1928 election is well taken, mere snobbism cannot fully account for the detestation of Smith on the part of many who, like Al, could claim a heritage from the wrong side of the tracks. The most militant of all the anti-Smith forces, the Klansmen, liked to think of themselves as plain and even poor people (which some of them were), "open to the charge of being 'hicks' and 'rubes' and 'drivers of second hand Fords.'" For such voters to concur with WCTU ladies from Houston, there had to be something more than simple social condescension to unite them. The common bond most frequently assumed has been anti-Catholicism. But the Woman's Christian Temperance Union had quite another primary concern, and the members of the Ku Klux Klan spent part of their energy in destroying whiskey stills. An inescapable political issue throughout the 1920s for any candidate, regardless of his church or his manners, was Prohibition.

Common causes which unite rather widely disparate kinds of Americans—anti-Masonry, Free Soil, free silver, world peace, and more recently antisubversion—are, of course, an old chapter in the Republic's history. When they have been comparatively short-lived or when they have not seemed clearly related to issues which are alive for a later generation, the emotions such movements can arouse have often seemed inexplicably intense. Robert Moats Miller has wisely noted: "Nothing is more diffi- cult than for an individual indifferent to a certain issue to appreciate that to others it might be of transcendent importance." It can only be said again that Prohibition *was* deemed to be of transcendent importance by millions of Americans, both "wet" and "dry"; the sheer bulk of serious public discussion of the issue during the 1920s is enough to document the point. Since the antiliquor crusade of the twentieth century emerged from nineteenth-century conflicts which pitted Protestant against Protestant, it would be begging the question to insist that the prohibitionists' case against Smith was nothing but a cover for anti-Catholicism. Hoover was "sound" on liquor; Smith was not. For many a voter, the issue was as simple as that.

Edmund A. Moore, in the able study of the 1928 election previously referred to, up to a point makes this same judgment: "There can be no doubt that the enforcement, by statute, of the ban on alcoholic beverages was an issue of great importance in its own right." But he warns us that "Prohibition . . . was often made to play hide-and-seek with the religious issue," and he suggests that the extensive debate on Prohibition may have been a sublimated version of a debate on Catholicism, frank discussion of which was "limited by a widespread sense of delicacy and shame."

But to speculate on what discussants *may* have meant—the "latent" as op- posed to the "manifest" content of their discussion, so to speak—is to play a very dangerous historiographic game indeed. Having in mind some of the imputations of religious prejudice in the 1960 campaign—as in, for example, the journalistic treatment of the West Virginia presidential primary—perhaps the historian of the 1928 campaign ought to be less con- cerned with searching out anti-Catholicism assumed to be masquerading as something else than with avoiding the error of assuming what might be called "anti-Catholicism by association." This effort, which would now be superfluous in the case of John Kennedy, is still necessary when discussing Al Smith.

And yet a further pitfall awaits the historian of Prohibition, after disentangling it from anti-Catholicism: the temptation to construe such a question in terms of equivalent *political* ideas, so that the "wets" be- come "liberal" and the "drys" become "conservative." This reading of the question then becomes assimilable to a liberal-versus-conservative reading of the Smith-Hoover campaign more generally, especially when one notices that four of the conservative "Solid South" states carried by Herbert Hoover were subsequently to be twice carried by Dwight Eisenhower, and three of them again in 1960 by Richard Nixon. But in the case of Prohibition, at least, these left-right categories of political ideology break down; as I have shown elsewhere, a progressive, social welfare, and even radical outlook pervaded the antiliquor movement, especially in its incipient stages and to some extent throughout its existence. So unquestionably liberal a journal as the *Christian Century* justified supporting Hoover in 1928 on prohibitionist grounds; and one social radical in 1932, finding the Democrats, the Republicans, and the Socialists either insufficiently liberal, insufficiently "dry," or both, by the process of elimination voted Communist!

Conversely, there were "wet" conservatives. Senator Oscar Underwood, for example, condemned the Eighteenth Amendment in his later years because it "challenged the integrity of the compact between the states" and compelled people "to live their lives in the mold prescribed by the power of government." The Alabama senator argued, furthermore, that the "drys" could no more force their interpretation of the Eighteenth Amendment on the Wets than the North could force its interpretation of the Fourteenth Amendment on the South. When one reflects that this same conservative southern senator had courageously denounced the Ku Klux Klan at the Democratic National Convention of 1924 and had thereby ruined his own chance to become a presidential nominee, the campaign of 1928 which followed becomes even harder to see in liberal-versus-conservative terms.

Yet Smith himself is persistently seen by his latter-day admirers as a liberal who became conservative only upon the failure of his liberal expectations. He was not always seen in this light, however, by his contemporaries. Walter Lippmann wrote in 1925: "[Smith] is really a perfectly conservative man about property. . . . He believes in the soundness of the established order. . . . He is what a conservative ought to be always if he knew his business." When one finds a *New York Times* story on June 27, 1928, the second day of the Democratic National Convention, headlined "Stocks up in 'Smith Market' as Raskob tells business it need not fear the governor," one begins to understand what Lippmann was talking about:

"Market leaders such as General Motors, United States Steel, Anaconda Copper, Allied Chemical and New York Central, had a sharp run-up. . . . Buying orders poured in so rapidly . . . that Wall Street began talking of a 'Smith market.' Friends of the governor were said to be actively in the market, prepared to demonstrate that the financial and business interests are not hostile to his candidacy."

One of these friends of the governor was John J. Raskob, whose remarks, the *Times* noted, apparently without irony, "frequently have stimulated buying enthusiasm in the stock market." Franklin Roosevelt, among others, had serious misgivings about Smith's choice of Raskob as Democratic national chairman, largely on account of this Wall Street taint—yet some of Smith's putative liberalism has rubbed off on the General Motors financier, who is described in Oscar Handlin's biography of Al Smith as "another poor boy who had come up in the world." Raskob grew up, Handlin writes, in "the free-and-easy atmosphere of Detroit where religious prejudice seemed altogether out of place." Remembering the notorious anti-Semitism of Henry Ford, who was president of the leading competitor of General Motors, one is a little surprised at hearing Detroit described as a city altogether free of religious prejudice; here is another indication that a straight liberal-conservative interpretation of the campaign of 1928 must be burdened with more ideological freight than it can carry.

Moore, in contrast to Handlin, sees Raskob's role in the campaign in terms not of liberalism but of expediency: the Democrats had to win some of the business community away from its prosperous love affair with Hoover Republicanism, and Raskob was their instrument for this purpose. But had not the candidacies of staunch Gold Standard advocate Alton B. Parker in 1904 and corporation counsel John W. Davis in 1924 demonstrated that Democratic attempts to beat Republican conservatism at its own game usually failed? Moore does note that Raskob's appointment as national chairman "seemed like an insult to the dry, Protestant, rural South." Was it not equally an insult to the Democratic party's anticorporate, antispeculative Progressives and liberals?

If, then, the campaign of 1928 will not reduce to a campaign between liberals and conservatives, snobs and plain people, or "wets" and "drys," are we left with Protestant against Catholic? Not necessarily. Let us return again to the contemporary assessment of Smith by Walter Lippmann: "The

Governor's more hasty friends show an intolerance when they believe that Al Smith is the victim of purely religious prejudice. . . . There is an opposition to Smith which is as authentic and, it seems to me, as poignant as his support. It is inspired by the feeling that the clamorous life of the city should not be acknowledged as the American ideal."

Closely allied to the image of the corner saloon in American folklore has been the image of the eastern city slicker. It is a venerable one; dissipated urban vice in contrast to abstemious rural virtue are themes as old in history as are cities themselves. In America, as witness Jefferson's *Notes on Virginia* and Royall Tyler's play *The Contrast*, they antedate the Constitution. There is also a long-standing tradition of the rural South and West perennially arrayed politically against the urban East, almost regardless of the specific political issues confronting America at any given moment. The anti-Smith country in the election of 1928 was, by and large, the old Bryan country—which suggests that the Prohibition issue, and the Klan issue, and possibly even the Catholic issue were surface stirrings of animosities of another kind. It may be noted in passing that this same trans-Mississippi Bryan country of 1896, which had become Hoover country by 1928, was to become Nixon country in 1960 and Goldwater country in the maneuverings which followed. Perhaps President Kennedy and Governor Smith had more in common as actors of an American political role than simply their religion, or their status as (by definition) liberal Democrats.

"The principal obstacle in Smith's way," wrote a contemporary observer of the preconvention maneuverings of 1928, "never becomes palpable. . . . It lies in the fact that to millions of Americans he . . . embodies something alien. Not something alien in race or religion, but something alien to themselves . . . something they do not understand and which they feel does not understand them. . . . Some of the perturbed Methodist clergymen in the South opposed to Smith's nomination unconsciously revealed what really moves them most profoundly . . . when they said he was 'New York minded.' " Had these words been written by one of those same perturbed Methodist clergymen, or indeed by any other Protestant, or even by a secularist liberal such as Lippmann, they could be cited as merely an unusually tortuous rationalization for anti-Catholicism. But they were written by a Catholic and were printed in the Catholic liberal weekly *Commonweal*. And, conscious that bogeymen are not slain by one magazine article, the writer, Charles Willis Thompson, returned to the fray some months later in the *Catholic World* with a piece entitled "The Tammany Monster." This second article was a ringing defense of the "monster" against attacks by the kind of outlanders (Thompson mentioned Iowa, Nebraska, Oklahoma, and Little Rock, Arkansas) who viewed the mysterious East and all its works as evil, saying "Tammany and Wall Street are the same thing, aren't they?"

Smith's own managers and friends were aware of this widespread fear of the urban East in the American hinterland. Norman Hapgood and Henry Moskowitz, in their campaign biography of Smith in 1927 (significantly titled *Up From the City Streets*) faced the problem squarely. The story of Al Smith, they wrote, "suggests that in the future our vast cities may do better by humanity than we have feared." Specifically, the politics characteristic of great cities, abhorred by some as machine or Tammany politics, might have creative possibilities undreamed of in the Mississippi Valley. Smith in particular "has been a product of the machine and . . . has remained a member of it, and at the same time has become a leader of the most progressive thought of the United States." Corner saloon politics, these authors argued, was not in essence very different from country store politics. Far from regarding "the machine" as oppressive and corrupt, the urban poor among whom Al Smith had grown up "were convinced that Tammany Hall was kind to them." Pressing this interpretation perhaps a shade too far in their enthusiasm, Hapgood and Moskowitz defined machine politics as "neighborliness—which on election day is translated into votes."

For the rural voter, who on successive days during the spring of 1928 might have seen headlines such as "Chicago's Election Starts with Kidnapping" and "Deneen Ticket Leads; His Candidate Slain," such a concept of big-city neighborliness was rather hard to take. New York was, of course, not Chicago, especially in 1928 when the Capone organization was near its peak; but to the rural mind one big city was much like another. With this problem in mind, local leaders in some rural areas—not all of them Democrats—strove to bridge the chasm between their constituents' world and Al Smith.

One of the most interesting of these attempts, particularly in light of what happened later in the campaign, was made by the Republican editor of the *Emporia Gazette*, William Allen White. Writing to Franklin D. Roosevelt on February 11, 1928, on behalf of the Kansas State Editorial Association,

White invited Al Smith to come out to Kansas, "the center of the world which Smith does not know and which does not know Smith." "Smith is supposed to have horns and a tail out west," he wrote, and a confrontation between the New York governor and a bipartisan group of western newspaper editors "would do more for him politically than any other one thing he might possibly do." Frank Freidel noted that Roosevelt tried to persuade Smith to accept this invitation but failed; in that failure may lie a subtle indication of one reason for the failure of Smith's entire campaign.

The aftermath of this friendly gesture was saddening and distasteful. Throughout his life, William Allen White was the kind of partisan who can be a man of good will toward the Opposition "three and a half years out of every four," as Franklin Roosevelt himself later put it. As the campaign grew hotter than it ever could have been in February, even in 1928, an organization man "regular" enough to have supported Harding and Coolidge when the time came could have been expected to be drawn into the fray against Smith, even though White credited him with "one of the important brains now functioning in American politics." But, as Professor Moore has shown at length in his study of the campaign, White's attacks on Smith went far beyond the generally acceptable limits of campaign behavior. White wrote that Smith's record as governor showed the New Yorker to be soft not only on Prohibition but also on gambling and prostitution. Worse, when he realized the enormity of such a charge when unproved, his retraction was grudging and ambiguous. It was, Moore concludes, a shocking lapse in a theretofore conspicuously honorable political career.

Professor Moore conjoins William Allen White's charges against the governor with those of the fundamentalist Baptist leader in New York City, Rev. John Roach Straton—a conjunction which strongly implies that White's and Straton's warfare with Smith came down essentially to the same thing, namely anti-Catholicism. White in this period of the campaign saw Al Smith as a threat to "the whole Puritan civilization which has built a sturdy, orderly nation," and Moore comments: "Of course one important facet of the 'whole Puritan civilization' was its staunchly Protestant character." Moore finds this attitude of the Kansas editor particularly "confused and distressing" because White, in a book which was already in press while these attacks were going on, "was about to present Smith in an essentially favorable light."

A rereading of *Masks in a Pageant*, the work referred to, led me to

33

a conclusion somewhat different from Professor Moore's. References to "Puritanism" and "a Puritan civilization" occur throughout White's writings in contexts having little or nothing to do with Smith or Catholicism. His apt characterization of Calvin Coolidge as "a Puritan in Babylon," for example, loses all its bite if the most cautious of all of America's presidents is made merely a *Protestant* in Babylon. What worried White far more than Al Smith's religious affiliation, or even his "wet" sympathies, was the old Jeffersonian bugbear of the great city as an enemy of liberty. In *Masks in a Pageant*, White was trying not only to reassure his readers about Smith but also to reassure himself about Smith's background.

William Allen White was aware that great cities had brought forth American presidents before, and he cited Theodore Roosevelt—whose faithful vassal he himself had been—and Chester A. Arthur. But neither of these two men "was purely urbanite" (recall Mark Hanna's "damn cowboy" epithet hurled at TR, for example), whereas Al Smith was "urbanite with an urbanity unstrained . . . city born, city bred, 'city broke,' city minded, and city hearted." White's urban reader might well have asked, why not? The Kansas editor did his best to agree: "There is no reason why the back alley cannot produce as good moral, spiritual, mental, and physical timber for politics as the backwoods. . . . The streets educated [Smith] as the woods and fields educated Lincoln." And yet, backwoods and back alley were inevitably headed for conflict in the twentieth century; "industrial democracy," White concluded, "was destined to "struggle for supremacy with . . . rural democracy—the America of our past."

As a determined political progressive, White was intellectually on the side of the new order; as a product of the Kansas frontier he was emotionally drawn to the old. The most revealing fact about the Al Smith sketch in White's *Masks in a Pageant* is that the author included it at the end of the book in a section titled "The Young Princes of Democracy"—and his other young prince was Mayor William "Big Bill" Thompson of Chicago. The Al Smith essay was, in the main, favorable to Smith, but Al and Big Bill were of the same species in White's mind. In the epigraph to that part of the book, White wrote: "When we have sloughed off our rural philosophy—our fundamental Puritanism—we shall crown the young princes. In the meantime the warning is plain: 'Put not your trust in princes!' "

With mistrust of White's sort rampant throughout Bryan country, it is understandable that practicing Democrats in the spring of 1928 cast about for a candidate who could hold Al Smith's constituents without alienating William Allen White's—ideally a Catholic who was not one of the young princes. Predictably, some of them found him, and in a state even more rural than Kansas. On March 4, Senator Thomas J. Walsh of Montana tossed his hat into the ring. On May 1, he was knocked out of the running in the California presidential primary, but in the meantime he had posed a major obstacle for the hypothesis of an "unwritten law" governing Catholic candidates. What is one to make of the fact that, in Professor Moore's words, "The two leading candidates for the Democratic nomination in 1928 were Catholic [and] one of them was nominated?" If the Walsh candidacy was a stalking-horse to divide the Catholic vote, as has been suggested, clearly the effort was unsuccessful; and if it was a serious bid for the presidency, then the "unwritten law" was already well on its way to being a dead letter. In either case, conclusions about toleration in American life more optimistic than those which have been customarily drawn for the 1920s would seem to be in order.

CHAPTER FOUR

The Forgotten Catholic Candidate

Thomas J. Walsh

On the eve of the Democratic National Convention of 1928, Bishop James M. Cannon of the Methodist Episcopal Church, South, published one last jeremiad against that convention's probable nominee. "Governor Smith," he wrote (in the *Nation*, a journal not usually consulted by southern Methodists), "is personally, ecclesiastically, aggressively, irreconcilably Wet"—a political adjective then applied to whole-hearted opponents of prohibition. "He was a frequenter of saloons while they existed," the bishop went on; "he put his foot on the brass rail and blew the foam off the glass"—and he then quoted a statement by *Nation* editor Oswald Garrison Villard in a manner which implied that Al Smith had not basically reformed. The New York governor was, Villard wrote, "ineradicably Tammany-branded . . . a pupil, a follower, a protege of Croker, Foley, and Murphy"; for thirty-three years he had been a worker and leader in an organization which the *Nation* itself had recently called "a society held together by the cohesive power of public plunder." Significantly, the bishop did not attack Smith's Catholicism directly; the Catholic Church, he noted, was "wet," and he certainly thought it "likely that Gov-

An earlier form of this essay appeared in the *Pacific Northwest Quarterly* 55 (January 1964): 1–8.

ernor Alfred E. Smith is influenced by the views of the Pope and cardinals on the subject of prohibition."

By the time this statement appeared in print, the prevention of Al Smith's nomination for president seemed most unlikely; on the page facing the bishop's essay, a news story from Democratic National Convention headquarters in Houston declared: "It's All Al Smith." But the kind of problem posed by Bishop James Cannon and his constituents had been worrying Democratic politicians, professional and amateur, for quite some time. The 1924 convention had impaled the party on the horns of a dilemma: no anti-Smith candidate could capture the loyalty of Smith's followers, and vice versa. But was there not a third alternative? The *Nation* titled Cannon's article "Al Smith: Catholic, Tammany, Wet." Could a candidate have been found to whom only part of this description would have applied, who would thus have been more "available," in the political sense, than Al Smith?

In 1932 such a candidate was to be nominated. Franklin D. Roosevelt was a New Yorker but not affiliated with Tammany, a "wet" but not a Catholic. Early in the campaign of 1928, a more novel shuffling of these adjectives had been attempted: a Catholic who was neither Tammany nor "wet." Such a candidate, it was pointed out, would have started from beginnings as humble as Al Smith's, but he would also be a resident of a rural state; he would be "a relentless foe of corruption and fraud, a bone-dry prohibitionist . . . a lover of the Constitution, and a devout Catholic who has no political enemies because of his faith." During the presidential primaries of 1928, there were those who hoped that they had found their man, as witness the above statement, which appeared in a *New York Times* feature story on the candidacy of Thomas J. Walsh, senior senator from Montana.

Let us examine certain of these specifications. A "bone-dry prohibitionist" Senator Walsh certainly was. One biographer writes that Walsh took the pledge when he made his First Communion and that he remained a "dry," "both personally and politically," throughout a long public career in a state where the mores were generally accounted to be wringing wet. J. Leonard Bates, a close and acute student of Walsh's career, suggested that this Catholic senator's persistence in prohibitionism can be accounted for "in part by his feeling that too many men (friends of his) had gone wrong in Montana on account of liquor."

But whatever the cause, Walsh's "dry" professions were taken at face value by other "drys." Josephus Daniels, for example, whose vigorous efforts to dry up the United States Navy in World War I were still painfully remembered in some quarters, came out for Walsh as his party's nominee. In the California presidential primary, where Walsh was described as being "as dry as McAdoo professes to be," the Anti-Saloon League backed the Walsh ticket against McAdoo, who had led the "dry" forces against Smith in 1924. Mrs. Ella Boole, the president of the Woman's Christian Temperance Union, endorsed the Walsh candidacy within a week of its announcement.

The adjective *Catholic* thus began to seem politically separable from the adjective *wet*. Hence, at a time when members of the (northern) Methodist Episcopal Church were formally pledging themselves to oppose "any man for president . . . who is not avowedly dry," their Board of Temperance, Prohibition, and Public Morals made a specific point of the acceptability of Senator Walsh. Conversely, as early as the spring of 1927 the chief Washington lobbyist of the Anti-Saloon League had been warned that if his organization did not take account of the possible candidacy of a "dry" Catholic such as Walsh there was a danger that the league and the whole prohibitionist cause would be branded as anti-Catholic. Even anti-Catholics themselves backhandedly conceded the point; a daily paper in La Grange, Georgia, grudgingly noted that "Mr. Walsh is less obnoxious by about 50 per cent than Mr. Smith, for while both are Catholics, Mr. Smith is a wet besides."

Speculating on the nature of the forthcoming Walsh campaign strategy, the *New York Times* editorialized: "It is expected that the campaign to bring about his nomination will be based on his adherence to the dry cause"—an accurate forecast, as witness the subsequent charge by a Walsh leader in California that "wet" Republicans were "registering in large numbers as Democrats in order to vote for Governor Smith." At least one newspaper in Walsh's home state claimed that the senator's sole object in entering the campaign was the defense of prohibition. The liberal Catholic weekly *Commonweal* declared that the California primaries were "not a test of Governor Smith's popularity" but rather a test of "whether rigorous addiction to prohibition is a virtue with Western Democrats." And Walsh himself was later to blame his defeat in those primaries on "thirsty Republicans and misguided Drys."

The liquor issue was not the only mark distinguishing one Catholic politician from another. The California organization to whose standard the Democratic faithful were being urged to rally was described as the "Walsh Dry-Progressive Anti-Tammany ticket." Through his prosecution of the Teapot Dome investigations, Senator Walsh had been typecast on the American scene as an anticorruptionist. J. Leonard Bates has shown that Walsh was more of a temporizer with the Powers of Darkness than Walsh campaign folklore would acknowledge, and historians of Montana have noted that there were disciplinary limits in Montana politics imposed by the Anaconda Copper Mining Company which not even a man of Walsh's stature could safely transgress. K. Ross Toole observed of the senator that "he walked the tightrope of senatorial liberalism and local conservatism with consummate skill."

Nevertheless, Walsh and his junior colleague in the Senate, Burton K. Wheeler, had been in the public eye for several years as punishers of evildoers in public life. The Teapot Dome story was still making headlines; the Senate committee itself was still holding hearings, and the second court trial of Harry F. Sinclair took place between April 9 and 21, 1928— a convenient time indeed for a Walsh presidential boom.

Lines of distinction which sophisticated political scientists and historians like to draw between big-business corruption and political-machine corruption are less clear to the layman; an American political tradition going back to Theodore Roosevelt and Lincoln Steffens links the malefactors of the corner saloon with the malefactors of great wealth. Senator Walsh's reputation as a "relentless foe of corruption and fraud" was thus, in some minds at least, readily translatable into a formal antithesis to Smith's reputation as a son of Tammany. Mark Sullivan, Walsh's most indefatigable champion, wrote in his nationally syndicated column: "If [Walsh] were elected president he would be his own man . . . and no one would suspect a private wire to Tammany Hall." (Montana was far enough away that the problem of a private wire to the Montana Power Company did not arise.) Sullivan went on to quote the *Colorado Springs Gazette*: "What an insult it would be . . . to nominate a lifelong member of Tammany Hall upon a platform demanding the purifying of elections!" Such sentiments were not confined to journalists or to westerners. A business broker in New York who admired Walsh declared: "Al. Smith is the head of an organization which has collected more graft than that involved in the Teapot Dome."

With some astonishment, people remembered that the same "dry," rural, Klan-minded Democrats who had blocked Al Smith's nomination during the 103-ballot ordeal which was the Democratic National Convention of 1924 had seemed very impressed by Walsh, who had been that raucous convention's calm and impartial presiding officer. Hearst man Arthur Brisbane had commented at the time: "If you think there is much dreadful religious prejudice in this country, just listen to that roaring welcome that Walsh gets and don't forget that he is a Roman Catholic. . . . Why don't they nominate Walsh for President?"

As a matter of fact, the senator had enjoyed a modest presidential boom in 1924. Walsh and most of the Montana delegation had voted for William Gibbs McAdoo, but when the exhausted forces of McAdoo and Al Smith had finally bowed out, and just before the convention had moved toward the selection of its distinguished but drab nominee, John W. Davis, to run against Calvin Coolidge, the courtesy vote for Chairman Walsh had climbed to the impressive total of 123. On the final ballot, just before the ritual motion to make the nomination unanimous, Walsh had picked up 28 votes from New York State—which meant that, at the end, some of the Smith men and some of the McAdoo men had been voting together for a westerner and a Catholic.

To drive the point home, a clamor for Walsh for vice-president had begun from the floor as soon as the nomination of John W. Davis was completed. "It appeared to spectators," a *Times* man remembered afterward, "that the demand for drafting Mr. Walsh was practically unanimous." Walsh stilled it only by recognizing himself as a delegate from Montana to move that the session be adjourned, and Senator Burton K. Wheeler later remembered the continuing pressure on Walsh to accept the 1924 vice-presidential nomination even after this dramatic refusal.

Partly on the strength of these 1924 episodes, Mark Sullivan was able to say in 1928 that Walsh was "a living refutation that Catholicism is a bar to popularity among Protestants in the United States." Understandably, some of those who had been most worried about the religious issue greeted the senator's bid for the presidential nomination with a feeling of relief. The influential Protestant weekly *Christian Century* editorially hoped that Walsh would win the Democratic nomination in 1928—and called his "A Clarifying Candidacy."

> [Walsh] is a Roman Catholic, but his membership in that church bears almost none of the popular connotations that make the Catholicism of Governor Smith such an issue. There is, in other words, a difference between a Mon-

tana Catholic and a Tammany Hall Catholic which the ordinary American voter feels, even though it may elude theological definition.

"If Walsh should be nominated," Sullivan wrote, "the voters will think about oil; whereas if Smith is nominated the voters will think about religion." At least one southern Methodist bishop declared on the eve of the election that he was against Smith but would have voted for Walsh. One is moved to ask: Had Walsh been nominated for president, how much of the southern vote—and the farm vote—might he have held for the Democrats in the face of a Hoover prosperity which even in 1928 was not very evident in the South or on the farm? It would seem to me to be pressing much too far the "unwritten law" thesis concerning Catholic candidates for president to maintain that none of the Americans who voted for Hoover as the lesser of two evils than Smith could have been persuaded to vote for Walsh as a lesser evil than Hoover.

On the other hand, it is conceivable that any Democratic gains earned by Walsh in the South and West might have been canceled out by the loss of some of Smith's urban constituency. The *New Republic*, for example, stated that in 1924 the senator from Montana might have been a suitable candidate but that in 1928

> his advantages as a candidate over Governor Smith are unimportant and his disadvantages are all-important. By nominating him, the Democratic party would forego its chances of carrying the eastern or middle western states. If it is going to take the risk of nominating a Catholic, it must obviously nominate a Catholic candidate who is strong in those neighborhoods in which Catholicism is strong.

There was also, of course, the possibility that Walsh was simply too late an entrant into the race. The venerable *Century Magazine* for March 1928, forecasting possible convention opponents to Governor Smith, did not even mention Senator Walsh. And *Commonweal*, on the eve of Walsh's preprimary campaigns, simply saw no alternative to Smith in sight: the New York governor was "about all there is of the Democratic [party]," and the national nominating convention at Houston would have "its choice between Peter Pan and Al Smith."

But there was a far more disquieting possibility. Was the Walsh candidacy entirely bona fide? Observers noted that his quest for delegates was being pushed seriously in only three states, all of them western (South Dakota, Montana, and California); they noted that, after all, Montana only had four electoral votes; they noted that, although Walsh was a well-preserved westerner who strode "into the Senate chamber like an Indian marathon runner" and was "obviously at the very height of his physical and mental powers," he was nearing the end of his sixty-eighth year, which in those times was considered rather late in the game for presidential candidates; they noted that another rural western "dry," Mrs. Nellie Tayloe Ross, governor of Wyoming, was supporting Smith and saying, "Prohibition has no place in the campaign"; above all, they remembered Walsh's long-standing friendship with William Gibbs McAdoo, the anti-Smith candidate of 1924, a friendship which had embarrassed Walsh in the Teapot Dome investigations—and some of them wondered audibly whether this whole affair of the Walsh candidacy was not a plot to kill off Al Smith.

Within a matter of days after Senator Walsh had filed, his campaign was described as a "stalking-horse" by a *New York Times* correspondent in the South, by the *New Republic*, and by the *Birmingham News*. The *Times* somewhat confusingly both editorialized that "the Walsh candidacy is to be spoken of with respect" and then characterized it as "obviously intended not to succeed." The columnist Frank Kent described the Montanan as "a good man misled" by "a certain element" anxious to divide Smith's support. Catholic journalists in particular were understandably skeptical. Charles Willis Thompson in *Commonweal* called Walsh's political activity "a mystery for which Mr. Walsh's dignified record affords no explanation," implying that the senator was deliberately letting himself be used. The *Catholic World* dismissed the entering of Walsh's name as "a particularly insincere and futile gesture"; McAdoo's declared support of Walsh was "the silliest argument of those who like to pretend that Smith's opponents are not moved to opposition by his religion."

Surely this is partisan overstatement. Are we to infer that Smith's *Catholic* opponent was "moved to opposition by his religion"? Or even that one Catholic politician would consciously and deliberately work with anti-Catholic forces to block another American Catholic's chances? The implications here are psychologically grotesque, and the burden of proof lies on Walsh's detractors. The senator himself, for whatever a politician's efforts to clear his own name may be worth, denied the stalking-horse charge categorically; in a letter to the Democratic state central committee back home in Montana, he wrote: "It is needless to assure those who know me as well as you do that I could not be prevailed upon to participate in any contest to help wreak vengeance on any man."

Indeed, far from their candidate's being inordinately self-seeking, Walsh's admirers were afraid lest he prove too self-effacing. A South Carolina newspaper noted with surprise of a typical Walsh speech: "In an hour and ten minutes not once did this United States Senator say 'I.'" Commenting on this, the loyal Mark Sullivan wrote ruefully: "The chief impediment to the kind of campaign organization and activity which would make Walsh formidable is Walsh himself." And a Montana newspaper friendly to Walsh said, after the senator had withdrawn from the race: "It matters not whether he would make a great president—greater even than Al Smith. All that appears to matter is that Al Smith is a charming man."

Senator Walsh announced his candidacy on March 4, 1928. His first clear-cut contest was in South Dakota, whose rather complicated primary-and-convention system finally awarded four national convention votes to Walsh, three to Smith. But at this point an extraordinary crisis developed in Walsh's own home state. The Montana Democratic state central committee endorsed Walsh—and simultaneously reelected their perennial national committeeman, J. Bruce Kremer, who had already come out for Smith. Kremer had a reputation in Montana as a hatchet man for the Company—that is, the Anaconda Copper Mining Company—because he had been an agent in the wartime harassment of Burton K. Wheeler for alleged subversion and in the firing of an economics professor at the University of Montana for advocating changes in the state's tax structure. In a Jefferson Day dinner speech in New York, Kremer praised Governor Smith as "a proponent of honest and incorruptible government," which in the ears of those who knew Montana, the Company, and Kremer, must have had a dreadfully ironic ring; nevertheless, this endorsement of Smith obviously created enormous difficulties for Thomas J. Walsh.

But the ACM, as the Anaconda Copper Mining Company was locally known (when not referred to simply as "The Company"), was not Walsh's only problem in Montana; there was also the senator's adherence to the "dry" cause. In 1924 an Al Smith man from the city of Butte had been elected to the Montana delegation to the Democratic National Convention, quite frankly on a beer platform. He had made a seconding speech for Smith at that convention, breaking an otherwise solid block of votes for McAdoo. Remembering Montana's 7-to-1 split for ballot after ballot in the ordeal of 1924, until all eight had finally gone for Walsh when McAdoo and Smith both withdrew, state politicians in 1928 realized that they were in a pretty dilemma indeed, a dilemma best summed up by the *Great Falls Tribune*:

> If Montana's delegation goes to Houston definitely and publicly instructed for Senator Walsh, it will be interpreted throughout [the East and South] to mean that Montana is opposed to Governor Smith—which, of course, is not true—and would lend strength to those who are endeavoring to split the party on the religious and prohibition issues. On the other hand, to send a delegation to Houston definitely and publicly instructed to vote for Governor Smith would be like a rebuke to Senator Walsh, for whom Montana Democrats have high regard.

The *Tribune*'s solution was an uninstructed delegation, but one which would be expected to vote for Walsh as long as his chances appeared reasonable. The paper stuck to this solution, but pro-Smith and pro-Walsh people talked of outright instruction of the delegation one way or the other, and out-of-state news stories carried headlines such as "Smith Men to Fight Walsh in Montana." A serious split in the state party seemed in the making. But the split was averted because of developments elsewhere.

The Montana Democratic State Convention was scheduled to meet on May 15; California held its presidential primary on May 1. Presidential primaries, then as before and afterward, were notorious as destroyers of presidential aspirations. Walsh lost disastrously, finishing a poor third behind Smith and the "wet" Protestant candidate, Senator James A. Reed of Missouri. The *Great Falls Tribune* loyally stayed by Montana's favorite son, declaring that his defeat did "not lessen Montana democracy's obligation to him." But the senator was more realistic: "Whatever hopes might have been indulged that in certain contingencies the Houston convention might deem it wise to make me its nominee," he said, "they can no longer reasonably be entertained." As soon as the candidate's wishes were known, the *Tribune* hailed "Walsh's good judgment" and promptly declared: "Montana is for Smith, now that Walsh is out of it"—as a good Democratic newspaper should have done in such circumstances.

In the excitement of a presidential election, the prenomination candidates are quickly forgotten; and doubly forgotten, in the light of Al Smith's subsequent defeat by Hoover, was the *Springfield Republican*'s prophecy: "If Governor Smith gains the presidency he will gain it largely on issues made real and vital by Thomas J. Walsh." A more lasting valedictory was Oswald Garrison Villard's in the *Nation*. He credited Walsh with having "at bottom a better mind and a better trained one, in some respects a wider vision" than Smith, and he predicted: "Some day a Catholic will—and must—find his way into the White House. The country may consider itself fortunate if that man should prove to be of the type of Thomas J. Walsh."

Franklin D. Roosevelt is reported to have told Burton K. Wheeler, who survived Walsh as a Montana senator for fourteen years, in a conversation in the summer of 1939, that "if there were an outstanding Catholic Democrat available—someone like my Montana colleague, the late Thomas J. Walsh, when he was 'a young man and vigorous'—he could possibly be elected in 1940." In the same conversation Roosevelt is supposed to have quoted George Cardinal Mundelein to the effect that " 'the Catholic they would elect would have to come out of the West and not from the sidewalks of New York.' "

Prophecy is a tricky business, and the region which eventually produced the available Catholic candidate turned out to be east, not west, of New York (though Bostonians sometimes feel as psychically distant from Manhattan as do far westerners). But in another respect it may be argued that it was less the endearing simplicity of Al Smith than the puritan detachment of Tom Walsh that reemerged in the administration of John Fitzgerald Kennedy.

CHAPTER FIVE

Prohibition and Democracy

*M*iddle America, wrote James H. Timberlake, enacted Prohibition "out of an earnest desire to revitalize and preserve American democracy." Like other efforts to revitalize and preserve democracy at about that same time—such as Woodrow Wilson's declaration of war against Germany—this crusade was destined for repudiation. The Eighteenth Amendment took effect at midnight on January 16, 1920, as a decade opened in which Americans soon realized that any formerly existing democratic common front had been shattered. Some in that decade affirmed their belief in a revitalized democracy while also insisting that if that goal were to be accomplished, Prohibition would have to go. Others, equally opposed to Prohibition, denied even the desirability of democracy's preservation and cited Prohibition as a dreadful example of the consequences of unsupervised democracy. Disillusion was a factor in the powerful and eventually successful drive for Prohibition repeal, and by the logic of hindsight we have tended to apply that disillusion retroactively, as a historical judgment of our own. Nevertheless, alongside the democratic "wet" liberals like Clarence Darrow and the antidemocratic

An earlier form of this essay appeared in the *Wisconsin Magazine of History* 56 (Spring 1973): 189–201, and later in *Another Part of the Twenties* (New York: Columbia University Press, 1977).

"wet" cynics like H. L. Mencken, throughout the twenties there were some "dry" Americans who maintained that by their efforts American democracy had not only been revitalized but also given a great push forward.

Harry S. Warner, writing in 1928 under the imprint of the World League Against Alcoholism, entitled one such argument *Prohibition: An Adventure in Freedom*. The Volstead Act, Warner contended, had not been imposed upon an uncomprehending electorate by a well-organized fanatic minority in a brief period of war hysteria, as "wet" folklore so often claimed. Quite the contrary; it was the climax of "one hundred years of trial and error," during which temperance forces had tried every other possible approach to liquor control and had found them all ineffective. Prohibition met all the tests of proper democratic action: the test of time, the test of full discussion, and the test of decisive majority expression (forty-six of the forty-eight states had, after all, ratified the constitutional change). By the time this "dry" rationale was written, Walter Lippmann had already published his cautionary essay *The Phantom Public*; and today, wiser in the ways of public relations, we may be more skeptical than Harry Warner was about the import of electoral majorities, however decisive. On the other hand, any historian who has labored in the vineyard of the twenties must conclude from the mountainous remains of "wet" versus "dry" polemic that Warner's test of full discussion, at least, is one which Prohibition passed with flying colors.

As a means of organizing the "dry" side of that discussion, the categories suggested in Joseph Gusfield's *Symbolic Crusade*, of "assimilative" against "coercive" social reformers—the one perceiving the drinker as a deviant who must be persuaded to accept the reformer's values, and the other judging the drinker as an enemy who must be prevented from flouting those values—seem to me altogether too simplistic, for they obscure the self-image of the reformer as underdog. As Harry Warner saw the matter, the "wets," by playing Goliath to the "drys' " David, had inadvertently boosted the temperance cause. The year-in, year-out hostility of the eastern metropolitan press and of the organized liquor interests, "with millions of dollars invested in wet news, publicity material, speakers and in the influencing of public officials, legitimately and illegitimately," had successfully "retarded prohibition," and thereby "helped to insure the democratic process against hasty action."

Warner was not alone in his judgment that Prohibition had been a political triumph of the popular over the powerful. In radical language jarringly out of phase with its usual dowager tones, then or today, the *Ladies' Home Journal* for March 1923 declared: "The prohibition embroilment is shaping its course as an inevitable class issue. The fashionable rich demand their rum as an inalienable class privilege," crying " 'To hell with the benefits to the poor there may be in prohibition!' " In a similar vein Roy A. Haynes, in his book *Prohibition Inside Out*, also published in 1923, expressed scorn for "the remnant of the old organization of manufacturers and dealers of liquor in pre-prohibition days, learning nothing by experience, forgetting nothing, wearing in its heart a Bourbon hope of its return to the throne of debauchery from which it was hurled by the wrath of the American people." Endorsed in a foreword by "the late President Harding"—an irony many Americans would not have perceived at the time—Haynes's book concluded: "It is the beverage liquor interests, the criminals, the vice-capitalists who *fear* we shall succeed. It is the leaders of the world who *wonder* if we shall succeed. It is the 'little people' of the world who *hope* we shall succeed."

Here the wisdom of hindsight may be a positive handicap. From a post-Depression perspective, the historian is aware that a great many of the "little people" who voted for Franklin Roosevelt in 1932 probably also voted for repeal the following year. The theme song of the 1932 Democratic national convention, "Happy Days Are Here Again," has often been described as prophetic of a forthcoming new deal for the American people, but to some in that joyous hall it may have meant primarily the prospect of legal beer. Moreover, in studies like Virginius Dabney's *Dry Messiah* or Andrew Sinclair's *Prohibition: The Era of Excess*, we have been reminded that the "wets" had, to say the least, no monopoly on high-handed or unethical behavior. On this point the "dry" advocates during the twenties were placed on the defensive. Still, they might have argued, one must put the matter into historical perspective; if "dry" politicians had often engaged in tactics similar to those of the "wets," perhaps it was a case of fighting firewater with fire. In effect, Harry Warner told his "wet" opponents in 1928, we have both played in the same game of marshalling public opinion for a democratic decision, and our side won. As Lord Bryce had put it long before in his *Modern Democracies*, "The prohibition movement has not proceeded from any one class or section of the community"; it had grown "mainly because it appealed to the moral and religious sentiments of the plain people." As such, Warner concluded, its victory called for democratic acquiescence by the "wet" minority.

Who were the members of this "wet" minority? Warner divided them into the "missed"—those whom the "drys" had not yet reached to educate or persuade—and the "opposition." In the latter category he grouped the "social drink users," whose position he dismissed as elitist and undemocratic; "the group with an alcoholic appetite," whose problem he saw as transitory ("most of these men are well along in life; they will pass on"); those with "adventure or bravado motives," which he also saw as transitory ("being prompted by adventure, it tends to be temporary . . . young men and women do grow older"); the "self-privileged," who chose for themselves which laws they would obey, a position Warner also saw as fundamentally undemocratic; and finally, "the trade, formerly legal, now illegal." For all the newfound affluence of entrepreneurs like Al Capone, Warner affirmed that drinking in America was doomed; the Noble Experiment was here to stay. Its remaining "wet" opponents, he conceded, were free to use the same methods of persuasion the "drys" had had to adopt before gaining the sanction of Constitution and law, but they must not engage in undemocratic shortcuts such as nullification.

But there remained the nagging question of personal liberty, even against decisions democratically made on behalf of decisive majorities. The Prohibition controversy illustrated the old dilemma so painfully recognized by Abraham Lincoln during the Civil War: "Must a government, of necessity, be too *strong* for the liberties of its own people, or too *weak* to maintain its own existence?" Prohibitionist Harry Warner tried to turn the argument in a different direction: "Is 'personal liberty,' not in the abstract but definitely in the lives of men, women, and children, greater where drink goes out, even with the aid of the heavy hand of the law, than it is where drink remains?" To support his own answer to that question, he cited a writer as far from the usual godly, churchgoing, "uptight" stereotype of the "dry" as could well have been imagined, namely George Bernard Shaw:

> If a natural choice between drunkenness and sobriety were possible, I should leave people free to choose. But when I seen enormous capitalist organizations pushing drink under people's noses at every corner and pocketing the price, whilst leaving me and others to pay the colossal damages, then I am prepared to smash that organization and make it as easy for a poor man to be sober if he wants as it is for his dog.

But what if a poor man considered that option and then, of his own free choice, rejected it? Even then, Warner contended, temperance could be construed as an affirmation of personal liberty rather than its negation. Far from being a suppression of individual freedom, Prohibition was "the liberation of the individual from the illusion of freedom that is conveyed by alcohol." In this respect, the "drys'" argument against liquor resembled the Marxists' argument against religion; the alcohol "high" was seen as a surrogate for effective action, preventing the exercise of any real freedom of decision. Further on in his polemic, Warner quoted former United Mine Workers president Tom L. Lewis as having said that "there is no easier way possible to make the unfortunate man, or the oppressed worker, content with his misfortune than a couple of glasses of beer." If the workingman in America of that period had largely left the church, as the statistics indicate he had, then perhaps religion had been displaced by a more powerful—or at least more congenial—opiate for the people!

Historically, Warner pointed out, the question of personal choice had been raised in the first place not by the "wets" but by their "dry" opponents. Paradoxically, prohibitionism had grown up in the first place among that sector of the population, the old-stock WASPs, which traditionally had been regarded as the most individualistic. Within the temperance movement itself, debate over the question of personal liberty had been intense ever since the time of Lyman Beecher, who for all the vehemence of his temperance views had opted for moral suasion and had opposed legal coercion. But times had changed. "No one," Warner asserted, "now would care to have such forms of personal liberty as the freedom to duel, to keep slaves, to sell narcotics to all who call, exist again freely. . . . They are out of date, and for the same reason that auto speeding is restricted in a crowded city." (On this last point the Flivver King himself concurred: "Booze," said Henry Ford, "had to go out when modern industry and the motor car came in.") Far from being nostalgic or reactionary, therefore, from the standpoint of "dry" apologists like Harry Warner the Prohibition movement "contemplates a new order of civilization."

The modern view, Warner argued—for all the world like an academic sociologist—is that the claims of the individual must be balanced against those of family and society. Man is not an autonomous atom; "he is also a member of a community, a citizen, a father, a taxpayer, a fellow worker. . . . Or he is an auto-driver . . . whose freedom and happiness are limited by the sobriety of other drivers." The trouble with the personal-liberty argument was that the consequences of excessive drink could "not be confined to the drinker; that the worst burdens fall, not upon him who becomes intoxicated, but upon those who suffer because of the toxic habits of others." In short, this "dry" advocate put down the "rugged individualism" of the drinker in much the same fashion that the New Deal's advocates would later put down the rugged individualism of that conscientious "dry" Herbert Hoover. If the "drys" did not realize that an effort to be one's brother's political keeper had sinister statist implications, neither did most of the New Dealers.

To be sure, this particular experiment in social control—or, if one prefers, social liberation—failed; and the "drys" themselves conceded that an important component in that failure was "the disintegration of popular support." But they tended to attribute that loss of support to public mis-understanding, abetted by well-financed "wet" propaganda. Here again our post-Repeal perspective can be a historiographic pitfall. Indeed, 3.2 beer was one of the earliest fruits of Franklin Roosevelt's Hundred Days, and Jim Farley did make ratification of the Twenty-first Amendment a matter of party regularity in the Democratic state organizations. But some "dry" observers at the time were inclined to see Repeal as the handiwork not of insurgent popular democracy but of the economic royalists.

"If the American people had had respect for all laws, good or bad, there would have been no Boston Tea Party." Sympathy with some of the crusades and confrontations of the 1960s may have inclined a later genera-tion to sympathize with such a statement from the 1920s. But as historians we must also carefully identify a quotation by its source, in this case the elder William Randolph Hearst, then at the height of his Red-baiting and Oriental-hating career, and a man not ordinarily identified in political folk-lore as a tribune of the people. Hearst said those provocative words on April 26, 1929, as he launched a temperance essay contest in the *New York American*. The first prize of $25,000 was won by Franklin Chase Hoyt, presiding judge of a children's court in New York City, who advocated leaving the Eighteenth Amendment intact but amending the Volstead Act to define intoxicating liquors as "all alcoholic products of distillation"—in effect a return to the old "ardent spirits" definition of Lyman Beecher and Benjamin Rush.

It is a truism that social action in America requires organization, and orga-nization costs money. Deets Pickett, a spokesman for the Methodist Board of Temperance, estimated afterward that of the total contributions received in 1929 by the Association Against the Prohibition Amendment (AAPA),

75 percent were given by only fifty-two men. Fletcher Dobyns, in a book entitled *The Amazing Story of Repeal,* published in 1940, dug a little farther into the historic antecedents of the AAPA. The association's first president, William H. Stayton, had been executive secretary of the old Navy League, an industrial elite group whose doings have been probed many times by progressive and leftist historians. In 1926, according to Dobyns, a new group took over the leadership of the AAPA while retaining Stayton as president. Prominent in this group were Pierre, Irénée, and Lammot DuPont; John J. Raskob of General Motors (in dissent, as usual, from Ford); and Charles H. Sabin, a director of sixteen large corporations and chairman of Guaranty Trust of New York, a Morgan bank. (Other, more obviously self-interested contributors included Fred Pabst, the Schaefer Brewing Company, Colonel Jacob Ruppert, W. Fred Anheuser, and August A. Busch.)

With telling effect, Dobyns quoted a letter dated March 24, 1928, from Wilmington, Delaware, by Pierre DuPont, addressed to William P. Smith, director of the AAPA:

> Dear Bill: I shall be glad if you will make known to the officials of the *Saturday Evening Post* my personal interest in the affairs of the Association Against the Prohibition Amendment, also in the interest of my brothers Irénée and Lammot. I feel that the *Saturday Evening Post* is intimately related to both the General Motors Corporation and the DuPont Company and that the aim of this paper is to promote the welfare of the people of the United States. As I feel that the prohibition movement has failed in its original aim and has become both a nuisance and a menace, I hope that the officials of the *Saturday Evening Post* will join in a move toward better things.

Dobyns also neatly reversed the "wets'" old argument that Prohibition had been foisted upon the masses by minority pressure during an abnormal wartime situation. It was, rather, the "wets," he contended, who had pushed Repeal through to ratification in 1933 while the Depression was still at its peak and the people desperate, ready to listen to any promise—before they had had a chance for (so to speak) sober second thoughts. They had been duped, Dobyns intimated, by the men of the AAPA, for whom Repeal was not a struggle for popular liberty but rather a "struggle to save themselves hundreds of millions of dollars by substituting for the income tax a liquor tax to be paid by the masses." Battling in 1930 against the rising tide of Repeal, the assistant pastor of one busy urban parish emphatically concurred: "The power of the church really unleashed can overcome any 40 billion dollar clique of business men who want to get revenue for the government and dodge their corporation taxes." Though he conceded that "good people who want prohibition have been fooled into voting against their own convictions," he argued that in the long run the popular will would prevail and that that will, in spite of apparent evidence to the contrary, was "dry."

Politically liberal historians nurtured under the New Deal may have overlooked some artlessly Marxist implications in this type of reasoning, perhaps in part because crusading radical bitterness against those "vested interests" which supported Repeal merged unexpectedly into Old Guard Republican bitterness against the Roosevelt administration, which actually accomplished Repeal. Fletcher Dobyns's case was argued with restraint and backed by substantial documentation, but for perspective it must be set alongside a similar book by Ernest Gordon published in 1943, *The Wrecking of the Eighteenth Amendment*, the tone of which was almost hysterically anti-FDR. Yet even that less savory tract for the times contained a lengthy chapter on "Wall Street and Repeal," followed by a chapter on "The Press and Prohibition." The latter takes on added significance in more recent years, marked as they have been by even greater exposure to mass-media manipulation. A cartoon by a liberal Methodist minister of the pre-Repeal period vividly captured that aspect of the controversy. It depicted a roly-poly figure labeled "The Real 'Repealer'" hiding behind a cadaverous dummy attired in a "Puritan" costume complete with high-crowned hat and buckled shoes. This scarecrow was labeled "Caricature of the Dry Cause."

In short, the victory for personal liberty contained in the Twenty-first Amendment was more ambiguous than it seemed; not all the right-wing elitism was on one side, nor was all the left-wing democratic liberalism on the other. In other words, the fight over Repeal was a more *normal* kind of American political controversy than historians—or the public—have usually assumed.

The AAPA's organizational heir, the American Liberty League, founded in August of 1934, shares in this historical ambiguity. The name Liberty League may have had a liberal connotation when these tycoons' energies were being directed toward the overthrow of Prohibition, but scant months later it carried quite another, as they were directed into a last-ditch defense of unhampered private enterprise against the assaults of the New

Deal. In particular we should remember that Al Smith, so symbolically important a political figure in the America of the twenties, was active both in the AAPA and the Liberty League. Sometimes his activity in the latter has been charged off to personal pique at Roosevelt over the outcome of the 1932 Democratic convention, and in any case historians like David Burner have sharply questioned whether the traditional clear-cut liberal image of the pre-1932 Al Smith can hold. But there is a chicken-and-egg problem here. Was Smith's activity in the American Liberty League merely a sign that his latent conservatism—sensed by Walter Lippmann as early as 1925—had at last come to the fore? Or did it show, rather, an urban liberal's intuitive concern that illiberalism might lurk behind the New Deal's liberal facade?

None of these ambiguities are resolved by the fact that the "wets," like the "drys," contrived to make their case as the underdog. "We are working against a highly organized, well-financed body of Drys," declared

55

Mrs. John B. Casserly on April 14, 1931, "who have made it their business to obtain control of the key positions in our whole system of government." This is, of course, a standard gambit of the "outs" against the "ins," of whatever stripe. Mrs. Casserly was speaking before a highly organized, well-financed body of "wets," the Women's Organization for National Prohibition Reform (WONPR). Its founder and president was Mrs. Charles H. Sabin, and her husband, as we have seen, was a leading figure both in the equivalent association for men and in the national business establishment. Other founders of the WONPR included Mrs. Pierre DuPont, Mrs. August Belmont, Mrs. J. Roland Harrison, Mrs. Coffin Van Rensselaer, and Mrs. R. Stuyvesant Pierrepont—hardly the representatives an American democrat in the Jackson-Bryan tradition would have chosen to typify "the little people of the world."

To "dry" apologist Fletcher Dobyns it was inconceivable "that the women of America had transferred their intellectual and spiritual allegiance from women like Frances E. Willard, Jane Addams, Evangeline Booth, Carrie Chapman Catt, and Ella Boole"—"dry" champions all—"to such women as Mrs. Sabin, Mrs. DuPont, Mrs. Belmont, and Mrs. Harriman." It was, rather, a public relations triumph engineered by fashionable society. "If . . . the members of this set have something they want to put over, they have only to issue invitations to teas and meetings at their houses, or request people to serve on committees with them, and the social climbers will fall all over themselves in the enthusiasm of their response." Once more the struggle of "wets" and "drys" was seen as a struggle of the classes and the masses, at least from the standpoint of the "drys."

In fact, one of the most effective weapons a WONPR spokeswoman could use was an elitist put-down of her opponents. "If the WCTU and the Anti-Saloon League had ever had opportunity to observe the power of an intelligent woman of the world," wrote Grace Root in 1934, "they must . . . have seen the Repeal handwriting on the wall as soon as Mrs. Sabin took leadership in the field against them." Driving the point home, Mrs. Root's book *Women and Repeal* contained a pair of photographs showing the presidents of the rival women's organizations. Mrs. Sabin of the Women's Organization for National Prohibition Reform, her well-groomed socialite good looks enhanced by the lighting and printing techniques also used at that time in portraits of film stars, contrasted most cruelly with Mrs. Boole of the Woman's Christian Temperance Union, whose robust countenance, split by a wide and toothy grin, branded her as the archetype of the Eternal Frump.

But had not the WCTU drawn from an elite leadership also, though perhaps from a less glamorous elite? Biographers of Frances Willard, for example, who headed the WCTU from 1879 until her death in 1898, have made much of her New England Puritan lineage, and many observers and historians of Prohibition have considered it a bourgeois attempt to impose WASP values upon the recalcitrant American masses. And yet, on the list of state officers and committees of the WONPR, the names were also overwhelmingly Old American. Meanwhile, the WCTU was losing some of its former elite status. In the state of Washington in 1910, writes Norman H. Clark, it "had attracted the wives of prominent physicians, lawyers, and men of commerce. In 1930, it could list only the wives of morticians, chiropractors, tradesmen, and ministers of minor distinction."

But the rivalry between the two women's organizations also went down to the grass roots. By 1930 the WONPR was able to challenge the WCTU for the allegiance of the same constituencies, and it was placing booths opposite the time-sanctioned WCTU booths at state and county fairs. One industrious member of the WONPR's Kentucky branch scored a breakthrough in the "dry" South by discovering in a second-hand store a scrapbook of newspaper clippings dating from 1887 that disclosed the antiprohibitionist views of the sainted Jefferson Davis. After verifying the sources, the Louisville *Courier-Journal* ran the story on page one, and the action seems to have been helpful to the "wet" cause throughout the domain of the old Confederacy. Mrs. Root suggested that her organization won support away from the WCTU in part because it presented a more attractive lifestyle: "Our women were more amiable and laughed with the crowd instead of preaching to them," though a cynic might have concluded that the power elite had merely learned a softer sell.

In any event, despite the sniping by "dry" defenders like Gordon and Dobyns—who in effect dismissed the women opponents of Prohibition as barflies—the activity of the WONPR clearly had destroyed a major component of the entire "dry" mystique: the notion that the women of America constituted a massive and undivided opposition to beverage alcohol. When Mrs. Sabin spoke on April 3, 1929, at a lunch given in her honor by the Women's National Republican Club and announced she had resigned as Republican national committeewoman because she wanted to work for a change in the prohibition law, she took note of that mystique: "It has been repeatedly said that the women of the country favored the prohibition law. I believe there are thousands who feel as I do." The president of the men's group, the AAPA, was quick to agree. "The women of America do not believe in prohibition," Henry H. Curran declared that same day. "They need only to be organized to make this perfectly clear." With the exasperating unconscious condescension so common in the male, Curran conceded that the ladies could even be permitted to do the organizing for themselves: "I understand that Mrs. Sabin's organization is to be independent, and that is right. Our association will help in every way possible."

Mrs. Root, who was official historian for the WONPR, noted that when the Nineteenth Amendment, giving women the right to vote, passed Congress in 1919, "not a woman's voice had ever been raised against Prohibition," whereas the WCTU at that time had been in business for fifty years. The Anti-Saloon League—run, of course, by men—generally supported woman suffrage in the preprohibition years on the assumption that women would overwhelmingly vote "dry." As the news of Mrs. Sabin's defection became known, one can imagine political professionals all across the land heaving a collective sigh of relief. In the words of Paul Conley and Andrew Sorensen, "as long as women kept a united voice in favor of Prohibition, no politician would dare cast a vote which would offend at least half of his electorate. Now that most formidable united front had been broken."

The impact of the WONPR could be attributed, of course, not only to its leaders' marital ties to the power elite but also to the "emancipation" of women during the twenties. Part of the disrepute in which the old-time saloon had been held, wrote Herbert Agar in the *English Review* for May 1931, "came from the fact that the saloon was a man's world, from which women were excluded, and which they therefore distrusted. In the speak-easy women are admitted on an equality with men." But from the standpoint of women's liberation it could be argued that the political price women had had to pay for this act of personal liberty was disastrously high: the loss of any fear by politicians that women's united support of Prohibition might be symptomatic of their potential as a bloc vote on *all* issues. It has been said, rightly or wrongly, that the women (in those states which had already given them the vote prior to the Nineteenth Amendment) re-elected Woodrow Wilson in 1916. Can they be plausibly said to have done the same for any of his successors?

Perhaps Ella Boole sensed that more was at stake than persuading American hostesses to serve unspiked fruit punch, although she engaged in that sort of activity also. But throughout her book *Give Prohibition Its Chance*, published in 1929, readers were forcefully reminded that the author spoke for the *Woman's* Christian Temperance Union, which for many years had engaged in activities—caucusing, lobbying, electioneering, direct action—for which American men had traditionally deemed women temperamentally unsuited, perhaps even biologically unfit. Midway through the book, Mrs. Boole played her trump card:

> A little girl . . . on returning from school one day said, "I don't like history." "Why?" asked the mother. The child answered "It is all about men. There is nothing in it about women." It is a fact that until women organized in societies of their own, there was little to record of woman's work except where women ruled their countries as queens.

So far as direct political rule was concerned, two women were elected governors in the decade of the twenties, both "drys." Is it entirely an accident that after that dry spell was broken, no woman would serve as governor of an American state for the following four decades?

If "woman power" perhaps suffered a setback in the struggles of the Dry Decade, the same may be said, even more tragically, of the alcoholic, who in this debate was simply lost in the shuffle. "Once prohibition was enacted," as Conley and Sorensen put it, "the drys saw the alcoholic only as a reminder of a bad dream that would soon disappear; to the wets, the alcoholic was an embarrassing source of dry propaganda." Nor did matters significantly improve after Repeal. Alcoholics Anonymous was founded in 1935 and enjoyed some spectacular successes with individuals who could be persuaded to go that route, but the appeal of that quasi-religious organization had some obvious built-in limitations. Otherwise, these authors concluded, "even today [1971], the care of the homeless alcoholic is still viewed in most cities as the exclusive province of the churches and missions." In other words, the care of these unfortunates had been relegated back to where it was prior to the Volstead Act and for centuries before that—to "the church and the jail."

Meanwhile, modern clinical psychology had begun to recognize that alcoholism was a public health problem, since individual therapy had been so staggeringly inadequate to the need; Conley and Sorensen cited one estimate that "if every psychiatrist and every social worker in the United States were to work in alcoholism there would not be enough to treat the alcoholics in the state of California." But Prohibition—for all its neglect of the individual alcoholic—paradoxically *was* an attempt to treat alcoholism as a public health problem, replacing individual treatment (for example, persuading people to "take the pledge") with a crude kind of preventive action.

Without forgiving or denying the mean-spiritedness, hypocrisy, legal repressiveness, and hysterical propaganda that so often marked the "drys'" cause, perhaps we can concede their point that Repeal overthrew this effort at prevention without putting anything in its place. In 1934, the year after the Noble Experiment ended, Deets Pickett wrote: "We come now face to face with the original problem, which is not Prohibition, but alcohol." Although the WASP churches had worked long and hard for Prohibition, and although the Anti-Saloon League had called itself "the Church in action against the saloon," in another sense the Eighteenth Amendment had been an attempt to secularize a kind of social concern that had hitherto been left in private and religious hands, and to make it the responsibility of the state—a transfer which had long since taken place in education and would soon, during the 1930s, take place in public welfare.

As early as 1884 Archbishop John Ireland, one of the rare Roman Catholic advocates of Prohibition, told the Citizens' Reform Association of Buffalo that "the state only can save us," because it alone was competent to control the sale of liquor, as distinguished from its consumption. In 1926 the Methodist *Christian Advocate*, militantly "dry," reasoned that the political logic of such a position led from local option to national control, using arguments not unlike those that "wet" political liberals would employ a decade later in dealing with other issues: "If New York may legally define intoxicants so as to break through the Amendment which prohibits the liquor traffic, why might not South Carolina—should she so desire, as most assuredly she does not—define 'involuntary servitude' in such terms as would nullify that other Prohibition Amendment which outlawed slavery?"

Although perhaps overly generous to the motives of some South Carolinians, this judgment does contain echoes of the quick dismissal of southern and Republican states-rights claims during the thirties and forties by ardent New Deal advocates, and it reminds us that the Noble Experiment was among other things an enormous augmentation of the power of the federal government. From our perspective on that experiment, which incorporates the decades since the twenties, post-Repeal and also post– New Deal, it may seem perfectly natural that a Liberty League would form, work vigorously to secure one form of personal liberty, and then savagely oppose the national government in defense of another. "Freedom" is a horse that everybody wants to ride, whatever their other ideological commitments. So in later years we would see a Barry Goldwater speech writer of 1964, Stephen Hess, become a New Leftist, and the rightist slogan "Extremism in the defense of liberty is no vice" transmute into a rallying cry for radical reform.

PART TWO

The Old-Time Religion in a New-Fangled World

CHAPTER SIX

The Pastoral Office
of the President

*T*he business was done at last: the oath sworn, the Bible closed, the crowd's three cheers acknowledged with a bow. The new president's stage fright was obvious, but the inaugural address had to be got through, and it was a time to put first things first. "It would be peculiarly improper," he declared in his second paragraph, "to omit in this first official act my fervent supplications to that Almighty Being who rules over the universe." In these devotions the chief executive included the assembled congressmen and, by implication, the American people: "In tendering this homage . . . I assure myself that it expresses your sentiments not less than my own."

Like much else that George Washington said and did as president of the United States, this was precedent setting. His thirty-third successor would launch a presidential administration with a formal Inauguration Prayer, and whereas the first president had merely "assured himself" that he and his countrymen were in agreement that such homage should be paid, Dwight Eisenhower would frankly invite the watching and listening

An earlier form of this essay appeared in *Theology Today* 25 (April 1968): 52–63.

millions to join him in the act of worship itself. In front of some television sets, in Republican homes at least, heads were in fact bowed.

From the standpoint of a conservative eighteenth-century critic of republican governments, which were expected to pull down religion along with law, property, and respect for one's betters, the conduct of both presidents would have been quite unexpected, as if the first magistrate should also act as *pontifex maximus*. The Constitution, to be sure, provided that no religious test should ever be required of anyone holding office or public trust under the United States; the prescribed inauguration oath itself had been given a carefully nonsectarian wording: "I do solemnly swear (or affirm)." But the Constitution began to be interpreted and transformed in the moment of its execution, and George Washington acted from the first as high priest of a national Establishment, using stately diction which somehow compounded the spirit of deistic Freemasonry with that of the *Book of Common Prayer*.

On New Year's Day, 1795, for example, he proclaimed a day of public thanksgiving, calling upon "all religious societies and denominations, and . . . all persons whomsoever" to petition the Deity "to preserve us from the arrogance of prosperity," and "to dispose us to merit the continuance of His favors by not abusing them." But meanwhile, in 1791, the states had ratified a Bill of Rights, the first article of which forbade "any law respecting an establishment of religion, or prohibiting free exercise thereof." Twentieth-century jurisprudence has strictly construed this article, assuming that freedom from establishment must mean the right of nonexercise. When the first president, therefore, called upon "all persons whomsoever" to worship on a set day, had he departed from his solemn oath to preserve, protect, and defend the Constitution (as amended)?

Certainly John Adams, Washington's heir and successor, continued the Washingtonian Establishment and added a few emphases of his own. In proclaiming April 25, 1799, as a fast day, the president urged "that the citizens on that day abstain as far as may be from their secular occupations, [and] devote the time to the sacred duties of religion in public and in private." Since such abstention on a weekday would have meant, presumably, the loss of that day's earnings, by meticulous construction a citizen might have claimed tangible (if also modest) standing to sue for a violation of the First Amendment, and the Fifth Amendment as well, which stated that no person could be "deprived of life, liberty, or property, without due process of law."

Was the national Establishment specifically Christian? In his inaugural address in 1797, Adams said that he came into the presidency "with a fixed resolution to consider a decent respect for Christianity among the best recommendations for the public service," in spite of the Constitution's ban on any "religious test" for fitness to hold a government job. And in some of his feast- and fast-day proclamations, John Adams used language ("beseeching Him . . . of His infinite grace, through the Redeemer of the World, freely to remit all our offenses and to incline us by His Holy Spirit to . . . sincere repentance and reformation") which could have been incorporated into any Trinitarian liturgy without altering a comma.

Like father, like son. John Quincy Adams, urging the House of Representatives in 1826 to share in the work of the first Pan-American Congress, told them it might be centuries before they would have another such opportunity "to dispense the promised blessings of the Redeemer of Mankind." And in his fourth annual message, the younger Adams skirted still closer to the edge of the establishment clause when he said, in a passing reference to the Indians, that "we have had the rare good fortune of teaching them the arts of civilization and the doctrines of Christianity." Indian responses to that tribute can well be imagined.

William Henry Harrison, or his ghostwriter Daniel Webster, went still further. A presidential inauguration, said Harrison in 1841 as he launched his brief reign, was a sufficiently solemn and important occasion "to justify me in expressing to my fellow-citizens a profound reverence for the Christian religion." And John Tyler, as he called upon the citizens to mourn Harrison's unexpected death a month later, made believers of them all by implicit fiat: "When a Christian people feel themselves to be overtaken by a great public calamity . . ." In the face of examples like these, what did it matter that the First Amendment forbade legislators to pass statutes preferring one religion over another, or none?

To be sure, Thomas Jefferson, who is ordinarily cited as the author of what has grown into the modern American doctrine of the separation of church and state, was more careful. During the eight years of his administration, references to God all but disappeared from the public messages and state papers. In his second inaugural in 1805, the Virginian explained why he had discontinued the proclamation of days of national thanksgiving and/or repentance: "In matters of religion I have considered that its free exercise is placed by the Constitution independent of the powers of the General Government. I have therefore undertaken on no occasion to prescribe . . . religious exercises." But under Jefferson's ally and hand-picked successor, James Madison, a longtime colleague in the struggle to separate church and state, the national Establishment was speedily restored.

Madison's first inaugural address, like George Washington's, began with a bow to "the guardianship and guidance of that Almighty Being whose power regulates the destiny of nations," and in his first annual message he asked God's blessing on the deliberations of Congress. By the summer of 1812 the proclamation of religious holidays was back in style, and the president set aside the third Thursday in August for "the public homage due" the Almighty and for prayer on behalf of Americans "that He would guide their public councils, animate their patriotism, and bestow His blessings on their arms" in the war which had just begun.

Canadians might more plausibly have discerned the blessing of God in the strong and saving arm of General Isaac Brock, and die-hard Federalist legislatures in New England voted fast days *against* "Mr. Madison's war." But, unabashed, the president in his second inaugural address declared that the War of 1812 was "stamped with that justice which invites the smiles of Heaven on the means of conducting it to a successful termination," an overoptimistic reading of the war news from Canada. Still Madison continued to designate religio-patriotic holidays, including January 12, 1815, on which date God would be asked to "inspire the enemy with dispositions favorable to a just and reasonable peace." The Peace of Ghent was signed on Christmas Eve, 1814, and afterward on January 8 the Americans at New Orleans won a smashing if superfluous victory. Heaven's timing may have been off.

When he got down to more local cases, Madison could be as scrupulous a separationist as Jefferson. On February 12, 1811, for example, he vetoed a bill to incorporate the Protestant Episcopal Church of Alexandria in the District of Columbia as a violation of the establishment clause; and in at least one of his war proclamations he tried to reconcile his political approach to religion with Jefferson's by limiting his recommendation "to all who shall be piously disposed." Likewise his successor, Jefferson's protege and Monticello neighbor James Monroe, sought in his first inaugural to balance a personal-national *confessio fidei* with the Jeffersonian doctrine of separation. He entered the presidential office with his "fervent prayers to the Almighty" for the continuation of "that protection which He has already so conspicuously displayed in our favor." On the other hand, "Who among us," Monroe rhetorically asked, had been "restrained from offering his vows in the mode which he prefers to the Divine Author of his being?" By implication, no one—but the position of the law-abiding citizen who acknowledged the existence of no such Author was not altogether constitutionally clear.

The turbulent upsurge which historians still unite in naming "Jacksonian democracy," however much they divide in their efforts to define it, saw no essential change in the religious, as distinguished from the political, Establishment. In good seasons and in bad, the official messages from Old Hickory invoked the blessing of God, who had granted, said the president in 1830, the "health, peace, and plenty" which the United States had enjoyed, and who, during an epidemic in 1832, had been pleased, said Jackson, "to mitigate its severity and lessen the number of its victims" as compared with the toll which the same pestilence had taken in Europe. It is an advance of sorts over the position taken by the first Adams, who in 1798 had accepted a similar outbreak of deadly disease as one of those afflictions which the Creator for his own purposes visits upon a people, in a judgment to be bowed to "with reverence and resignation."

Some contemporaries of Andrew Jackson evidently thought that divine favor toward the nation also extended to the person of the president himself. On June 20, 1835, in the Capitol rotunda, a would-be assassin fired a pistol at Jackson from a range of some two yards. The exploding percussion cap failed to ignite a well-prepared charge of powder and balls and, so we are told by a pious caption writer for an illustration of the scene, the weapon's inexplicable failure "excited the religious fervor of the people as a providential miracle." Perhaps they missed the homiletic point here being made, for the story continued that when the assassin produced a second pistol, the aged chief executive took after him with a cane.

But the God who bestowed peace and plenty with one hand and sowed pestilence and war with the other could as readily take a president's life as spare it. Only six years after Andrew Jackson's narrow escape, William Henry Harrison became the first president to die in office. John Tyler, summoning Americans "of all religious denominations" to a day of fasting and prayer, reflected that the passing of a president so soon after his ordination was "peculiarly calculated . . . to impress all minds with a sense of the uncertainty of human things and of the dependence of nations, as well as individuals, upon our Heavenly Parent." Some months afterward, Tyler had occasion to strike down an act of Congress which Harrison almost certainly would have signed had he been alive, and in his veto message the new president noted that he sat in Harrison's place "by the occurrence of a contingency provided for in the Constitution and arising under an impressive dispensation of Providence."

Here Tyler seemed to imply that God could be enlisted on His high priest's side even in a controversy with equally God-fearing representatives and senators. Indeed, from the outset there had been a temptation in these Establishment sermons to include under heaven's protection not only the United States considered as a nation or a people—or a form of government—but also at times the government of the day. Proclaiming a fast day in 1799, with the Alien and Sedition Acts in full swing, President John Adams had prayed to "the Most High God" that "He would withhold us from unreasonable discontent, from disunion, faction, sedition, and insurrection." Unfortunately for the elder Adams, one of the campaign issues which shortly thereafter ousted his political party from office forever was the extent and meaning of the word *unreasonable*. Most heads of the Establishment since John Adams's time have tried to keep their formal devotion to deity and their informal allegiance to party in separate, Sabbath-tight compartments, but there were some interesting leakages.

Thus in 1825, in a message in which adherents of a latter-day Great Society could find much comfort, the junior President Adams wrote that "moral, political, intellectual improvements are duties assigned by the Author of our Existence to social no less than to individual man," and that "for the fulfillment of those duties governments are invested with power." Even today a philosophic opponent of Big Government might consider such statements outrageously partisan. For many of John Quincy Adams's contemporaries in 1825, the God-given duties of political man lay in quite another direction.

Jackson, for example, rounded out his presidency with a farewell address in which he spelled out a philosophy in sharp contrast to the dictum of John Quincy Adams that "liberty is power." The ideal polity, said Andrew Jackson in one of his messages to Congress, was one which demonstrated not only that "the people can govern themselves" but also that they could do so through "a machinery . . . so simple and economical as scarcely to be felt." And whereas the second Adams had declared that for a government not to exercise its powers for the general welfare "would be to hide in the earth the talent committed to our charge" (cf. Matt. 25:25–30), the hero of New Orleans prayed that God would "so direct our deliberations and overrule our acts as to make us instrumental in securing a result so dear to mankind," namely, a government limited in scope to "a few subjects of general interest not calculated to restrict human liberty"—presumably in spite of all the Adamses and Henry Clays who would have had it otherwise.

The line between the interests of the commonwealth as a whole and a leader's own partisan concerns is not always easy to draw. When President Jackson issued his no-nonsense proclamation to the people of South Carolina during the nullification crisis of 1832, he called upon God's "wise providence" to inspire in the would-be nullifiers "a returning veneration for that Union which, if we may dare to penetrate His designs, He has chosen as the only means [Unam Sanctam?] of attaining the high destinies to which we may reasonably aspire." Was he, then, addressing the potential leaders of a schismatic church? Or only some fellow southern politicians with whom he had had a falling out? To carry the nullification story into its next chapter, were the Confederate secessionists of 1860 heretics as well as traitors? And what was to be the policy of a president, ex officio pontiff, toward "Our separated brethren"?

Questions like these were to burden Abraham Lincoln, who acknowledged toward the close of the Civil War that Unionists and Confederates "both read the same Bible and pray to the same God." Nor was that God altogether on one side: "The prayers of both could not be answered. That of neither has been answered fully. The Almighty has His own purposes." Lincoln's answer to the terrible question of Job, as starkly Calvinistic as any sermon by Jonathan Edwards, was in sharp contrast to the more typical presidential assurances that the crops flourished and the people multiplied because God smiled on and blessed America. If Jefferson had been the Establishment's Ikhnaton, purging the national faith of superstition and bigotry, Abraham Lincoln was its Deutero-Isaiah, reminding a people that to be chosen is to suffer. It is this tragic vision which saves and gives bite to the famous "malice toward none" statement that followed, which otherwise might have seemed a lofty platitude.

In the Gilded Age—a period of American history not usually associated with enlightened secularism—a serious effort was made to check the drift toward Godliness. In his annual message to Congress on December 7, 1875, President Ulysses S. Grant proposed a constitutional amendment which would have required the states to establish free compulsory public education for all children and would have forbidden the teaching in such schools of any doctrine about ultimate reality, "religious, atheistic, or pagan." To discourage the creation of separate parallel schools which might teach such tenets, he wanted the amendment to declare "that all church property shall bear its own proportion of taxation." Historians of good will have often brushed this proposal aside as nothing but covert anti-Catholicism. Still, the taxation of churches as a logical conclusion from the First Amendment has in recent years been talked of so seriously as to suggest that in neglecting this "Grant Amendment" proposal we may have overlooked a historical precedent of some importance.

In any case, and whatever his personal religious or nonreligious stance may have been, Grant took no steps to compromise the presidential pastorate itself. Quite the contrary. In that same year, 1875, he (or the secretary of state acting in his name) proclaimed a Thanksgiving "in accordance with a practice at once wise and beautiful," and recommended, in words very much like those of the first Adams, that "the people of the United States, abstaining from all secular pursuits and from their accustomed avocations, do assemble in their respective places of worship." Thanksgiving Day, sanctified as an annual event under Lincoln, is in a sense America's one original contribution to the liturgical year of the church. By Grover Cleveland's time its function as a governmental profession of faith was recognized as such by the representatives of other, older establishments. "What difference is there," wrote a visiting French prelate in 1887, "between this beautiful proclamation of a state leader and the decree of a Catholic bishop?"

The Christian character of the American Establishment has no doubt been modified by the pluralistic culture of the twentieth century; today it is at most Judeo-Christian. But it has not, thereby, necessarily ceased to be an establishment. (Dwight Eisenhower unintentionally gave the national church its way out of the dilemma posed by pluralism when he declared that "our government makes no sense unless it is founded in a deeply felt religious faith—and I don't care what it is.") Franklin Roosevelt's first inaugural and many of his other addresses are studded with references to the Scriptures and *The Book of Common Prayer* references, and FDR could turn partisan differences to religious account quite as much as John Quincy Adams or Jackson. Think, for example, of his daring metaphor implicitly comparing certain of his opponents with the money changers whom Christ drove out of the temple, or of his memorable characterization of the moral and political difference between humane Democrats and rigid Republicans: "Governments can err, Presidents do make mistakes, but the immortal Dante tells us that divine justice weighs the sins of the cold-blooded and the sins of the warm-hearted in different scales."

It is doubtful whether the Supreme Court, in its modern concern for religious separation and freedom, could even begin to touch the Establishment at this level. The "establishment of religion" clause in the First Amendment means, according to Justice Hugo Black, that no government, state or federal, "can pass laws which aid one religion, aid all religions, or prefer one religion over another," and that "no tax in any amount . . . can be levied to support any religious activities or institutions, whatever they may be called." This reasoning has been used to stop the mouthing of simple prayers by kindergarteners, but could the courts have enjoined FDR from including in his war message against Japan that passionate and ungrammatical plea: "So help us God"? As for public ceremonies, merely to have added to the Protestant, Orthodox, Catholic, and Jewish clergy whose presence had become de rigueur at such functions, a Zen Buddhist, a Black Muslim, and perhaps Dr. Timothy Leary would hardly have met the Jeffersonian purist's objection to "laws which aid one religion, aid all religions, or prefer one religion over another." Would there be space on an inauguration platform for the kind of soul who dwelt in the Harvard of another day, where (as George Santayana once observed) you could almost be an atheist if you were sufficiently troubled about it?

Of course, establishments can and do carry on after the culture of a people has become thoroughly secular. Sometimes they remain fruitful in scholarship and good works, as have the national churches of Great Britain and Scandinavia. In that event, our presidential pastors' religious observances might become merely a convention, mere "piety along the Potomac." Still, that is not so very far from where the civic religion of ancient Rome came out in its metropolitan age. The god-emperor of the day might make his devotions to philosophy, or Sol Invictus, or Mithras, or Christ. Each new faith duly received its niche in the government-approved shrine, and all that the good citizen really had to do was burn a little incense before the emperor's bust. This was his civic duty, and as for religion, "the free exercise thereof" was otherwise pretty much his own affair. Those who insisted on getting themselves crucified or sent to the arena in spite of this reasonable arrangement seemed not so much subversive as willfully wrongheaded. The last pagan emperor referred to them in all sincerity as atheists.

CHAPTER SEVEN

The Idea of Progress in American Protestant Thought, 1930-1960

*I*n hope that sends a shining ray/far down the future's broadening way . . ." Quoting these lines from a well-known hymn by the Social Gospel pioneer Washington Gladden, Clarence Reidenbach, a Congregationalist minister in Holyoke, Massachusetts, addressed himself late in 1930 to the question of the meaning of the New Year: "Was Dr. Gladden right? Is life really a broadening way?" Or, to put the matter in the language of a classic of intellectual history, is "the idea of progress"—in J. B. Bury's words, the idea "that civilization has moved, is moving, and will move in a desirable direction"—a valid description of social reality? Reidenbach had no doubt that it was. "I have at least two great reasons for optimism" that the future is in fact a broadening way, he continued. "One is my confidence in God . . . the other is that history shows progress."

Confirmation of a belief in "the future's broadening way" could have been found in abundance among Reidenbach's American Protestant contemporaries. "I believe in the heritage of the past, . . . in the challenge of the present and the promise of the future," a recent graduate of a midwest-

An earlier form of this essay appeared in *Church History* 32 (March 1963):75–91.

ern Methodist college affirmed in 1932. "I believe in the possibilities for
the good life which are within myself and within all my fellow men. . . . I
believe in the coming of the cooperative commonwealth of all mankind."
The widely influential magazine *Christian Century* likewise faced the world
of 1931 affirmatively: "We *can* have a new world if we want it!" its editors
declared. Unitarians reaffirmed their traditional evolutionary optimism:
"All human institutions are . . . in process of change," said the American
Unitarian Association's moderator, George R. Dodson, in a 1933 address.
"They are being altered so as better to suit our needs." And more than
simply institutions were in the process of change: "The world itself is in
the making, and we know what o'clock it is in humanity's great day."

Not only could American Protestants still be progressive in the early
1930s, they could also still identify their progressivism with their Protestantism. Thus the president of the Federal Council of the Churches of
Christ in America could address that body on December 6, 1933—the
twenty-fifth anniversary of its founding—on the subject "Protestant Convictions and Progress." Protestantism, said President Albert Beaven (citing
the history of the organizing of that council itself, at the national, state,
and local levels, to prove his point), "represents . . . the principle of liberty, which . . . is the very essence of modern progress." "Democracy and
Protestantism have come and proceeded together," Dwight Bradley wrote
in the *Christian Century* early in 1932. "It is apparent beyond legitimate
question that the development of mankind, the very evolution of the race,
tends directly toward individualistic democracy, and follows the lines of
authentic Protestant leadership."

But this particular Protestant position was a difficult one to sustain
in the thirties, for the reason that progress itself was beginning to fall into
ill repute. J. B. Bury himself, the historian of the idea of progress, had
warned that "the process of change, for which Progress is the optimistic
name," might one day dethrone progress itself. "A day will come," Bury
had written on the final page of his study, "when a new idea will usurp
its place." Bury expected such a day to come only "in the revolution of
centuries," but the kind of events that were following on what H. G. Wells
in his *Outline of History* called simply "the catastrophe of 1914" seemed to
warn that the day of such a dethronement might be more imminent than
anybody except perhaps Henry Adams had anticipated.

The World War (as it was called then) had been interpreted "progres-
sively" for a time; crassly, as in the sixth-grade American history textbook

by Wilbur Fisk Gordy, whose chapter on that war was entitled "Democracy Triumphs over Autocracy"; and more eloquently in some of the justifications of Woodrow Wilson's belief in a "war to end war." But the succeeding age of revolutionary nationalist dictatorships made such a thesis hard to defend. On the Continent it had already been suggested that the "future's way" which broadened out from the war not only might not be progressive but might indeed be regressive; the twenties were years of considerable vogue for Spengler's *The Decline of the West*—a vogue not without its influence in America, as witness the last chapter of Joseph Wood Krutch's melancholy little book *The Modern Temper*. Krutch, of course, wrote from a secularist position (at that time, at least), but Christians could also learn from Spengler, especially after the lapse of a few more terrible years. In 1930, for example, the dean of the College of Religion at Butler University wrote that the gloomy German prophet "irritated me terribly at first and I vowed to have nothing to do with him. Later the course of world events made me turn to him again. . . . Today his prophecy of doom for Western civilization does not appear half so preposterous as it did five years ago."

To be sure, many Americans in the twenties and thirties escaped from Spengler's pessimism by declaring, in effect: "But that sort of thing only happens in the Old World." Richard Hofstadter noted that isolated America had traditionally seen herself as "a kind of non-Europe or anti-Europe." Thus in an age of European collapse, isolationist Americans continued to believe in historical progress by defining it in narrow nationalist terms: whatever happened to Europe, America at least remained the land of progress. But such hopes of an isolationist progressivism were dashed by the Great Depression. Recoiling in disillusion from their experience of the war, Americans had looked forward with Herbert Hoover to the time when, with the help of God, they would be within sight of the abolition of poverty from their nation, a progressive enough goal. Now, after the Crash, they looked around at America's Hoovervilles and sang, "Brother, can you spare a dime?" Progressive America, it appeared, was no more immune than Europe from retreat, retrenchment, and despair.

Religion itself was caught up in the prevailing disillusion and despair. To the formal attack on the church unleashed by critics like H. L. Mencken—perhaps the most formidable polemicist of his kind since Voltaire—was added a serious loss of morale within the religious camp itself. Robert T. Handy has convincingly characterized the decade 1925–1935 for the Protestant churches of that period as "the American religious depression," a time of slump, loss of prestige, and a failure of nerve. Meanwhile, among the Protestant theologians of Europe, there was emerging out of the agonies of the times a "crisis theology" which was a far cry from the evolutionary liberalism of their nineteenth-century forebears—and this far-from-progressive theology was beginning to find American hearers, in the unprogressive situation in which they now found themselves. Karl Barth's *The Word of God and the Word of Man*, for example, appeared in English in 1928. Douglas Horton, his translator, was able to write: "People in general have heard Professor Barth gladly because he seems to understand their inner needs." Though dissenting from Barth, Paul Tillich similarly seemed to understand the inner needs of people for whom "liberalism and fundamentalism" had become—the words are his translator's—"equally intolerable," the former in part because of its "naïve faith in progress."

So, when American Protestants of the sort from whom I quoted at the outset reaffirmed their belief in progress, it was in the teeth of considerable argument to the contrary. But sometimes they reversed the sword's point; the greatest danger to progress, they insisted, came from those who denied it. In reviewing Reinhold Niebuhr's *Moral Man and Immoral Society*, for example, Theodore C. Hume argued that "to remove the morally creative factor in social life which we call religious idealism" (but which Niebuhr would have called, pejoratively, "liberal optimism") "would do much to hasten the doom which Niebuhr fears may soon be upon us." Indeed, Hume implied that Niebuhr's antiliberal and antiprogressive theology might even be heretical: "To call the book fully Christian in tone is to travesty the heart of Jesus' message to the world."

Writers like Hume implied that the disillusion variously expressed by Spengler, Barth, and the brothers Niebuhr amounted to no more than hypochondriac pains in a body social which in fact would enjoy progressive good health if it were only aware of the fact. But what of events themselves? Did not the succession of tragedies since 1914 demonstrate that the prophets of disillusion were articulating the real pains of a real illness? That some writers in 1931 and 1932 could still answer "no" surely demonstrates that hope springs eternal, including the hope that the future was not a narrowing way.

Clarence Reidenbach, for example (the progressive first quoted in this chapter), took cognizance of the two examples most frequently cited by critics in refutation of progress—world war and depression—and nevertheless declared that "we are morally better" than our ancestors; nay, more, "the original disciples of Jesus were obtuse," presumably by comparison to ourselves. The wars of today were no more terrible than those of antiquity—"you can die just as painfully by spears as by poison gas"—and, unlike ancient man, modern man had the hope of peace through social order, as in the League of Nations: "There is a spirit of peace stirring among us, and that spirit is growing a body." In any case, war flouts modern rationality: "It is to the point that we know now that if we go on having wars, we shall not only be criminals; we shall also be fools." Similarly with the Great Crash; conceding the Depression to be "the greatest social crisis since the war," and "a disease that will be fatal, if unchecked," Reidenbach concluded with desperate optimism: "But it is quite likely that somebody will have an idea."

It is perhaps not surprising to find a liberal Congregationalist clergyman solving problems as grievous as war and social disorder in such rationalistic terms, but quite unexpectedly, even so deeply conservative a journal as the *Living Church* could face a war scare of the period in a progressive and optimistic mood. "Peace Education," its editors suggested in 1931, could create a situation in which "Christian governments find that they cannot rely upon the support of their citizens in any war that cannot be squared with an enlightened Christian conscience," and when (not if) such governments limit armaments as a result, "the millennium will be distinctly nearer at hand." Similarly, in *The Churchman*, the "low-church" spokesman for the same denomination, Joseph Fort Newton maintained that, while "any civilization may advance in one direction and retrograde [*sic*] in another," our very perception of this fact constitutes a clear and permanent gain:

> Perhaps the greatest moral advance that has come about is—that wrong is now seen to be wrong, although done by the king, the church, or the state. Such brutality as Cromwell was guilty of at Drogheda would be a disgrace to the Turks of today. Surely a man whose life has spanned nearly all of this advance must be an incorrigible pessimist not to trust God and the future.

But again it must be said that the rush of events was making a position like Newton's increasingly difficult to maintain. Perhaps it was arguable that the Turks in Armenia had not out-Cromwelled Cromwell, but what is one to say of the Germans after Dachau and Buchenwald? Or, for that matter, of the Americans after Hamburg and Hiroshima? The First World

War, Walter M. Horton was to write after experiencing the second, was only the beginning: the American churches at the close of the former war "did not yet know the depth of the world-crisis they were facing. They supposed the war to have been a temporary halt in the progress of Christian civilization, not the beginning of its breakup." Perhaps it is significant that the *Christian Century*, which had published Theodore Hume's adverse review of *Moral Man and Immoral Society*, only two years afterward carried a review of another book by Reinhold Niebuhr which praised its "good wholesome pessimism." "Its aim," editor Charles Clayton Morrison wrote of Niebuhr's *Reflections on the End of an Era*, "is to dispel the romantic illusions about life and to set religion in a context of realism where it must function under conditions of limitation, unattainment and defeat, instead of depending for its vitality upon the optimistic presuppositions of progress and attainment."

However the readers of such a review might quarrel over the adjective "wholesome," pessimistic Reinhold Niebuhr's new book undoubtedly was. "Our western society is obviously in the process of disintegration," he categorically declared. "It lives under the peril of a new war which it seems powerless to avert" (as indeed it did) "and it suffers from serious dislocations in its economic processes which it cannot overcome." To one familiar with the affluence of latter-day America, Britain, and the Common Market countries, that last statement might seem dated, but the next sentence could have been written yesterday—or tomorrow: "Though it is generally known that another war will prove suicidal to the whole of western culture it is no longer certain that fear of the possibility of such a suicide will avert the war."

Thus far the thesis set forth by Niebuhr was not necessarily incompatible with progressivism—of the catastrophic sort for whose advocates things have to get a lot worse before they can get any better. Even his rash prediction that the New Deal was bound to fail, as "the vague liberalism of the Roosevelt administration" disintegrated "into a more obvious conservatism and radicalism," was no more than the Marxists—good progressives too, in their fashion—had said and were continuing to say. But Niebuhr set himself against "both the bourgeois idea of progress and the Marxian idea of salvation through catastrophe." The Marxist was ultimately as optimistic as the capitalist and therefore in the long run as self-deluding: "The communist faith that communist oligarchs will not make a selfish use of their power belongs in the same category of illusions which aristocracies of the past have nourished. . . . Aristocracies . . . have always been corrupted in the end by the poison of power."

It is true that the book "brightens toward the end," as one reviewer noted, but the hope which brightens these reflections is not the shining ray of progress. It is "the assurance of grace." And the experience of that assurance—"the apprehension of the absolute from the perspective of the relative"—is a kind of consolation which can "have no meaning to the modern man and the modern spirit." For the modern spirit is (by intention, at least) rational and prosaic, whereas "the idea of grace can be stated adequately only in mythical terms." The modern spirit is progressive in that it seeks to solve "problems of man in nature and man in society" in such a way that they do not recur, whereas such problems ought to be seen as "perennial problems of the human spirit, and not merely as injustices of an era." Although he carefully distinguished his theological position from that of the Barthians, Niebuhr like Barth reached back to and beyond Luther for a radical reaffirmation of the doctrine of justification by faith—"the sinner is 'justified' even though his sin is not overcome" (*Simul justus et peccator*)—which is a long way indeed from the "idea of progress."

But some readers of these unprogressive *Reflections* were not convinced. "The author . . . has decidedly limited his perspective," one reviewer objected. "He seems unaware of the actual operation of the corrective forces" which were already at work restoring civilization to an even keel. The New Deal in particular gave progressivism a new lease on life in America. President Roosevelt stubbornly declined to be pessimistic—"a whole nation . . . is full of cheer once more," he insisted in a 1936 campaign speech—and the effect was felt among American Protestant churchmen. "Neo-orthodox arguments," Donald Meyer observed, were "frustrated by . . . liberalism's practical success." Paradoxically, even when the war came which Niebuhr had predicted would "prove suicidal to the whole of western culture," it unexpectedly gave renewed sanction to a progressive philosophy of history. The rehabilitation of words like *progress* and *reaction* by the positive program of the New Deal was confirmed, in most American minds, by the crusade against Nazi Germany.

The Marxists for many years had been calling fascism "the last stage of capitalism" and therefore antiprogressive; now they were joined by other kinds of progressives, who saw the military decision to prevent a Nazi-dominated world as being at least a decision between the possibility of progress and its impossibility. Ralph E. Flanders, later a United States senator from Vermont, told a regional laymen's meeting that "Germany under Hitler openly and purposefully seeks to destroy [the essentials] of Christian civilization," a civilization which "it does not do to discount . . . by recounting its weaknesses and failures." Our awareness of these short-comings, "to which our ancestors were blind or resigned, is no cause for contempt of our progress. It is an evidence of progress."

The founding of the journal *Christianity and Crisis* in protest against the "plague on both your houses" brand of pacifism to which the *Christian Century* had come by 1940, represented a decision that a future under the United Nations would be at least relatively more progressive than one under the Axis, and a group of distinguished American clergymen, including Methodist bishop Francis McConnell, Episcopal bishop Henry St. George Tucker, Federal Council president Luther A. Weigle, and Henry P. Van Dusen, among others, made such a progressivist judgment the basis for a public declaration that "this war must be won by the United Nations." At stake, they said, was "our Christian concept of man's destiny, and our opportunity for years to come, to work toward a larger earthly fulfillment of that destiny." "We are members of a human race," the chaplain to the 1942 Congregational General Council told that body, "which has done some noble things on this earth, and we purpose to be a part of the unending procession of men who will continue to better it."

But as the war drew to its fiery close and people pondered the meaning of such things as obliteration bombing, calls for total extermination, and the making of souvenirs out of the bones of fallen enemy soldiers, the debate was resumed. On the one hand, for example, a Christmas editorial for 1944 in the Congregationalist journal *Advance* maintained that "man's inherent selfishness had been grossly exaggerated, his capacity for generosity minimized. The nations of the earth are commonly pictured as more aggressive than they are." Consequently, since "the people sincerely want peace," the prospects were excellent that they might get it. President Roosevelt again threw his weight on the side of progress; on the day of his death he was working on the manuscript of a radio address which was to have concluded: "The only limit to our realization of tomorrow will be our doubts of today. Let us move forward with strong and active faith." On the other hand, Drew Middleton, fresh from observing the rubble of Berlin, wrote (in the *New York Times*) that "the end of Western urban civilization is no longer an empty phrase but a terrible fact already within the grasp of mankind," and the editors of the *Christian Century* were moved to wonder whether Middleton had his verb tenses straight. "*Has* Western civilization survived this war?" they asked in all seriousness. If not, "there lies before the church a period of such hardship and change"—but hardly, in the usual sense, progress—"as even its boldest prophets have not yet envisaged."

The end of the Second World War was consequently marked by what may have been the most somber victory celebration in the history of humankind. On the deck of U.S.S. *Missouri* in Tokyo Bay, Douglas Mac-Arthur, the leader of the victorious Allied forces in the Pacific, warned friend and foe alike: "We have had our last chance." Nor was this simply a call for secular world order: "The problem is basically theological. . . . It must be of the spirit if we are to save the flesh." Even more soberly, Reinhold Niebuhr wrote on the day after V-J Day: "The victory over Japan leaves a strange disquiet and lack of satisfaction." He reminded his fellow Americans of "the prophetic warnings to the nations of old, that nations which become proud because they were divine instruments must in turn stand under the divine judgment and be destroyed." "Strange paradox," Walter M. Horton wrote two years later, "that modern science should so recently have been used to prove that . . . the 'progress of mankind onward and upward forever' was assured," and should now have brought us into a new world whose end could be expected "at almost any time." It followed that "the basic assumption of modernism (progress) has been undercut by . . . events."

For some progressives, therefore, the Bomb simply meant the end. H. G. Wells, for example, closed out a long lifetime of writing and think-ing by formally adopting the pessimism which theretofore had occasionally glimmered through the militantly optimistic progressivism of his many books: "The human story has already come to an end and . . . *Homo sapiens*, as he has been pleased to call himself, is in his present form played out. The stars in their courses have turned against him." Human history is neither progressive nor providential nor cyclical but simply meaningless; for "that congruence with mind, which man has attributed to the secular process, is not really there at all." Hence, "the attempt to trace a pattern of any sort is absolutely futile." Of the terrifying little book which embodied this judgment, *Mind at the End of Its Tether*, Reinhold Niebuhr wrote: "The spiritual pilgrimage of Mr. Wells is an almost perfect record in miniature of the spiritual pilgrimage of our age."

For a secular optimist-turned-pessimist like Wells, such a statement ended the matter. "The utmost that mind can do . . . its last expiring thrust," he wrote, "is to demonstrate that the door closes upon us for evermore." But for the Christian there was a further difficulty. In the grim year 1962 an American doctoral candidate in theology at Oxford was to write: "Christ is the Lord of history, we say. . . . Can Christ be the Lord of a human enterprise which is about to put an end to itself?"

One way of answering this question would be to deny that the historical process has any transcendent meaning. From an existential premise similar to that of H. G. Wells—"We find ourselves more or less at the end of the modern rope. It has worn too thin to give hopeful support"—Karl Löwith came to a similar conclusion about pattern or meaning: "To the critical mind, neither a providential design nor a natural law of progressive development is discernible in the tragic human comedy of all times." Professing Christianity, Löwith could fellow-travel with unbelief on this one vital point: "Religious faith is so little at variance with skepticism that both are rather united by their common opposition to the presumptions of a settled knowledge." The idea of progress is such a presumption, and "the skeptic and the believer have a common cause against the easy reading of history and its meaning." Thus, as a Christian, Karl Löwith's answer to the question of whether Christ can be the Lord of history would be, "The message of the New Testament is not an appeal to historical action but to repentance. . . . The story of salvation, as embodied in Jesus Christ, redeems and dismantles, as it were, the hopeless history of the world"— atomic bombs to the contrary notwithstanding.

But many Protestants nurtured in a progressive historical tradition could not accept so radically transcendent a thesis. Kenneth Scott Latourette, reviewing Löwith's book *Meaning in History* for the *New York Times*, challenged his antiprogressivism: "It is at least debatable whether '. . . the empirical history after Christ is qualitatively not different from the history before Christ.' " And, from the perspective of his own monumental writings on nineteenth-century Christianity, Latourette declared: "It is highly doubtful that 'Christianity . . . as a world religion is a complete failure.' " Elaborating these views in response to the theme of the Second Assembly of the World Council of Churches at Evanston, Illinois, in 1954, "Christ the Hope of the World," Latourette wrote, "Judged from the scope of the entire human scene and the course of history to our day, Christ and his Church are making themselves more and more felt and have never been more potent than in our time." And in the same symposium F. Ernest Stoeffler wrote: "We cannot help but feel that our Western civilization has moved forward in its general approximation of the ideals of the Christian ethic. . . . In that sense we have made progress."

Another answer to the question "Can Christ be the Lord of a human enterprise which is about to put an end to itself?" would be to say, But the enterprise need not end. Such a response to the challenge of nuclear war does much to explain the Arnold Toynbee vogue which sprang up in America (and elsewhere) following the publication of volumes 1 through 6 of *A Study of History* in the Somervell abridgement in 1947. For H. G. Wells's door that closes upon us for evermore, Toynbee substituted his celebrated metaphor of the cliff, in which civilizations are like mountain climbers, ascending the cliff in a rhythm of "challenge-and-response." Thereby Toynbee appeared to have contrived a philosophy of history which was both progressive and providential at the same time; human beings retained their power of autonomous action, yet their capacity to respond to crisis was a gift of God: "The divine spark of creative power is still alive in us, and, if we have the grace to kindle it into flame, then the stars in their courses cannot defeat our efforts to attain the goal of human endeavour."

Toynbee became enough of a prophet in America that his cliff-climbing civilizations were converted (by the inspired pen of Abner Dean) into cartoon characters for a spread in *Life*, and the mentor himself made the cover of *Time*. But some saw the whole phenomenon as one more deplorable example of what Professor Sidney Hook had called "the new failure of nerve." One of Toynbee's American reviewers, Harry Elmer Barnes, sarcastically commented that "the Neo-Medicine Man seems to be coming into his own." More important for our present purpose, Toynbee's system of civilizations did not hold out quite the answer that progressive Protestant Americans were looking for. His assumptions were not particularly Protestant. Since Protestants were shortly to be writing and speaking of a "post-Protestant era," that might not have been so bad. But also, his assumptions were not particularly Christian, as the four succeeding volumes were to make painfully clear; and while Americans were beginning to flirt fairly seriously with Eastern religious ideas, notably Zen Buddhism, they were a long way from the idiosyncrasies of a faith that could break forth in a litany which interspersed Latin Christian liturgical phrases with prayers to Buddha, Isis, Mithras, Muhammad, Zarathustra, and even Lucretius.

In any case, "the association of the two ideas of civilization and progress," which Professor Bury had thought of as "taken for granted" by modern man, was certainly not taken for granted by Toynbee. If there is progress in history, it is at the *expense* of civilizations, which suffer and die so that man's soul can go marching on. The metaphor of the cliff dissolves into a metaphor of a chariot, which is religion, and "the wheels on which it mounts toward Heaven may be the periodic downfall of civilizations on Earth." This was hardly what most of Toynbee's admirers had in mind. "Since civilization is more or less subsidiary to religion," H.C.F. Bell wrote in reviewing *Civilization on Trial*, "the crisis we are going through may contribute to religious evolution in the end. But this seems cold comfort when one thinks of planes droning between Bizonia and Berlin."

It is interesting to note that Professor Bell was both a professional historian and a practicing Catholic. One of the most disconcerting features of the anti- or perhaps post-progressive position which many Protestants found themselves driven to after the Second World War was that it was not fully shared by Protestantism's venerable adversary. On his elevation to the pontificate, Pope John XXIII proceeded briskly to reverse the Pius IX antiprogressive stereotype. Summoning a Second Vatican Council to take up where the "reactionary" pontiff had left off, Pope John opened the conclave with a speech in which he took strong exception to "prophets of gloom who . . . say that our era, in comparison with past eras, is getting worse." Such pessimists, His Holiness declared, "behave as though they had learned nothing from history, which is nonetheless the teacher of life." He even had a good word for "the marvelous progress of the discoveries of human genius," and he predicted "a new order of human relations." "Providential" rather than "progressive"? Perhaps, but when one finds an opening address to a comparable non-Catholic gathering, the World Council of Churches Assembly at Evanston, declaring "It is just because it has made so much progress that mankind has reached the point beyond which it must not go," one wonders how it was that Protestantism could have become identified with progressivism in the first place.

Nor were Roman Catholics the only ones still finding some operational validity in the idea of progress; there were also the inescapable Russians. In the article "Notes on the Meaning of History" in a Soviet historical journal in 1961, N. I. Konrad observed that "the theory of progress . . . has always been subjected to criticism." For all the world like Bury, Konrad pointed out "the dogmatic nature of the very concept of progress . . . or, in the final analysis, the debatable nature of what is considered progressive." In restaging this debate, Konrad gave the antiprogressives their due: "The replacement of hot pincers by electric current in torture was made possible by the vast advance in science and technology. . . . Does this mean progress?" And his answer to this kind of question reminds us of the kinds of answers which Protestant Americans had given for a time and had now begun to abandon:

> All that is dark in history, the ocean of sorrows and suffering to which man has been, and continues to be, subjected . . . all this did happen and does happen. But the truly great achievement of mankind and perhaps the highest manifestation of progress is the fact that people *did* discern this, and called evil evil, coercion coercion, and crime crime. . . . The development of the understanding of that which had to be evaluated as evil is . . . proof of progress.

Whereas the discovery of the magnitude of evil in the world was being advanced by some American Protestants as an argument *against* progress!

The Russian concluded on a frankly utopian note. The Greeks and Romans, the ancient Chinese, and other peoples had had a dream of a "golden age," or a "happy land." "The idea of this end, expressed in various images, has never left mankind and has inspired it to struggle against whatever blocked the achievement of an ideal state of society, worthy of man." Compare Reinhold Niebuhr, in *The Self and the Dramas of History* (1955): "We can only hope . . . that we may have the chance of being purged of our illusions and, in a more modest mood, dedicate our great energies and virtues to the building of a tolerable world community." The Soviet historian, presumably a materialist, wrote of an ideal state; the American Christian theologian wrote of illusions. As possible philosophies of history, Konrad saw the options as "the theory of the closed cycle" and "the theory of progress," with no Christian interpretation as a third possibility. Niebuhr saw "the real alternative to the Christian faith" available to all secular thinkers as "the idea that history is itself Christ, which is to say that historical development is redemptive." If each writer was in some sense representative of thought on his own side of the Iron Curtain, then the cold war had become a good deal more subtle and complex than any of us had bargained for.

CHAPTER EIGHT

The Negro and Methodist Union

The schism in the Methodist Episcopal Church in 1844 and its reunion in 1939 fall into a pattern remarkably similar to that of the great schism and reunion of the United States. The antislavery movement possessed religious overtones of the evangelical temper characteristic of Methodism, and the centralized—constitutional, if you will—structure of Methodism exposed it to federal-versus-regional stresses similar to those that divided the nation. There is the significant difference that the northern and southern Methodists parted amicably and did not become involved in partisan bitterness until after the adjournment of their last General Conference together, but otherwise the parallel is complete: general acceptance of the principle of emancipation by the founders both of church and nation; with the renascence of slavery, the recession of this view, marked by a series of compromises in the General Conference as in the Congress; the rise, and unpopularity of, militant abolitionism;

An earlier form of this essay appeared in *Church History* 21 (March 1952): 55–70. At the time of the controversy described in this article, the word *Negro* rather than *black* or *African-American* was the preferred term. One's task in the classroom when I commenced teaching was to persuade insensitive white students to spell it with a capital N. I have edited this 1952 article with these circumstances in mind.

a dramatic revival of partisan concern, marked by an acute constitutional debate; growing sectional irreconcilability; schism; conflict—and an eventual resolution of the breach *in terms of the tacit recognition by the North of the principle of segregation.*

All the phases of this historical parallel, as far as the clerical side of it is concerned, have been adequately explored except for the last mentioned. The slavery breach in Methodism has been well covered in John N. Norwood's *The Schism in the Methodist Episcopal Church.* The intricate history of the negotiations, commissions, and conferences which led to the union of the northern and southern wings of the former ME Church with the Methodist Protestant Church in 1939 has been traced by John M. Moore in *The Long Road to Methodist Union.* But Bishop Moore's major emphasis was upon the constitutional process of separation and union rather than upon the dynamics of slavery and segregation on which the issue of separation and union really turned. Moreover, as a partisan participant in the union of the churches, he naturally stressed the elements making for harmony over those making for disagreement, and as a bishop of the former ME Church, South, his inclination was to regard segregation as a settled question. It is my intention in this essay to indicate that the question of segregation in the church, as in the nation, does not down quite so easily.

The debate over ratification of the Plan of Union in the (northern) Methodist Episcopal Church turned on the status of blacks in the new united church. Bishop Moore summarizes and dismisses this debate in one paragraph:

> The antagonism to the Negro Jurisdictional Conference forcibly expressed by certain white leaders and violently stressed by certain Negro leaders, and the reasons which they gave for their antagonism, recruited for a time the opposition in the South, especially in those sections where the membership of Negroes in the Church at all, and particularly in the General Conference, was strongly opposed. The Negro was made the chief obstacle to union by both groups, but for opposite reasons.

Bishop Moore's chief interest in the black members of the ME Church was evidently their function as a *casus belli* for the southern opposition— that is to say, as a problem which had to be solved prior to the union of the northern and southern white Methodists. But when one considers black Methodists as a community within Methodism, with religious and secular aspirations of its own worthy of being taken seriously, one is confronted with historical questions which Moore did not answer: What features of this

Negro Jurisdictional Conference were there to produce "violent" opposition? How large a following was represented by "certain Negro leaders"? Why did the reasons for this opposition produce, in turn, a negative reaction at the South? It is my hope that the evidence submitted herein will throw light on some of these points.

The crisis in Methodism in 1844 was precipitated by a conflict in the itinerant episcopacy; so, indirectly, was the crisis in the 1930s. The immediate cause of the schism had been the suspension by the General Conference of a slaveholding bishop, and Collins Denny, Sr., the leader of the modern southern opposition to union, stated his objections in 1911 as follows: "It is stated that Bishops . . . should circulate throughout the Church. . . . If one of the Conferences should elect a Negro Bishop to preside over the whole Church, there would be no Methodism in the South for him to preside over. We cannot possibly subject our people to that possibility."

The prevention of that possibility could have been achieved in either of two ways: by removing all blacks and hence all potential black bishops from the rolls of the united Methodist Church, or by constitutionally restricting the activity of bishops so that no "Negro bishop should circulate throughout the Church." The first view was held by many, if not most, southern Methodist advocates of church union down to about 1920 when the North elected its first non-missionary black bishops; it was the official position, for example, of the Oklahoma City General Conference of the Church, South, in 1914. In view of the vigorous black church life which had developed in the Methodist Episcopal Church after the Civil War, this was never a practicable basis for church union. "It is clear to those who know the loyalty and devotion of the masses of the [N]egro ministry and membership of our church that [if they do leave it] they must be *forced out*," said Bishop Thirkield in 1916. The idea, however, never quite died; Bishop Moore, for example, continued to advocate the separation of the black Methodists even after union had been consummated with their inclusion, and doubtless it long lingered in southern circles of the united Methodist Church.

The other method of meeting southern objections consisted of the creation of Jurisdictional Conferences, midway in authority between the General and the Annual Conference. The boundaries of all but one of these conferences would be geographic; the other would be based on race. The Jurisdictional Conferences, including the Negro Jurisdiction, would elect the bishops, who had theretofore been chosen by the entire church. This would involve a breakdown of the traditional Methodist itinerant episcopacy, required by the *Discipline* to travel "throughout the Connection," but because the work of the bishops since before the turn of the century had already been administratively divided into Episcopal Areas, the practical difference in itinerancy would be slight. Indeed, inasmuch as a great deal of the "Negro work" of the northern church was grouped into two such Episcopal Areas already, presided over after 1920 by black bishops, the reader may wonder wherein the proposed jurisdictional plan differed sufficiently from the existing situation in the northern church to warrant opposition to one and support of the other. This is discussed at greater length below; for the moment, let me observe only that in the northern church prior to unification the presiding bishops of these Episcopal Areas were still elected by the General Conference of the church as a whole. This meant that black and white delegates were obliged to consult together in the election of both black and white bishops. It was to be argued in behalf of the Jurisdictional Plan that the black members would be better off under it because they would be assured of bishops of their own choosing; but the growing integrationist party among black Americans concluded that the loss in interracial relationships would offset the gain in black autonomy under the new arrangement.

After two false starts at unification in 1920 and 1924, the last of many Joint Commissions of the ME Church, the ME Church, South, and the Methodist Protestant Church on December 12, 1935, released the text of the Plan of Union, which was to become the basis of the actual merger in 1939. Acceptance of the jurisdictional idea was explicit; there were to be five geographical jurisdictions (Northeastern, Southeastern, North Central, South Central, and Western), and one based upon color, the Central. I am fully aware that the Plan represented the unanimous opinion of the commissioners, two of whom were black. I submit, however, that the size of an opposition is often less important than its nature and that the opinion of the black commissioners, admittedly able men, was unrepresentative of their people, as demonstrated by the ultimate outcome of the debate.

The clearest contemporary discussion of the merits and defects of the Plan of Union from an African-American standpoint appeared in *The Crisis*, the official journal of the National Association for the Advancement of Colored People, in an article by two black ministers of the Methodist Episcopal church entitled "Methodist Union and the Negro." This is sufficiently comprehensive to deserve summarizing here:

Arguments in favor of the plan included the assertion that the Jurisdictional Conference was "largely administrative"; it did not differ in principle from the organization for convenience of certain non-English-speaking Methodists in America into German, Swedish, and Norwegian-Danish Annual Conferences—or from "the existence of separate Negro [local] churches, separate Negro Annual Conferences, and separate Negro Episcopal Areas." The General Conference, the supreme governing body of the church, remained unsegregated. It was true that the General Conference would no longer *elect* the bishops, white and black, who would preside over it, but this would work to the advantage of the blacks by enabling them in their separate jurisdiction to elect their own leaders rather than having their votes "swallowed up" in a mixed jurisdiction. Since it was constitutionally provided that all jurisdictions, including the Central (Negro) and the Southeastern, should have equal representation on the administrative boards of the church, the plan "would increase points of contact with the white Methodists of the South."

Arguments against the plan included a challenge to this last statement. The plan was "a deliberate move to reduce the contact with the Negro to a minimum." The analogy between the existing segregation pattern in the ME Church and the proposed Negro Jurisdiction was historically inaccurate; the creation of the black congregations and Annual Conferences had been "on the basis of a 'mutual understanding,' to enable the blacks to make the most of the situation" that society at large had imposed upon race relations. "The new plan differs from the present arrangement in that it would write into the very constitution of the church the article of segregation." As an example of the increased restriction on racial mobility in the church under the plan, if it should be desired to transfer a black congregation out of a black Annual Conference into the appropriate white Annual Conference covering that geographic area, the consent of both Jurisdictional Conferences involved would have to be obtained. This meant, in other words, that the Plan of Union made it, for all practical purposes, constitutionally impossible for blacks to crack the color line in those parts of the Methodist Church located in the South even if a local situation developed which favored it.

The issue of segregation, however, was by no means the entire story.

Behind the floor debates at the northern and southern General Conferences lay the driving force of the Ecumenical Movement. Others have discussed this remarkable reversal of the tendency toward fission that was historically characteristic of Protestantism in a thorough fashion beyond the scope of this essay. I shall here only indicate the somewhat uncritical nature of this trend by pointing out that most discussion of the state of Christianity by Christians took it for granted that the divided character of American Protestantism was an evil. One heard little reference to the social and religious vigor of sectarianism. There will be something to be said on this point in my concluding remarks.

American Methodist ecumenicalism in particular was augmented by considerations arising out of the Social Gospel. In the various crises of the age, its leaders called for religious unity in order to make a concerted attack on evil. A particularly effective summation of this ecumenical basis for unification sentiment in both North and South is contained in the Episcopal Address to the Southern General Conference of 1938:

> The problems of our world are too great and grave to be met by any one branch of the Christian faith. We must minimize our differences, magnify the cardinal tenets that unite, and consolidate our common spiritual resources if we are to stem the tide of secularism that is sweeping across the world. No compromise of essential values is involved in joining with evangelical Christians in every nation and presenting a solid front against the common enemies that oppose the Church everywhere.

The final General Conference of the (northern) Methodist Episcopal Church met at Columbus, Ohio, on May 1, 1936, to transact its quadrennial affairs and to pass upon the Plan of Union. The Episcopal Address, the traditional message from all the bishops to the constituency, included a thoughtful discussion of the conflict between the social and individual gospel then raging in the church, pronouncements on various social issues (including a forthright paragraph on "the Negro"), and an emphatic endorsement of the Plan of Union in terms explicitly ecumenical. Changes on this ecumenical theme continued to be rung throughout the conference. The president of the Federal Council of Churches declared that "the evils of this world are too great for any sort of a divided Church." Bishop Ainsworth, fraternal delegate from the ME Church, South, linked ecumenicalism with the church's social message: "The solidarity of mankind is being hammered into us. . . . Mankind must be one or we will soon be none, and Christianity must rebuild the world on the basis of brotherhood. . . . United Methodism must lead the way." The fraternal delegate from the British Methodist Church saw the world potentiality of American Methodism in the context of the moral force of America in collective security. "There isn't a bridge in America built by the forces of evil that can withstand the tramp, tramp of eight million Methodists," was the cry of President Broomfield of the Methodist Protestant Church. And Bishop Edwin Holt Hughes, summing up the work of the conference in his address just before adjournment, called the merger "the blessed example that may providentially result in other needed mergers in Protestantism. . . . Your overwhelming vote . . . has been succeeded by an increasing assurance that in this great matter we have done the will of God."

It should be borne in mind that the Plan of Union was presented to the Churches to be accepted or rejected *as a whole*; many delegates who had reservations against the arrangement with respect to the black members but who were immersed in this ecumenical atmosphere therefore voted for the Plan as a greater good. Important objections, however, were raised on the ground that no end was sufficiently high to warrant the violation of minority rights for its attainment. *The Christian Century* editorialized: "From the Christian standpoint, the determining element should not be what a minority under great pressure is willing to take, but what the majority, in the light of its responsibility to the minority, must feel under obligation to offer."

This was entirely in keeping with the conclusion to which northern Methodists had come in 1916, that "the Negroes themselves [should] confer about, agree to, and confirm whatever decision is made." By this criterion, if the reaction of the secular African-American press is any indication of contemporary black opinion, the merger of 1939 was clearly a mistake. The headline on the front page of the *Pittsburgh Courier*, then the most widely circulated black newspaper, in its next issue after the northern Methodist vote on Unification, was characteristic: "Race Protest Ignored as Ohio Methodists Vote for Merger." *The Crisis*, the official organ of the NAACP—then considered a comparatively conservative organization—ran an editorial entitled "Jim Crow for Jesus." The Philadelphia *Tribune* was even more caustic: "God watched and followed the proceedings with keen interest; when the conference insulted His intelligence by approving segregation of Negroes in His name, He took a walk." If General Conference voting strength was in any sense representative, the pattern of opposition extended to the black members of the ME Church. In a caucus held the Saturday evening before debate began, 33 of 44 black delegates present asked David D. Jones as their spokesman to " 'protest in a mild, but manly, way against this Plan of Unification.' "

The opposition at the northern church's General Conference, however, was not confined to blacks. In spite of the ecumenical considerations which kept many white delegates on the side of church union, a small but determined group stood with the majority of the black delegation in voting against ratification of the Plan of Union. The most outstanding of these in my opinion was Lewis O. Hartman, chairman of the New England Annual Conference delegation and editor of the small but influential independent Methodist weekly *Zion's Herald*, which, then as later, bore a relation to the rest of the Methodist press somewhat resembling that of *The Nation* to the rest of the American press. (It is a matter of historical fitness that we not only find New England once again a center of intransigence on the "Negro question" just as it had been at an earlier point in Methodist and national history but also find *Zion's Herald* playing a role comparable to its own militant abolitionist stand of a century before.) Hartman campaigned editorially against the union with the ME Church, South, from the moment it became apparent that the jurisdictional agreement was to be the basis of that union, and while he accepted the verdict of the majority and was eventually elected to serve the united Methodist Church as a bishop, to the end of his life he remained convinced that the merger had been a mistake.

It was most fitting, then, that Hartman should lead off the debate on the actual resolution. He made it plain at the outset that he was in favor of the general principle of church union:

> We are faced not with a clear-cut choice between an absolute good and an absolute evil; rather, we are presented with two "goods," one the great desirability of Unification and the other the equally great desirability of keeping clear of the very appearance of the evil of race discrimination. . . . I cannot bring myself to endorse unification at the price of the Negro.

His most important contribution to the discussion was to remind the conference that the world social mission of the church, which had been cited by the advocates of union as an argument for the Plan, could also be used against it:

It has seemed to me that . . . the whole issue has been approached too much from the angle of organization and administration and too little from the less tangible, but equally important viewpoint of . . . the effect of the possible passage of the Plan of Unification upon our prophecy and our witness before a listening world. . . . It is possible to unite and pile up a great total of millions of members and yet lose our spiritual power.

Hartman was followed in the debate by Harold P. Sloan, who defended the plan as an enlargement of black opportunity, "not . . . discrimination against the Negro, but . . . discrimination in favor of the Negro," protecting blacks from being outnumbered and hence unable to have an effective say in the Church.

Ernest F. Tittle made a rebuttal to this: "To be sure, by segregating Negroes in a Negro Conference we give them political opportunities which they would not possess as minority groups within our white conferences; but we take away from them the experience of Christian brotherhood which, in my judgment, is far more important"—a tacit recognition that racial antagonism works both ways. Dr. Tittle also made the point that Methodists in this matter were lagging behind other churchmen and also behind secular organizations:

The Protestant Episcopal Church has not felt it necessary to do it [segregate black members] . . . Southeastern share-croppers, black and white, are forming a union . . . and they are asking "Is it possible that an organization without any religious profession of faith can transcend a historic, irrational, un-Christian prejudice, whereas the Christian Church cannot do so?"

Black speakers were heard on both sides of the question. David D. Jones, president of Bennett College in North Carolina, called the Plan "segregation in the ugliest way, because it is couched in such pious terms." Matthew Davage, president of Clark University in Atlanta, countered that the plan had "not been thrust upon us," that "two of the ablest men in our group," Bishop Robert E. Jones and President Willis J. King of Gammon Seminary, had been on the Joint Commission which formulated the plan and had concurred in the jurisdictional arrangement. A more telling point was that black participation, even restricted to the General Conference and administrative board level, in a church which would include southern whites, would make the Methodist blacks "the only members of our race having real organic relationship with influential white leaders of the

South." But opponents of the union explained away this minority black support for the plan, and also that of white leaders whose social liberalism was unquestionable, such as Bishop Francis McConnell, as "the outcome of a process of rationalization and wishful thinking induced by an almost irresistible enthusiasm for unification."

After some two hours of debate a delegate moved the previous question, which had the effect of preventing the introduction of an amendment which would have put the conference on record as in favor of the Plan of Union but with a reservation against the Negro Jurisdictional Conference. The fate of this amendment, had it been offered, is of course problematical, but in view of the heavy vote in favor of the plan as it stood and the fact that the amendment would have left the ME Church with a different plan from that presented to the other two constituting Churches, thereby jeopardizing the merger, I believe that the amendment would have been voted down. The vote of the General Conference of the Methodist Episcopal Church was: 470 for the Plan, 83 against. Of the 47 black delegates present and voting, 11 cast their ballots for, 36 against. "When the vote was announced," the correspondent of the *Christian Century* reported, "the conference arose and broke forth into singing, 'We're marching to Zion.' Many people of the colored race did not rise and did not sing."

"You may adopt this Plan. We are powerless to prevent it," David D. Jones, the spokesman for the majority of black delegates, had said in the debate. "All we can do is to appeal to time." With unification a fait accompli as far as the northern church was concerned, many of its black members seem to have resigned themselves to the inevitable. Edgar A. Love's statement on May 12 typifies this view: "You have adopted by an overwhelming majority, in the face of a pronounced objection to this Plan by a great majority of Negro delegates, this plan. . . . We are going into this new setup graciously and with the avowed purpose of making Unification, as far as we are concerned, a success."

But expressions of opposition continued. Lorenzo H. King, pastor of St. Mark's Methodist Church in Harlem, preached a sermon on Methodist unification which was printed and circulated. "Under this 'Plan,' he said, "every other race group in America can join, and move with freedom in any section of the Methodist Church, except the Negro. . . . This 'Plan' will emasculate the Christian gospel of its moral imperative." The protests became more strident as it became increasingly apparent that the ratification of the plan would inevitably be sustained. In fact, the vote in favor of the plan by the ministerial and lay delegates to the Annual Conferences was proportionately more decisive even than that of the General Conference—17,239 to 1,862, or about 9 to 1.

With the northern church committed to unification, the desire to hasten the completion of ratification became evident in the Methodist Episcopal Church, South. At their 1936 sessions, 25 of the 38 Annual Conferences comprising that church petitioned their College of Bishops to submit the Plan of Union for their approval the following year—so that Annual Conference action would be complete *before* the South's General Conference met, thus hastening the process of union. This was accordingly done; the ministers and lay delegates to the Annual Conferences of 1937 accepted the Plan of Union by 7,650 votes to 1,247. The Plan was thereby placed before the General Conference of the ME Church, South, for final action.

The Episcopal Address to that final Southern General Conference, which convened in Birmingham, Alabama, on April 28, 1938, was appropriately devoted in large part to a historical review of the achievements of the Church South, since it was anticipated that that church would shortly lose its separate identity. As with the Northern Episcopal Address of two years before, the document made pronouncements on sundry social questions, including a remarkable statement on "the Negro" which bears favorable comparison with the northern declaration on the same subject, and argued for the Plan of Union in ecumenical language which I have already quoted. Echoes of ecumenicity continued to be heard in the subsequent floor debate. "Our native people think that all Christians are brethren," asserted a missionary to the Congo. "Now, what would they think of us . . . if they could be . . . told that we must continue to be separate? . . . I will be ashamed to go back to the Congo next year if we are going to go back again as Southern Methodists." "The condition of the world is too serious for three great churches to be tied hand and foot," said George H. Lamar. Harry Denman, evangelist, predicted "a great spiritual awakening in America" as a result of union.

But in the southern church, too, voices were raised in opposition. Two were those of bishops, Collins Denny and Warren A. Candler, who took a step unprecedented in Methodist history by declining to sign the Episcopal Address. A statement by them in opposition to the Plan of Union was published alongside the address in the General Conference *Journal*. But the debate itself was on the whole a model of courtesy and good humor, partly because the result was recognizably a foregone conclusion, and the opposition pinned its hopes on a legal issue. It was agreed on motion of T. D. Ellis, the floor leader for the proponents of unification, that the previous question would not be moved until all who wished to speak in opposition had had their say. Thereby a debate which had taken up some two hours at the northern General Conference took all day in the more leisurely atmosphere of the South.

The southern opposition focused upon what the northern and western majority in the united church might force upon the South. The resolution of the North's General Conference of 1932 committing future conferences to accept invitations only from cities where black delegates would receive equal treatment in hotels and restaurants was a particularly sore point; in recognition of the element of sacrifice in the South's decision for unification, it should be pointed out that entry into the united church meant forfeiting the possibility of a General Conference in any city in the South for the foreseeable future. Fear was expressed that the membership loss because of individual unwillingness to become associated with black churchmen and women in any way would destroy Methodism in the South—just as fear had been expressed that the membership loss because of an unwillingness to accept segregation in any way would destroy black Methodism in the North. A delegate viewed with alarm "the Communistic organization of the Northern Church," by which he evidently meant its qualified racial integration. One delegate challenged ecumenicalism in terms that surprisingly resembled Hartman's as expressed at the northern General Conference: "I am fearful that this merger is too big, and history says that when a church becomes a grounded estate, it become more or less in harmony with the worries of that day and loses the power to lift men heavenward."

But the significance of the southern debate lies not in the nature of the opposition, which ultimately turned out to be even more inconsiderable numerically than in the northern church, but in what was said on behalf of the majority. For in rebutting the arguments of the enemies of unification, its advocates asserted the very claim that the northern opposition had advanced as an argument *against* unification, namely, that the Negro jurisdictional plan safeguarded, if it did not actually advance, segregation. Clare Purcell of the North Alabama Conference said:

> If next Sunday morning . . . a Negro comes down and says "I would like to join your church," what can I tell him? Where will I have legal authority to say, "You cannot come into this church?" I would have absolutely no grounds upon which to stand, but if you adopt this Plan, I can tactfully suggest to him that he would be more at home in his own communion as provided in the Central Jurisdiction of this plan.

This, and statements like the following, would seem to clinch the case for the negative in the North:

> The General Conference . . . is confined to legislate on those matters which are distinctly connectional and those only. They can change the number and boundaries only upon the consent of the majority of the annual conferences in each jurisdiction. Under that rule they can't possibly put anybody in that we don't want.

"We are in this Plan, brethren," said T. D. Ellis in his speech formally closing the debate, "preserving every essential ideal that we have in the South on the Negro question." His fellow delegates agreed with him by a roll call vote of 434 to 26.

This was not quite all, for a legal objection to the plan had been raised. The Judicial Council of the ME Church, South, ruled the merger valid, but the dissidents, unwilling to accept defeat, attempted to prevent the property of several local churches from passing into the hands of the new Methodist Church which came into existence in 1939, and thereby transferred the controversy to the civil courts. (The division of the Methodist Book Concern between North and South in 1851 by order of the United States Supreme Court comes to mind. It is an interesting historical observation on the pattern of church-state relations in the United States that both the schism and the reunion of American Methodism ultimately required the seal of federal adjudication.) The courts eventually ruled that neither the property nor the name Methodist Episcopal Church, South, could be claimed by the dissenting group. Having lost its bid for control of part or all of the material and spiritual assets of the ME Church, South, the opposition nevertheless remained alive, in a new religious body known as the Southern Methodist Church—whose membership a decade later of 6,327, chiefly in South Carolina, was not enough to disturb the slumber of the eight and a half million members of the Methodist Church.

The Uniting Conference of the three branches of Methodism met in Kansas City on April 26, 1939 to complete unification. This conference was largely procedural in nature; the question of union had been settled at the General and Annual Conferences of the constituting churches. In an impressive ceremony, the Methodist Episcopal Church, the Methodist Episcopal Church, South, and the Methodist Protestant Church formally passed into history, and what became simply the Methodist Church was born. This is not to say that the question of church and race was thereby settled. On the contrary, it continued to come up, notably at the General Conference of 1944—one hundred years after the church had divided over another phase of the same issue.

One of the least satisfactory aspects of the relationship between Methodism and black Americans, for example, was at the level of the local church—about which very little has been said in this essay because there is very little to say. Frank S. Loescher showed, in his study *The Protestant Churches and the Negro* (1948), that this malady was characteristic of American Protestantism: "A survey of almost 16,000 churches in six denominations has failed to discover a single 'white' church with an 'open' or mixed membership in areas undergoing transition [i.e., in areas where blacks were moving in and whites were moving out, as on the periphery of Harlem]. It is only when colored members are in the majority that the membership in transition areas is open."

This situation, as far as northern Methodism was concerned, admittedly antedated unification, but it had been on an ad hoc basis, and the entrance of all but 7,000 of the 316,000 Negro members of the ME Church into the Central Jurisdiction did not merely perpetuate segregation—it rendered its modification, at the level of local-church mobility, almost impossible.

At the Annual Conference level, results of movements for integration were mixed. On the one hand, it was provided in 1948 that all new "Negro work" in the vicinity of New York City would be under the New York and New York East Conferences of the Northeastern Jurisdiction instead of under the Delaware Conference of the Central Jurisdiction, as had previously been provided, but here the precedent of mixed Annual Conferences already existed. On the other hand, a similar move by the Detroit Conference, inviting black local churches in from the coterminous Lexington Conference of the Negro Jurisdiction, failed to win majority approval in the *white* North Central Jurisdiction, which included Detroit—a striking example of the effectiveness of the new constitutional segregation even in the North. On the whole, the overwhelming majority of black members of the Methodist Church could echo the judgment of *The Crisis* that "separation by statute . . . remains in force virtually forever." The sacrifice in the principle and practice of racial toleration in the North was considerable, as charged by blacks and confirmed by southern whites in the debates. (This was the prime fact which had been glossed over in all accounts of Unification prior to the present essay's first appearance in 1952.)

Much could nevertheless be done in the field of race relations within the Methodist Church as it now stood. Both the ME Church and the ME Church, South, had, in their way, long traditions of ministry to blacks. At the top level of church administration, the southern members of the new Council of Bishops were uniformly courteous to the black bishops; racial equality prevailed at General Conference and on the administrative boards. Some of the most articulate black members of the Methodist Church were not members of the Central Jurisdiction, and while their numbers were small, population shifts could change the social picture entirely, inasmuch as New England and the Far West were not included in the Central Jurisdiction at all. A most encouraging sign in 1952 was the invitation by the Southern California Annual Conference to Bishop Alexander P. Shaw, a black, to preside over it. And the General Conference of 1948 adopted a statement looking to the eventual end of racial discrimination in the church:

> The principle of racial discrimination is in clear violation of the Christian belief in the fatherhood of God, the brotherhood of man, and the Kingdom of God, the proclamation of which in word and life is our gospel. We therefore have no choice but to denote it as unchristian and to renounce it as evil. *This we do without equivocation.*
>
> We therefore recommend:
>
> That every Methodist, and every Methodist church, conference, and institution accept the achievement of full fellowship in our churches as a vital responsibility.
>
> We are not unmindful of the difficulties to which we summon The Methodist Church in this matter.

While there is a great gulf fixed between a resolution and its embodiment in legislation, this was at least on the record as a standard for self-criticism, and for those who had stood in opposition to unification on the grounds of Christian brotherhood it represented a modest moral victory. Eventually it would lead to substantive legislation, for the black Central Jurisdiction now no longer exists.

Against the forthright words of the 1948 General Conference resolution, unfortunately, must be set a factor which was implicit in the arguments of the opposition: the obscuring of the church's witness in the world by its augmented size. Even before the merger, friendly critics were calling it the "Methodist Statistical Church." After the Uniting Conference, the church's social message tended to bog down in an impersonal—and essentially secular—administrative bureaucracy.

The advocates of unification, of course, as we have seen, regarded the increase in combined numbers as an increase in effectiveness, as a means to the better bearing of an ecumenical witness. But this in turn suggests that the Ecumenical Movement, at least in its American form, needs closer scrutiny. Even though the Central Jurisdiction proved ultimately to be no barrier to the integration of blacks into the Methodist Church—it may, in fact, prove, in the long run, to have been the best means to such integration—the fact that an important minority considered that it was wronged and was so emphatically overridden by the majority would still be relevant in a critique of unification. The obsessive chant "eight million Methodists" which accompanied and followed unification betrayed an acceptance of the tenet "My heart is pure because my strength is as the strength of ten," which is hardly characteristic of Christianity at its best.

A fact of surpassing historical interest has, in my opinion, emerged from this discussion: an implicit splitting of the Social Gospel movement. The old Social Gospel in America, as defined by H. F. May to exclude conservative "Christian stewardship" on the one hand and radical "Christian socialism" on the other, was one coherent program, to be accepted or rejected as such. The Ecumenical Movement in its American phase had been closely related to the Social Gospel—indeed, C. H. Hopkins titled his account of the rise of the Federal Council of Churches "The Churches Federate for Social Action." Yet here we find this socially oriented ecumenical drift in American Methodism at odds with another social issue confronting the church—not merely the race question but the general problem of the rights of minorities. Had this church become so secularized as to have fallen into the ideology of "compulsory consensus," which remains a present danger in American society? The issue is obviously more complex than the rise or decline of the Social Gospel; a qualitative change was involved. The New Theology's criticism of the social order—so much more drastic, in essence, than that of the casually optimistic liberals of the Progressive–Social Gospel era—might well have been transferred to a criticism of social ecumenicalism, which could become a source of spiritual pride quite as insidious as any other kind. An instance of this, it seems to me, was the argument by speakers at the Methodist General Conferences of 1936 and 1938 that the church union would facilitate a "revival" of secular America; they should have devoted their attention to a revival of Methodism. For not only was the segregation of blacks not in keeping with the spirit and work of John Wesley and Francis Asbury, but more generally some such radical reexamination would have had to precede any rekindling of the historic crusading spirit of Methodism, conspicuously obscured in recent years.

CHAPTER NINE

The Fundamentalist Defense of the Faith

*T*he shambling defense attorney, hooking a thumb under one of his red galluses, with his other hand held out for inspection a lump of rock laden with fossil shells. When he claimed, in defiance of Bible chronology, that the relic was ten million years old, the large, balding, wide-mouthed man on the witness stand retorted: "It is better to trust in the Rock of Ages than to know the ages of the rocks," and an excited member of the audience shouted, "Amen!" But the year was not 1925, and this scene was not played out in Dayton, Tennessee, during the trial of *Tennessee* v. *John Thomas Scopes*. It took place thirty years later when a land-grant college troupe put on the play *Inherit the Wind*, with its re-creation of the celebrated "monkey trial," in their home state, and that "Amen," however disconcertingly it might have rung in the ear of an eastern liberal intellectual, was also "audience involvement" to a degree that the theater aims at but does not always attain.

Equally spontaneous was a line uttered on a fine spring day in 1962

An earlier form of this essay appeared in *Change and Continuity in Twentieth-Century America: The 1920s*, edited by John Braeman, Robert H. Bremner, and David Brody (Columbus: Ohio State University Press, 1968), 179–214.

by one of a group of university students who were gathered at the river, not for baptisms and prayers, but for that most modish of New Frontier recreations, waterskiing. Strengthened by a Lutheran confirmation textbook, with its assurance that God had "created the many species of plants and animals," which were "not the result of a natural development from a single form, as claimed by the evolutionary theory," one young woman pointed a painted toenail at some green algae at the water's edge and declared, "I'm glad I don't have to believe we're descended from *that*."

These incidents suggest that historians of fundamentalism, myself included, erred when describing that movement as a spent or dying force. But Thomas C. Oden, a seminary professor who taught in a region of the United States where "the fastest-growing religious communities" were "not the defensive 'status quo' churches of culture-Protestantism (Presbyterian, Methodist, Disciples, and others) but such aggressive fundamentalist groups as the Churches of Christ, Pentecostals, and Jehovah's Witnesses," reminded us once again in 1962 that "world views already discarded by the intelligentsia have a way of perpetuating themselves far beyond their expected life span." Biblical fundamentalism "maintains remarkable grass-roots strength among the organization men and the industrialized mass society of the 20th century," Oden wrote, and "it would be a sad illusion for liberal Protestantism"—and for the secular academic intellectual, he should have added—"to imagine seriously that fundamentalism is dead."

Perhaps the continuing power of the movement appeared most vividly when one looked away from the conventional old-line Protestant denominations and observed, in almost any American city, the proliferations of Assemblies of God, "holiness" churches, gospel missions, Bible tabernacles, Soul-Saving Stations, and *iglesias pentecostales*, often housed in storefront churches characteristic of Michael Harrington's poverty-stricken "other America," but also (and increasingly) erecting churches of substantial architecture or purchasing older houses of worship that had originally been built for "mainstream" congregations. And in the mainstream itself there was the phenomenon of Billy Graham hobnobbing with presidents and exchanging pleasantries before the camera with comedians and talk-show hosts.

It is hard to imagine Billy Sunday playing quite so urbane a role, and it is therefore sometimes suggested that the latter-day evangelist ought to be distinguished from his predecessors by some such term as *neofundamen-*

talism. But Billy Graham attended three fundamentalist colleges, taking his major in anthropology from professors who taught him that the theory of evolution was false; and one has but to observe the man in action, with the Book as his only stage prop and with his almost liturgical reiteration "The Bible teaches us . . ." to be reminded that the prefix *neo-* qualifies the word *fundamentalism* a good deal less than it does the word *orthodoxy*.

Moreover, the intent faces picked out of the crowd in the telecast of a Graham crusade were as likely to be those of people from Cleveland or Boston as they were to be those of people from "down south" or "out west." The Southern Baptist Convention, in which Graham was ordained, had long since broken out of the South to plant flourishing new congregations as far afield from the classic Bible Belt as Hawaii, Alaska, and Maine. In the sixties it surpassed the combined northern and southern membership of the Methodist Church and became the largest Protestant denomination in the United States, still numbering many a fundamentalist, young and old, in its ranks, many of them in positions of denominational power. As for fundamentalism "out west," the Lutheran Church–Missouri Synod, among the major Lutheran bodies in America the one in which resistance to the theory of evolution was most stoutly maintained, not only remained an important social and political force in many midwestern and High Plains states but also, like the southern Baptists, had new parishes thriving everywhere, including such unlikely places as southern New England and suburbia.

Nor was continuing conservatism limited to clergymen. Anticlerical liberalism (in America as elsewhere) perennially imagines a democratic and commonsensical people who would rid themselves quickly of religious bigotry and backwardness were it not for the machinations of reactionary priestcraft. There is more than a touch of this in Stanley Kramer's filmed version of *Inherit the Wind*, for example. But a Methodist pastor, writing in 1957 of "the cleavage between the beliefs of the average church-goer and his minister," insisted that it was the *clergy* of his generation, educated by the seminaries "far beyond the understanding and religious position of the laity," whose personal religious convictions were often "far more liberal and unorthodox than they would dare to admit in public"—a judgment which, if valid, would suggest that fundamentalism at midcentury may have been even more pervasive than the mere persistence of preaching that relies for its proof on the biblical text would indicate.

Surprise, and sometimes alarm, at the vitality of "that old-time religion"—and particularly at its adoption by the young—characterized intellectuals' encounters with fundamentalism from the beginning. One pilgrim from New York's Union Theological Seminary who had traveled in the South in the summer of 1964 spoke with obvious concern about having met "persons who had renounced the training they had once received [as Episcopalians, no less] . . . in favor of a biblical and ethical fundamentalism strong enough to chill the heart of anyone who dreamed that an advance had been made beyond the Scopes Trial."

The Scopes trial in its day had similarly produced a rude awakening in some quarters. "We thought that forty years ago in America religion had become adjusted to the evolutionary theory," the president of Brown University wrote in 1923, "as it was adjusted in the sixteenth century to the far more startling Copernican theory." Instead, he noted by way of current example, "in one college a new professor happened in his first lecture casually to use the terrifying word 'Evolution.' Whereupon the whole class hissed him." In 1927 Granville Hicks interviewed Hillyer Straton, son of one of the leading fundamentalist pulpit performers of the day, and was taken aback to learn that along one sector of the battle line no "revolt of youth" was taking place: "Half my crowd Sunday evenings are under twenty-five," the youthful minister declared. "Do you think the modern generation is bound for the dogs?" Hicks asked him. Young Straton smiled—and well he might, as an enthusiastic student minister with a busy Philadelphia parish turning out for two preaching services every Sunday—and replied, "That's where Father and I disagree."

In the first article of a series on "The War in the Churches," published in 1923, Rollin Lynde Hartt painted a portrait of the liberal intellectuals, many of them "dwellers in apartments looking out across the Gothic quadrangle[s] of famous theological seminaries," who vibrated between "underestimating the enemy's strength" (or his intelligence) on the one hand, and on the other, giving way to panic and perhaps to compensatory overestimates of fundamentalism's strength when they experienced the movement in its raw and vigorous reality; or discovered, as Glenn Frank did in the thick of the fight, that orthodox leaders seemed to have a "much better sense of generalship than liberals. . . . The Fundamentalists have succeeded in giving the liberal and intelligent leaders of the church the appearance of renegades." Hartt thought it significant that "fundamentalist" and "modernist" each accused the other of being heavily subsidized—an explanation that permitted both sides to escape the logical dilemma of how a view regarded as unpopular should seem to be so widely accepted.

Much of the liberal polemic of the twenties contained the ambivalent notion that fundamentalism was both dying in ill repute and at the same time dangerously threatening to prevail. Harry Elmer Barnes, for example, a liberal by the canons of the twenties, asserted in the preface to *The Twilight of Christianity* that fundamentalism had "burned its bridges behind it" and that it was "only a matter of time until it must decay and disintegrate." Two hundred pages later, however, he was not so sure: "The situation is likely to get worse, as the figures indicate that the sects harboring the Fundamentalists are those which are growing most rapidly." In like manner Kirsopp Lake, a professor in the Harvard Divinity School, conceding fundamentalism's "energy, determination, organization, and . . . clearly intelligible position," predicted that in the long run the modernist view of religion would no doubt prevail, but it might be a very long run indeed: "If any one of the . . . parties wins completely and speedily, it is likely to be the Fundamentalists." And in *Religion in Human Affairs*, a book intended as a text for university courses in sociology, Clifford Kirkpatrick prophesied: "Doubtless each successive generation will contain a smaller and smaller proportion of aggressive Fundamentalists," but he then recalled how the scientific-minded nineteenth century had somehow produced Joseph Smith and Mary Baker Eddy, and he wondered, "Who can tell what religious leaders, prophets, and messiahs will arise to lead men back to the old ways of thought" in the twentieth or twenty-first centuries.

Stewart Cole, the first historian of fundamentalism, concluded his study with the observation that the recent controversy in the church had "changed few minds." Probably there remained in 1931 "as many conservative believers as there were two decades ago." Cole criticized the liberals of his day for having "resorted to the logical rather than the psychological method" in evaluating the faith of their orthodox brethren. They had weighed fundamentalist doctrines in the balance of science and scholarship and had found them "contrary to genuinely modern beliefs," Cole concluded, and then they had committed the intellectual's characteristic blunder of assuming that if only other people's thought processes were informed and enlightened, general agreement would result. But to bring Protestant churchgoers "abreast of the problems and ideals that characterize the age," Cole predicted, would be "an exceedingly heavy educational task" for the next generation of church leaders—a task which, judging by the continuing strength of fundamentalism, those leaders failed to accomplish. Indeed, the problem for the historian of the twenties is not so much one of accounting for the later decline of fundamentalism, as Cole, Norman Furniss, and Ray Ginger assumed in their historical treatments of it, as it is one of discerning elements in the movement that account for its continuing vitality.

The showdown between fundamentalism and modernism had long been in the making. Sixty-six years had elapsed between the publication of Darwin's *Origin of Species* and its constitutional testing (so to speak) in the Scopes trial. But as early as 1873, Charles Hodge, the formidable Princeton theologian, had rhetorically asked, "What is Darwinism?" and answered, "It is Atheism." On the other side of the fence, Phillips Brooks had written from Boston in 1887 that he was "more and more sure that the dogmatic theology in which I was brought up"—well before the Civil War, since Brooks was born in 1835 and ordained deacon in 1859—"was wrong." A biographer of Phillips Brooks added a footnote detailing the issues over which his subject had diverged from that dogmatic theology, and these turn out to have included "its literal theory of inspiration and its conception of Scripture as a whole; its indifference to intellectual culture; its insistence upon the necessity of acknowledging a theory of the Atonement"; and its tendency to limit church fellowship to the "elect"—all adding up to a dissent from a point of view that unmistakably foreshadowed modern fundamentalism.

The heresy trials that shook Protestant churches, particularly their theological seminaries, in the 1880s and 1890s are also a part of this story; and it must be noted of those earlier controversies that by and large the modernists had won. Going further than mere modernism in his attacks on orthodoxy had been the itinerant freethinker Robert G. Ingersoll, as archetypal a figure of the Gilded Age as the shoe-salesman-turned-evangelist Dwight L. Moody; and while the multitudes at Moody's public meetings were singing Ira Sankey's gospel hymns, a host of critics, more systematic if less eloquent than Ingersoll, had quietly been thinking out a worldview that left little if any place for "that old-time religion." In short, the world in which the famous "five points" of fundamentalism were put forth in 1895 was a world that subjected all such concepts to devastating attack—sometimes in sorrow, sometimes in anger, sometimes even by inadvertence, but always unremitting and inescapable.

There is a sense in which it can be said that without modernism—and the anticlerical scientism that went beyond it—there could have been no fundamentalism, in precisely the sense that without the New Deal–New Frontier—and the anticapitalist philosophies that went beyond them—there could have been no Goldwater Republicanism. Fundamentalism was not *simply* "the old-time religion"; the mere affirmation of an inherited tradition is not at all the same thing as the affirmation of that tradition (or a more or less reasonable facsimile) after it has gone through a period of public eclipse by a rival faith. One can thus speak of fundamentalism as "new" in the twentieth century, despite the relative antiquity of orthodox Protestantism, in the same way that one can speak of a "new" American right in the time of the cold war despite the relative antiquity of orthodox laissez faire economics.

It would be easy to push this parallel one step further and simply identify fundamentalism as the religious version of radical rightism. The continuing vitality of the one could be seen as a function of the recurrent upsurges of the other, and we could settle back into the familiar groove of an economic or psychosocial interpretation of history. To put the matter into fundamentalist language, "Ye shall know them by their fruits" (Matt. 7:16), and by that test there is clear evidence for the identification. To make the point, one has only to compare William Bell Riley in 1926, labeling "those professors in our modern universities who . . . in their devotion to the Darwinian theory dare to dethrone God" as "the outstanding leaders today" of "Sovietism," with itinerant ultrarightist Helen Wood Birnie in 1960, lecturing on the presumed atheist and materialist views of American college and high school teachers as "Communism's Secret Weapon" and testifying that she had withdrawn her two boys from "the godless public schools" lest they be taught the theory of evolution. The line of evolutionary descent from Riley (and Billy Sunday and outright fascist Gerald Winrod) to Mrs. Birnie (and Billy James Hargis and Harvey Springer of the Christian Anti-Communist Crusade) is all too clear. There were even survivors from one generation of right-wingers to the next: witness the career of Gerald L. K. Smith, who was twenty-seven years old at the time of the Scopes trial and who was still going strong in the presidential election campaign of 1964, in which "for the first time in my mature life," this extremist declared, "a major political party has nominated a candidate for President worthy of respect."

But descent and overlap do not quite add up to identity. Some latter-day fundamentalists bitterly resented being equated with the political far right; thus John W. Bradbury, editor of the *Watchman-Examiner*, a paper that in the fifties, as in the twenties, was a bastion of biblical evangelicalism, complained in 1952 of "religious vigilantes" who "cannot be classified . . . with the original Fundamentalists. They may appropriate the name, but they know not the spirit of the movement." In any case, it would be a historiographical error to extrapolate backward from the "apparently cordial marriage" between the radical right and fundamentalist religion in the more recent years and assume therefore that all that it is necessary to say about the meaning of fundamentalism in the twenties has been said.

The most systematic defense of the basic fundamentalist tenets may be found in twelve paperback volumes of essays published and distributed between 1909 and 1914 under the overall title *The Fundamentals: A Testimony to the Truth*. At that time such spokesmen for Protestant social concern as Shailer Mathews and Washington Gladden, Walter Rauschenbusch and Josiah Strong, most of them modernists in their theology, were enjoying a considerable vogue. What did the framers of *The Fundamentals* think of the Social Gospel? The answer is difficult to find since nearly all of the several dozen essays in *The Fundamentals* were characterized less by right- or left-wing views than by the absence of political discussion altogether. Their apolitical quality contrasts sharply with the neofundamentalism of more recent years. In the earlier fundamentalist writers' comparative disregard for the burning public questions of their day—the welfare of workers, the control of the trusts, the purity of food and elections—it is tempting to find a kind of conservatism by default. This, however, would be an argument *ex silentio*, and any such argument runs certain risks. In the discourse of *all* preachers, be they fundamentalist or modernist, social liberal or social reactionary—or none of these—there is necessarily much that is of a purely devotional, doctrinal, or pastoral nature. The reader from outside the faith under consideration, for whom most of the material may have no meaning, is prone to skim it and dig down for the occasional nugget of sociopolitical comment, assuming that this is the heart of the matter; indeed, the assembling of many such nuggets may well have inclined historians to view the liberal Social Gospel ministry before 1914 as having been even more activist than in fact it was.

But we do not have to proceed entirely by inference. The comparative neglect in *The Fundamentals* of political and economic issues does not go quite to the point of total silence. Unfortunately for our present purpose, the little that we do find of this sort of thing in *The Fundamen-*

tals is somewhat inconclusive, even contradictory—until we reach the last article of the closing volume of the series. In this final item, *The Fundamentals* suddenly got to the point. The article was entitled "The Church and Socialism." The author, Charles Erdman, was the son of William J. Erdman, one of the founders of the Moody Bible Institute in Chicago and himself a professor at Princeton Theological Seminary, one of the most important American intellectual fountainheads of fundamentalism, and a member of the editorial committee having general supervision over publication of *The Fundamentals*. Here at the end, the reader might surmise, the "two Christian laymen," Lyman and Milton Stewart, who had patiently and anonymously supported the venture with their California oil earnings, could at last have expected their due. But if a Christian defense of free enterprise was what the Stewart brothers expected for their money, so to speak, that was not what they got. There were those in the church, Erdman admitted, "quite comfortable under what they regard as orthodox preaching, even though they know their wealth has come from the watering of stocks and from wrecking railroads, and from grinding the faces of the poor." But, he bluntly declared, "The supposed orthodoxy of such preaching is probably defective in its statements of the social teachings of the Gospels. One might be a social bandit and buccaneer and yet believe in the virgin birth and resurrection of Christ; yet one cannot be a Christian unless he believes . . . [that] to live for Christ means to live for Him in every sphere and relationship of life, whether employee or employer, capitalist or laborer, stock-holder or wage-earner." As for socialism—a term that until comparatively recently had "suggested a dream of fanatics"— Erdman continued, it now embodied "the creed and hope of intelligent millions" as a "serious protest . . . against the defects of the present economic system, against special privilege and entrenched injustice, against prevalent poverty, and hunger, and despair."

A "New American Rightist" of a later day would have found such a critique of socialism outrageously disappointing if not downright subversive, and in such a context it would seem as logical to equate this early mode of fundamentalist thinking with radical social protest as to equate it with the reactionary right—as logical and as meaningless, for in deepest essence this was not what the fundamentalist controversy was about. "Christianity is a religion; Socialism is an economic theory, or a political proposal," Erdman argued. It followed that "a man may be an ardent

Socialist and a sincere Christian, or he may be a true Christian and a determined opponent of Socialism." The major social thrust of fundamentalism, in its earliest years at least, was neither liberal nor conservative in the political sense. Rather, it foreshadowed a position like that which was to emerge in the thirties among churchmen decidedly not fundamentalist in their outlook: "Let the Church be the Church," or as Erdman put it, "The Church is committed to no one social order. . . . It is opposed to the wrongs and injustice of every system."

Fundamentalism was not predestined from its inception to play a rightist role in America. Dogmatic as the authors of *The Fundamentals* were, they were not so graceless but that one of them could warn against "the temptation to feel as if we belonged to a superior order of Christians," and in sharp contrast to the anxieties and angers of the radical right of a later day, the tone of these essays is in general quite as much marked by love for God and man as it is by hate for the devil and modernists. It is a spirit best summed up in the reply of a prominent evangelist to a well-bred young lady who balked at going out as a missionary to the "dirty Chinese": "I do not think the question whether or not you love the Chinese is the one to be considered; it seems to me that the real question is whether or not you love the Lord."

One does not need to be a religious believer to be moved, for example, by the testimony of Philip Mauro, a wealthy and successful but unhappy Manhattan attorney who learned his religion "from the company of exceedingly plain, humble people, of little education, to whom I regarded myself as immeasurably superior," and whose meetings "from the ordinary standpoint would have been pronounced decidedly dull." The pages of *The Fundamentals* are filled with this kind of discourse, both as testimony and as advice, and on occasion, as when Reuben Torrey, the dean of the Los Angeles Bible Institute, echoed a slogan associated also with the essentially liberal John R. Mott ("the evangelization of the world in the present generation"), the purposes of fundamentalism and of the Social Gospel could fuse.

Not even the blustering nationalism of World War I, which found vehement religious voice in Billy Sunday's notorious "damn-the-Germans" crusade in New York City in the spring of 1917, would entirely shoulder aside this humane and universalist side of fundamentalism. James M. Gray, dean of the Moody Bible Institute in Chicago, where most of the editorial work on *The Fundamentals* had been done, wrote in July 1917 of a German pastor whom he had planned to bring to Moody when the war intervened:

> He is doing his best today to minister to the German soldiers, and to promote the interest of his fatherland I doubt not, and I expect to do the same for my country. But I love that man still and he loves me; and when this cruel war is over, one of the earliest exchanges of brotherly love I have in mind is to bring him here. . . . [In the meantime] the German Christian is serving Christ in obeying his government and the American Christian is doing the same, and *Christ is able to keep them both and to make them stand.* Nor is either of them required to pray for victory [but rather] for the will of God to be done.

Such utterances in wartime were, of course, exceedingly rare from men of any faith except the foundering one of socialism, and in the red haze of generalized intolerance that hung so ominously over the postwar years, they became if anything even more rare—which suggests that fundamentalism may have been not so much one of the causes of that wartime and postwar intolerance, as has so often been assumed, as one of its victims. If the war unleashed hate, it also unleashed disillusionment. Fully to have accepted 100 percent Americanism as a fighting faith would have involved subscribing to the American ideology of ongoing and inevitable progress, and progress, as J. B. Bury was about to point out, had been searching more than a century for a rationale and had finally found one in Darwinian evolution. One way out of the resulting dilemma for fundamentalists was to find in the war itself a convincing demonstration that the progressives— and, by implication, Darwin as well—had been wrong.

Many nonfundamentalists also felt this particular disillusionment. George W. Richards, who would one day write on the topic *Beyond Fundamentalism and Modernism*, wrote in 1923 that the war years had reminded men of "the proximity of savagery to culture. . . . It matters little whether man wears skins or broadcloth, so long as the heart is unchanged." But it was the fundamentalist who was prepared to follow this logic most uninhibitedly to its conclusion: "Darwinism had saturated the war-lords with all the catchwords essential to the prosecution of their designs," Alfred W. McCann asserted, "and the people . . . were prepared to follow to the end, little dreaming of the carnage, starvation and disease toward which their 'progressive' evolution was now thundering its flight."

The reference to "the war-lords" suggests the World War I propaganda stereotype of the "Hun," although McCann noted that his German villains (Ernst Haeckel was a favorite) had their French and British counterparts. But other fundamentalists had felt a challenge from Germany long before American national interest became involved. They quite correctly saw their position undermined not only by the theory of evolution but also by modern critical study of the Bible, an impressive amount of which had been done in German universities. Their warfare against German historical scholarship easily broadened into a more general attack on *Kultur*. The Nietzschean superman, or the propagandists' caricature of him, was a bogeyman for fundamentalists long before he became one for George Creel and Woodrow Wilson.

"It is notorious to what length the German fancy can go in the direction of the subjective and the conjectural," wrote a contributor to the first volume of *The Fundamentals*. German biblical criticism, the same essayist observed (with some truth) "deals with the writers and readers of the ancient Orient as if they were modern German professors." This same note of quasi-philosophical objection to the Teutonic penchant for "hypothesis-weaving and speculation" runs through other pages of *The Fundamentals*. One contributor, for example, wittily satirized the skeptical extremism of certain German biblical scholars by applying their kind of reductionist logic to a contemporary figure, to "prove" that Theodore Roosevelt had, like Jesus of Nazareth, never really existed! The Peerless Leader of the anti-evolution forces might not have been at home in a discussion at quite so sophisticated a level, but he had heard of Nietzsche; and at the Scopes trial Bryan conjoined the Nietzschean superman's transvaluation of values to Darwinism and hurled back at Clarence Darrow the latter's plea for extenuation in another celebrated trial, made on the ground that "the teachings of Nietzsche made [Nathan] Leopold a murderer."

At both the metaphysical and the moral level, fundamentalists continued to see Germany as the fountainhead of what they were opposing. When Hitler came to power, some American fundamentalists would view the Nazi government as the logical outcome of a century of godless German modernism and would declare, in effect, "We told you so."

At the same time, however, the fundamentalists were more open-minded in their attitude toward Germany than latter-day right-wingers were regarding the Communist "menace." Thus J. Gresham Machen, himself a former graduate student at Marburg and Göttingen and by all odds intellectually the ablest major spokesman for fundamentalism, urged a protege who was contemplating a year of study abroad in the mid-twenties to spend all of his time in Germany: "At most of the universities you will be living in a highly stimulating intellectual atmosphere that will be entirely foreign to Christianity," he wrote; "not altogether an easy experience" for an orthodox young man but one that would give him "the satisfaction of having come into firsthand contact with those forces which underlie all the doctrinal indifferentism in Great Britain and this country." It would be a rare bird indeed among right-wingers since World War II who would have urged a student to spend a year in Moscow or Beijing, or Havana, to become acquainted at firsthand with the other side!

But even more incongruous than Machen (whom Walter Lippmann called "a scholar and a gentleman") as a progenitor for the radical right of our day was the arch-fundamentalist of them all, William Jennings Bryan. In the apostolic succession of the Democratic party from Andrew Jackson to Franklin D. Roosevelt, Bryan has often been an embarrassment to the academic liberal, and never more so than in the anti-evolution campaign. Indeed, he has been judged by a double standard so that we are inclined, for example, to remember that he went to Dayton in 1925 to prosecute a schoolteacher and to forget that he went to the Presbyterian General Assembly in 1920 to prosecute his own denomination's war profiteers. But the Great Commoner saw his public career as one internally consistent whole; he felt that his crusades against the scientists and the Higher Critics, like his crusades against the hard-money men and the militarists, were on behalf of popular democracy. Well along in the pages of *In His Image*, his own special-creationist tract, Bryan reaffirmed his lifelong credo: "I fear the plutocracy of wealth; I respect the aristocracy of learning; but I thank God for the democracy of the heart."

But that, in the opinion of more than a few of his contemporary critics, was precisely what was the matter with Bryan: not that he attacked the principle of "one man, one vote" but that he defended it. The anti-evolution campaign was seen by some of them as a characteristically bad example of popular, one person–one vote democracy in action. Thus the antics of William Bell Riley, debating the theory of evolution against all comers but packing the meetings with loyal fundamentalists so that his defense of the Bible would be voted to have won, and of John Roach Straton, reacting to the American Museum of Natural History's exhibit on the Age of Man with what amounted to a demand for "equal time" for an exhibit of "The Bible

Story of Creation," only served to confirm H. L. Mencken's opinion that "the mob has made its superstitions official." Five years after the Scopes trial, Mencken wrote in praise of the civilized rule of enlightened skeptics during the eighteenth century and lamented the subsequent "spread of the democratic pestilence," the results of which in the United States, "where democracy has been carried further than anywhere else," included "such obscenities as Comstockery, Prohibition, and the laws against the teaching of evolution."

The dilemma posed here was one not for fundamentalists and their opponents only but for representative government itself. "Can the public school, at this stage of the world's history, be dedicated to a literal interpretation of Genesis . . . ? Can the religious frame of mind which this assumes be imposed by law upon educators and pupils?" No, said the liberal Catholic journalist Michael Williams, covering the Scopes trial for *Commonweal*. Yes, said Benedict Elder, editor of the Catholic diocesan newspaper in Louisville: "If the citizens believe that the Bible is true, the state has no right to employ instructors . . . to teach . . . that the Bible is not true." State schools had to be controlled by the state "and not by any professional group—however learned," Elder went on. "After all, the common judgment of the plain people is not to be scorned." Such also was Bryan's conviction when at one point in the Scopes trial he cried, "Your Honor, it isn't proper to bring experts in here to try to defeat the purpose of the people."

At this point in discussions of fundamentalism by liberals and modernists it was (and is) customary to shift from categories of left and right to categories of intellect and ignorance. Thus Clarence Darrow replied to Bryan that the logic of his argument amounted to saying, "It is a crime to know more than I know." And it is further customary to equate these in turn with urban and rural life: one person's vote is the full equivalent of another's provided that both are equidistant from the centers of modern thought and culture. Walter Lippmann, for example, readily embraced a rural-vs.-urban interpretation of fundamentalism as the most practical way of arguing it down without falling into the illiberal assumption that the people ought to be governed by their betters:

> The deep and abiding traditions of religion belong to the countryside. . . .
> The omnipotence of God means something to men who submit daily to the
> cycles of the weather and the mysterious power of nature. But the city man

puts his faith in furnaces to keep out the cold, is proudly aware of what bad sewage his ancestors endured, and of how ignorantly they believed that God, who made Adam at 9 A.M. on October 23 in the year 4004 B.C., was concerned with the behavior of Adam's children.

One of the most persistent and persuasive of the interpretations of fundamentalism set it in a wider context of rural-urban conflict in America, akin to the crusades against Demon Rum and Al Smith, and perhaps also to the prenomination struggles of 1964 between Barry Goldwater and those personalities within the Republican party whom the senator was wont to term the "fat cats back East." John Washington Butler, author of the Tennessee anti-evolution law, was moved to run for the legislature and introduce his bill in large part because a girl from his hometown had gone away to college and had come back believing in evolution and not believing in God; this episode has often been cited as a demonstration of the role in the evolution controversy of "cultural lag"—a concept, popular in the 1920s, which is still too frequently employed by historians.

Such an interpretation of fundamentalism, like the politico-ideological one, must be applied with caution. To be sure, a certain willful ignorance does pervade much fundamentalist discourse, and to be sure, the record of the Scopes trial—that symbolic heart of the entire controversy—fairly crackles with resentment at the way Chicago (personified in Clarence Darrow) and New York (personified in Dudley Field Malone) were interfering in the private affairs of Dayton, Tennessee. But every tale of a country boy or girl being ruined, intellectually or otherwise, by the liberal ways of a metropolitan university could be matched by testimony to the contrary, such as that of Harry Emerson Fosdick, next to Darrow the prime target of fundamentalist wrath in the twenties. Discovering the theory of evolution toward the end of his freshman year in college in 1897, young Fosdick had announced to his family "as impressively as I could manage it: 'I have made up my mind that I believe in evolution,'" only to have the wind taken out of his undergraduate sails by his father's reply: "Well, I believed in that before you were born."

A Methodist minister who came out of a hamlet that was culturally even more remote from modern America than Dayton to earn a B.A. degree in 1922 and a theological degree in 1925, the year Darrow took on Bryan, later recalled no tension or conflict between a rural upbringing and an exposure to modern science in college. The theory of evolution, this liberal clergyman wrote in 1936, "did not disturb my thinking at all, for it was the most natural explanation of the world of Nature I had known." Thus one country dweller, as Lippmann suggests, might sense in the powers of nature beyond his own control a transcendent Power behind them, which would drive him into fundamentalist religion, but evidently another country dweller could have found in his own firsthand acquaintance with the living things of field and forest a world of experience for which the theory of evolution gave him a fully satisfying explanation. "The study of evolution seemed perfectly natural," the same minister wrote after his retirement in 1962. "The fundamentalism of the [hometown] church must have passed me by. I never did have to get rid of it."

When one uncovers the intellectual roots of the fundamentalist controversy in the warfare of science and theology in the nineteenth century, the cultural-lag hypothesis—with urban high-brows all ranged on one side and rural low-brows all on the other—becomes even harder to sustain as a universal proposition. For on this assumption what is one to make of John Wesley Powell, growing up in a village and educated in one-room schoolhouses and a library-laboratory housed in a private dwelling, then roaming the riverbanks of an Illinois barely a generation away from the frontier, and in the process insensibly making a first-rate geologist of himself? Free inquiry has never been wholly confined to the intellectual and cultural centers of the nation. In our age of dependence upon large university libraries and astronomically expensive laboratories, we are prone to forget the number of Americans over the years in both town and country who contrived to educate themselves catch-as-catch-can.

And just as there have always been instances of intellect at work in the American countryside (think of Edwards ministering to the Stockbridge Indians while writing *Freedom of the Will*), so there have been important revivalist and biblical-literalist manifestations in town. Fundamentalism in the 1920s claimed many a strategic city pulpit, from Boston's venerable Park Street Church to W. B. Riley's home base in Minneapolis. The *New Republic* commented on this paradox in an obituary on the "Fundamentalist Pope" of Manhattan, John Roach Straton: "In spirit, he was a Baptist of the old school, attached to the letter of the Old Testament; in technique he was a New Yorker of the twentieth century." A man who "planned a skyscraper church as a shrine for doctrines in which he believed as literally as did the tent-dwelling patriarchs to whom they were first proclaimed in

Palestine" and who preached the old-time religion over that most modern of gadgets, the radio, Straton "was typical of a persistent contrast in our national life."

A further difficulty for a purely rural-urban interpretation of the fundamentalist controversy is its international dimension. When Bryan took off his coat in the blazing July heat of Tennessee and "revealed the fact that he was not wearing galluses but a belt, an article of apparel affected only by advanced dressers and advanced thinkers," the drama would seem to have been about as far from the spirit of old Europe as it was possible to get; but of the three million copies of *The Fundamentals* that had been distributed by 1914, approximately one-third had gone outside the United States, half to the British Isles and the balance to the European continent and the rest of the planet. Even if we assume that most of these overseas recipients were British or American Protestant mission workers, no generalization about the American self-made man, the American rural mind, or the American hostility to scholarship entirely suffices to cover the subject.

Does fundamentalism, then, come down to unadorned anti-intellectualism, regardless of race, political creed, nationality, or regional origin? Once again, *The Fundamentals* are a major interpretive obstacle. These articles are, most of them, sober. Only one or two of them are really ranting in tone, and the level of the argument on the whole is only a hair more illogical than academic discourse in general—which, indeed, much of it is; a high proportion of the authors were professors of theology, many of them in respectable institutions, and only a small proportion of them could have been classed merely as vulgar evangelists. Even if we dismissed these essays as irrelevant for understanding the fundamentalism of the twenties, there would still remain the enigma of J. Gresham Machen, who was not only a man of impeccable scholarship himself but one who turned the sword's point around in the twenties and accused the liberals of low-browism. "We are opposed with all our might," Machen vowed in 1924, "to the passionate anti-intellectualism of the modernist Church." The entire first chapter of his book *What Is Faith?* (1925) was a polemic against "the intellectual decadence of the day," not only in the church but also in secular education, with its "absurd pedagogic theories which . . . depreciate . . . the labor of learning facts."

But how could a plea for high standards of intellectual enterprise be reconciled with a categorical rejection of the findings of modern science? The fundamentalist who did not retreat into *credo quia absurdem*—an answer that a Machen would have rejected as contemptuously as a Mencken—was forced into the assumption that someday, somehow, the whole evolutionary edifice must topple for lack of sufficient evidence and that science itself would conclude that Darwin had been wrong. In the twenties this did not seem as forlorn a hope as it does today. Alfred McCann in *God—or Gorilla?* argued that scientists' attempts to reconstruct man's subhuman ancestors from fossil remnants were at best hopes and at worst forgeries, and in his first chapter went with a debater's unerring instinct to the Piltdown Man, which, of course, eventually did prove to be a fabrication. We should bear in mind, too, that the provenance of *Pithecanthropus*, the Trinil or Java Apeman, was not finally established until 1939, and that Rhodesia Man had a hole in his skull that for years was believed to have been made by a bullet! This was later shown to have been the bite of a primeval hyena, but in the meantime it afforded people like McCann much fun at the evolutionists' expense.

As for Darwin's theory of the origin of species by natural selection, it had fallen on evil days. "Discussions of evolution came to an end," the British geneticist William Bateson told the American Association for the Advancement of Science in 1921, "primarily because it was obvious that no progress was being made. . . . Variations of many kinds, often considerable, we daily witness, but no origin of species." Noting Bateson's indiscreet remark that "when such confessions are made the enemies of science see their chance," and ignoring his insistence that "what has been learned [about evolution] constitutes progress upon which we shall never have to go back," fundamentalists wrote sermons and editorials and whole books whose thesis was that the evolutionists were dogmatizing to cover up their own ignorance. From this point of view, the classic warfare between science and theology anticlimactically came down to a case of my faith versus yours. "It was . . . remarkable," one contributor to *The Fundamentals* had written, "that men of trained intellect should have so promptly accepted at face value [Darwin's] two principal works, in which the expression, 'we may well suppose,' occurs over eight hundred times."

The defender of evolution was put in an awkward position by this kind of attack. If he denied that any such tentativeness or doubts existed among the world's experts, a William Bateson—professionally aware that the mechanism of natural selection seemed to have proven unsatisfactory as an explanation of evolution and that the mechanism of genetic mutation was as yet very imperfectly understood—quite properly could be quoted in rebuttal. If he affirmed that supposition, inference, hypothesis is the way science operates, a McCann was ready with the Baconian observation that "science deals with facts known to be facts, and not with opinions supported by conjecture, speculation, assumptions, or theoretical connecting links."

If there is a culture lag in operation here, it is one not between science and superstition, but between nineteenth-century science and twentieth-century science. In the words of A. Hunter Dupree, "The quest for 'hard things' in science seemed a reasonable enterprise in the nineteenth century; it is madness in the twentieth." When fundamentalists and evolutionists tried to reduce the issues between them to "hard things," the contending parties sounded startlingly alike. For contenders battling over what they took to be "hard things," the kinds of armistice terms proposed by modernism—that science deals with facts and religion with values, or that evolution deals with the "how" of man's origin and the Bible with the "why"—were rejected on both sides as illogical compromises or dishonest evasions. American Catholicism probably came the closest to a workable *via media* that anyone achieved in the 1920s on the evolution question, but it was the editor of the *Catholic World* who challenged "anybody to convey to a class the arguments for the evolution of man without revealing, I will not say his own scientific conclusions, but his own theology." In the 1960s we became acquainted with the concept of a social and religious "mainstream," but in the twenties the liberals and conservatives, religiously if not politically, were more inclined to insist that one climb out upon the stream's right or left bank.

It is interesting that although the word *fundamentalism* is still used to describe a recognizable entity (e.g., the sermons of Billy Graham), the word *modernism* has all but dropped out of the American Protestant vocabulary. And in retrospect many of the modernist compromises do sound curiously empty. Thus Edward Scribner Ames, for forty years pastor of University Church (Disciples of Christ), Chicago, wrote of Christianity as being on the verge of a new "great epoch," which he described variously as "the religion of the spirit, as social Christianity, and as the religion of democracy." But by *spirit* he seemingly meant nothing more transcendental than the glow of good-fellowship, as in the term *school spirit*. In fact, he made the parallel explicit: "Our college is our Virgin Mother, to whom we address songs and sentiments of genuine affection." Fundamentalists were quick to deride the shallowness of this kind of Christianity—"You could take the 'C' out of YMCA and nobody would ever notice the difference"—and to warn of its total inadequacy for the great crises in life: "For mere popular lectures it is still serviceable; but . . . when despair at the loss of all one has loved takes possession of the mind . . . when one is on a sick-bed and death approaches . . . just at this time when its help is most needed, this modern religion utterly fails." Or as Lippmann put it, "A man cannot cheat about faith."

All of which suggests that the fundamentalists may, after all, have been doing just what they thought they were doing: not merely defending a political ideology, however much some of them talked of the American way of life—for the Jehovah's Witnesses, equally literal in their interpretation of Scripture, were refusing to salute the flag; not only defending an economic system, however much oil money was poured into the dissemination of *The Fundamentals*—for other oil money built Riverside Church and housed Dr. Fosdick therein; not simply defending the countryside against the city—for the "old-time religion" early discovered, and has perpetuated, an evangelistic style of city-based revivals; not even essentially defending ignorance against intellect—for the claims of intellect in the ivory tower were scarcely lived up to in the encounter in the courtroom that merely pitted authority against authority, "the Bible teaches" against "science says"; but also, and chiefly, defending what the fundamentalists honestly believed was all that gave meaning to life, "the faith once delivered to the saints."

Although for many people living through the twenties science had, in the words of Joseph Wood Krutch, "not only won from us a confidence in her methods, but also made it well-nigh impossible for us to believe in any others," this does not detract from the high seriousness of the fundamentalist defense of the faith. Krutch himself—one of the apostles of the gospel of science—acknowledged that the findings of science had indeed robbed human life of its intrinsic value: "We have grown used . . . to a Godless universe, but we are not yet accustomed to one which is loveless as well, and only when we have so become shall we realize what atheism really means." The terrifying darkness of this passage, I have found, still has power to kindle in student readers its author's despair; and from it one can understand why some clung to fundamentalism in the twenties: God help them, they could do no other.

CHAPTER TEN

Science and the Death of God

*T*he question "Is God dead?" is a more venerable one than some who asked it during the 1960s were aware. Many centuries ago, the Psalmist declared: "The fool hath said in his heart, there is no God." The pioneer philosopher of science Lucretius—no fool—acknowledged that there might indeed be gods out there somewhere, serene and indifferent, but he had no patience with those persons who "supposed that the gods designed all things for the sake of men." In contrast to the theist's grand claim that in the beginning God by an act of will created the heavens and the earth, the sturdy Roman aristocrat proposed an evolutionary view almost deliberately ugly in its naturalism: "Thus then the ponderous mass of earth was formed with close-cohering body and all the slime of the world so to speak slid down by its weight to the lowest point and settled at the bottom like dregs."

Constantine, Saint Augustine, and the Middle Ages (to telescope a great deal of Western history) are commonly supposed to have put a stop to all such impieties, but as the Middle Ages waned, the old heterodoxies surfaced again. John Herman Randall, in his widely used textbook *The*

An earlier form of this essay appeared in *The American Scholar* 42 (Summer 1973): 406–21.

Making of the Modern Mind, suggested that the first "modern" symptoms of God's fatal illness may have been diagnosed in the fifteenth century by the sometime Dominican friar Giordano Bruno, who revived the Lucretian concept of infinite space and thereby broke open the tidy cosmopolis in which God and man had previously dealt together. By the time of the Copernican and Cartesian revolutions, Randall intimated, the God whom medieval man had worshipped was indeed mortally stricken:

> Throughout the whole vast windy stretches of infinity, in stone and plant and animal, nowhere in the universe was there another being like man, nowhere a being who felt and suffered, loved and feared and hoped, who thought and knew. Man was alone, quite alone, in a vast and complex cosmic machine. . . . Of all that medieval world, one thing alone was left . . . the faith in a Creator in whose image man was made, in a wise and loving Father who had built all this vast machinery for the good of man.

By the seventeenth century, even that last bastion was under siege. Quoting (perhaps too selectively) from Spinoza, Randall concluded: "Gone is the wise and loving Father, to whom man can appeal in prayer; irretrievably gone is the great Friend behind the world who cares."

That this Father and Friend was irretrievably gone was not equally clear to all of his children. The generations that followed Spinoza's, who heard the atheist polemics of d'Holbach and the anticlerical strictures of Voltaire, knew also the warm consolations of German pietism and of Wesleyan Methodism. According to Randall, it was left for the nineteenth century to finish off the "fond remnant of the Christian epic." The century of Darwin, who seemed to reduce man's soul to the caperings of a naked ape, and of Wundt, who seemed to reduce it to a series of electrochemical discharges inside man's skull, heard from Nietzsche the very words the mass media seemed to think had been first spoken only yesterday: "God is dead." "It has been the great effort of the time to establish a mathematical equation between an instructed mind and an abandoned faith," wrote the best-selling American religious novelist Elizabeth Stuart Phelps in 1886. "We learned that we were not men, but protoplasm. We learned that we were not spirits but chemical combinations. . . . We learned that the drama of Hamlet and the Ode to Immortality were secretions of the gray matter of the brain."

Harmonizers of science with religion were on the scene also, to be sure. In the 1880s, on Sunday evenings in the Old Chapel at Yale, Professor James Dwight Dana told the students that the theory of evolution did not overthrow the story of creation as found in the first chapter of Genesis, "except perhaps in one or two details." The college pastor listened with approval and then dismissed the congregation with a scientific benediction: "You see, gentlemen, that when the right kind of a man of science and the right kind of a theologian come together there is no dispute between science and religion." The trouble with this kind of "peaceful coexistence" proposal, however, was that the scientists, and especially the publicists and popularizers of science, would not let the theologians alone. When one clergyman denied in 1876 that there was any conflict between true science and true religion, Edward L. Youmans, crusading editor of the *Popular Science Monthly*, replied that the clash was "natural and inevitable . . . because science is driving on . . . regardless of anything but the truth it aims to teach, while the religious world is full of anxiety and dread about what is going to happen as a result."

From a different perspective, Friedrich Engels came to the same conclusion. "In the history of modern natural science," Engels wrote in the *Dialectics of Nature*,

> God is treated by his defenders as Frederick-William III was treated by his generals and officials in the Jena campaign. One division of the army after another lays down its arms, one fortress after another capitulates before the march of science, until at last the whole infinite realm of nature is conquered . . . and there is no place left in it for the Creator.

Moreover, from a Marxist point of view the harmonizers of religion with science were no better than the out-and-out reactionaries. "God is nowhere treated worse than by the natural scientists who believe in him," Engels gibed, tracing the humiliating retreats of God's defenders from Newton to "his last great Don Quixote, Agassiz," and ending with Tyndall, who "forbids Him any entry into nature and relegates Him to the world of emotional processes, only admitting Him because, after all, there must be somebody who knows more about all these things (nature) than John Tyndall!"

In wider circles, beyond the special audience of *Popular Science Monthly* and outside the special outlook of Marxism, crusaders against God may have received a more respectful hearing then than they have in the twentieth century. During those Victorian years "the Great Infidel,"

Robert G. Ingersoll, was denouncing the Bible with humor and passion: "They may say I will be damned if I do not believe that, and I tell them I will if I do." In 1876, Ingersoll took time out from his freethinking evangel to deliver the nominating speech for James G. Blaine at the Republican National Convention. It is difficult to imagine so avowed a religious radical placing a serious presidential contender's name in nomination at a major-party convention held in the Roaring Twenties, or even in the Swinging Sixties. Again, that staunch evangelical William E. Gladstone took time out from his politicking to refute the Biblical heterodoxies of T. H. Huxley. I doubt that Richard Nixon during his out-of-office years would have considered the "God is dead" theologians dangerous enough to have penned twenty-page tracts against them.

To be sure, in some quarters the churches were marching on from strength to strength. If Robert Ingersoll packed in the crowds, so did Dwight L. Moody; if writers for Youmans's *Popular Science Monthly* urged that we cleanse ourselves from "the leprosy of the miraculous which taints men's minds," Mary Baker Eddy championed the miraculous in a startling new way. Martin Marty has called our attention to "the extent of the evangelical triumph" in post–Civil War America, particularly in contrast to Europe: "Wherever one turned, signs of progress, growth, and success could be documented. . . . All these signs were impressive to partisans of Christianity and seemed oppressive and overpowering to its antagonists." Foes of organized religion who claimed that millions of Americans privately agreed with them may therefore have been indulging in wishful thinking. "It was the best of times, it was the worst of times," Charles Dickens wisely observed when writing of another strife-torn period. Speaking specifically of America's Gilded Age, William R. Hutchison has suggested that "the culture as usual was getting more religious and more secular at the same time. . . . Faith was both growing and declining," and the historian's problem is to figure out the special form for that age of "our perennial paradox."

In *The Spiritual Crisis of the Gilded Age* I argued that there were, in fact, special elements in the American (and British) religious situation a century ago, such that the question "Is God dead?" may have been asked then in a far more searching way than was possible in the 1920s or even in the 1960s. For example, in our own century conflict of this kind has sometimes been muffled by relativism: you may be right, I could be wrong, so if you don't criticize my faith, I won't find fault with yours. In his more genial moods even H. L. Mencken sometimes masked his basic hostility toward religion with a kind of personal tact: "We must respect the other fellow's religion, but only in the sense and to the extent that we respect his theory that his wife is beautiful and his children smart." But much of nineteenth-century thought was still monistic, both philosophically and morally; truth, whether conceived of religiously or irreligiously, was *truth*, and its defender was obligated to combat the purveyor of falsehood, come what may. Just as the evangelist urgently felt the duty of asking anyone he met, "Have you been saved?" rather than tactfully letting him go his own way, so also a counterevangelist like Ingersoll quite naturally carried the fight into the enemy camp: "The agnostic does not simply say, 'I do not know.' He goes another step, and he says, with great emphasis, that *you* do not know." Paradoxically—as Bertrand Russell's great essay "A Free Man's Worship" was to make clear—the rejection of traditional religion had itself become "religious."

Another complication in the conflict between "knowledge" and faith during America's Gilded Age (or in England's Victorian Age) was the period's notorious literalism: "Facts, facts, facts!" cried Mr. Gradgrind on the opening pages of Dickens's *Hard Times*. In his essay "The Place of Science in Modern Civilization," Thorstein Veblen would argue in 1906 that the culture of modernity had become "peculiarly matter of fact"; it was, to use Veblen's arresting adjective, *opaque*. The growing body of impersonal factual knowledge plus the insensate discipline of the machine increasingly gave industrial man a worldview in which intangible reality had no place. Three decades earlier, the Anglo-Catholic apologist James DeKoven anticipated the reasoning of the great Norwegian-American renegade. "The visible encroaches on the invisible," DeKoven confessed in 1878. "Between us and God appear to come laws, and forces, and powers, the duration and extent of which we can grasp and measure. . . . What, then, if these laws begin to take to us the place of God?" In his Lowell Lectures of 1894, the British scientist and evangelist Henry Drummond put the question into a still more troublesome form: "If God is only to be left to the gaps in our knowledge, where shall we be when these gaps are filled up? And if they are never to be filled up, is God only to be found in the disorders of the world?"

It gave no relief to such inquirers that in the coming century philosophy was destined to become less monistic and science less literalist, even though some of them had already realized that the palpable material world upon which their science seemed to rest was not quite a fact in Mr. Grad-grind's sense of that word. Noting as early as 1873 the overthrow of what had been classic textbook distinctions between substances that could be weighed and more imponderable substances such as light, electricity, and magnetism, E. A. Sears, a contributor to the Methodist *Christian Advocate*, wrote: "Matter has no ultimate units, but is divisible to the point where it vanishes from human perception"—not a bad description of what goes on in a particle accelerator. Nevertheless, the notion that one must perforce choose between fact, which is demonstrably true, and fiction, which is by definition false, dies hard. In this particular area the typical churchman, no matter how learned, was just another unspecialized layman, and usually his unchurched opponent was no less an amateur. One reason for the ste-rility and thinness of much modernist Protestant thinking in the twentieth century is that thinkers who prided themselves on being up to date were continuing perforce to live off the intellectual capital of the Gilded Age.

They were not always aware that that was what they were doing. In any era, the young who categorically reject all the crimes and follies of their elders quite unknowingly use many weapons that were forged in the arsenals of other elders. Never was this more true than in the decade of the twenties, with its strange polarity between nostalgia for normalcy and hunger for novelty, and as a result much of the detail of the science-versus-religion debate in that period has quite properly been forgotten. Those more familiar with their elders' deeds than most of their own generation, however—men like John Herman Randall, for example, whose *Making of the Modern Mind* was published in 1926—were capable of producing "tracts for the times" that retain a certain timelessness to this day.

They preached their gospel in an age when religion, at the popular level, was more obviously on the defensive than it had been during the Gilded Age. The upward statistical march of the churches ever since the federal census of 1790 took a sharp downward turn; mainstream WASP denominations showed an actual net membership decline. Robert T. Handy has aptly and convincingly characterized the decade from 1925 to 1935 as "The American Religious Depression," and Philip Gibbs's novel *The Age of Reason* (1928) strongly implied a British equivalent. If skeptics and icono-clasts did not go about nominating presidential candidates, they churned out a spate of books whose volume and readership were impressive. A short span of months between 1929 and 1930 saw the publication, for example, of *A Preface to Morals*, by Walter Lippmann; *The Twilight of Christianity*, a thoroughgoing positivist tract by Harry Elmer Barnes; *The Modern Temper*, by Joseph Wood Krutch; *Treatise on the Gods*, a typical foray by H. L. Mencken; and from within the religious camp itself, *Theism and the Modern Mood* by the Protestant theologian Walter Marshall Horton, who confessed to his own personal theistic creed but conceded that in general, at the time he was writing, "the fact of a decline of faith in God seems undeniable." Horton blamed the situation to a great extent on World War I:

> Before the war, we found it easy to believe in a smiling and benignant Providence, rolling on the chariot of Progress from victory to victory, and from bliss to bliss. During the war, we read our Hebrew prophets, and with a sense of tragic exaltation looked out upon a world where a stern but righteous Providence was bringing down a well-earned retribution upon the heads of the wicked. Since the war, we prefer to take our history naturalistically, in the mood of *The Bridge of San Luis Rey*. . . . We are inclined to turn savagely upon anyone who tries, after the great fiasco of the war, once more to "justify the ways of God to men."

This is an argument that many ethically sensitive persons continue to find persuasive.

In the middle of our century an even more world-convulsing conflict would lead the American Jewish theologian Richard L. Rubenstein to argue that after Auschwitz the God who must be affirmed "in order to remain faithful to both tradition and contemporary Jewish experience" would have to be "a willful, cosmic sadist who repays the love offered by his tortured believers with criminally obscene 'punishments.'" Yet ancient Assyria's national policy, as destructive in its own way as that of modern Nazi Germany—and as effective, in that at one stroke it cut the twelve tribes of ancient Israel down to two—had not prevented the rise of Israel's prophetic theist tradition in the first place. On the Protestant side represented by men like Walter Horton, it should be similarly noted that the confessions of the Reformers were first made in the midst of frightful wars of annihilation, culminating in a Thirty Years War that is said to have left the population of Germany reduced by two-thirds. Although we must take full account of what H. G. Wells called simply "the international catastrophe of 1914" as a causal explanation for the spiritual malaise of the twenties, we must also raise again the question of theistic religion's inherent credibility, a question that can be asked both in the best of times and in the worst.

But at once a major obstacle arises for anyone who would ask that question seriously: the scientific and philosophic issues so searchingly aired in the seventeenth, eighteenth, and nineteenth centuries have in the twentieth become difficult, at times even impossible, for nonscientists to discuss. J. Robert Oppenheimer, in one of his last published essays, speculated as to "why the views of Copernicus, the discoveries of Galileo, the understanding and syntheses of Newton, should so greatly have resonated throughout European society, so greatly altered the words with which men spoke of themselves and their destiny," whereas the same can hardly be said of the views of Niels Bohr, the discoveries of Heisenberg, or the understanding and syntheses of Einstein. Oppenheimer's answer was that the errors revealed by physics and mathematics and astronomy in the sixteenth and seventeenth centuries had been "errors common to the thought, the doctrine, the very form and hope of European culture"; therefore, "when they were revealed, the thought of Europe was altered." In contrast, "the errors that relativity and quantum theory have corrected were physicists' errors, shared a little, of course, by our colleagues in related subjects." Appalling as have been some of the practical consequences of those corrections, such as the hydrogen bomb, the concrete demonstration over Hiroshima of the validity of $E = MC^2$ did not carry with it also a demonstration of how our intellectual conception of the universe had been altered by relativity—a word that the unspecialized theistic apologist often confuses with *relativism*. Much the same observation can be made of evolutionary theory, whose reception had been such a traumatic experience for the nineteenth century. Oppenheimer pointed out the stark "contrast between the impact of the views of Darwin, and the almost total lack of general interest in Mendel's discovery of binomial coefficients in the populations of succeeding generations of peas."

Was God's fatal illness, then, so elusive to diagnose that the theologians, trapped on the wrong side of C. P. Snow's Two Cultures, were unable to proclaim the death of God until after the event had occurred? Or—as many theologians and some scientists insisted—were the findings of Einstein and Bohr *less* lethal to traditional religious belief than the findings of Darwin at first had seemed? When the theist hesitantly attempted to appropriate the new science for his own purposes, the antitheist was quick to scout any such argument. "Don't let the Einstein-twisters catch you here!" with their assumption "that the discovery of the identity of matter and energy breaks down eighteenth-century materialism and reopens the way for mystical myth-making," H. P. Lovecraft wrote in 1929:

> What these feeble-minded theists are howling about as a sudden victory for themselves is really the materialist's trump card. . . . Matter indeed has been shown to be a passing phase of energy . . . but what is this save a perfect confirmation of the basic essentials of Haeckelian monism? Thus the materialist, now using that title in an historical sense only, emerges strengthened in his position as an atheistical (or agnostic) monist. He has sounded space a little deeper, and found . . . simply a profounder disintegration, and a profounder mechanistic impersonality.

Surely in 1929, the writer concluded, God was dead—or at best, as for Lucretius, inaccessible. "Here we are," Lovecraft continued, "and yonder yawns the universe. If there be indeed any central governor, any set of standards, or any final goal, we can never hope to get even the faintest inkling of any of these things."

But as evidence for this sweepingly negative credo, Lovecraft counseled his correspondent to "read what Harlow Shapley, A. S. Eddington, J. H. Jeans, or any contemporary astrophysicist has to say," and from a God-killer's standpoint, the choice of these authorities in particular was ironically inapt. Arthur Eddington, a practicing member of the Society of Friends, had already delivered his Gifford Lectures for 1927 at the University of Edinburgh, published as *The Nature of the Physical World*, and had come out four-square for mystical religion. In 1932 Sir James Jeans argued that, contrary to all materialist expectations, "the stream of knowledge is heading toward a nonmechanical reality; the universe begins to look more like a great thought than like a great machine." And Harlow Shapley eventually joined with a group of church laymen, clergy from various denominations, and scientists from several disciplines to meet periodically on Star Island for summer retreats. Out of their discussions would grow an Institute of Religion in an Age of Science, dedicated to the proposition "that science, in a wide sense, could enrich the holdings of religion, and that religion could perhaps ennoble the concepts of science." This was a striking departure from the view, widely held in the nineteenth century, that the only proper relationship between science and theology was one of warfare.

Admittedly, the terms of the debate had subtly changed. Religion for some of these savants was a very broad concept indeed. Albert Einstein, whose unique blend of saintly simplicity and mathematical profundity so haunted the twentieth-century popular imagination, ringingly declared in 1940 that "science without religion is lame, religion without science is blind"; science could only be created by men "thoroughly imbued with the aspiration towards truth and understanding," an aspiration that "springs from the sphere of religion." Yet Einstein seems also to have read the Almighty's death notices: "In their struggle for the ethical good," he asserted, "teachers of religion must have the stature to give up the doctrine of a personal God." Did this mean that God was dead, exactly? "A conviction, akin to religious feeling, of the rationality or intelligibility of the world lies behind all scientific work of a high order," Einstein declared on another occasion. "This firm belief, a belief bound up with deep feeling, in a superior mind that reveals itself in the world of experience, represents my conception of God."

Some scientists, of course, rejected both the acknowledged theism of a Jeans or an Eddington and the more cryptic confession of an Einstein. "Like bed bugs in the cracks of walls and furniture, miracles lurk in the lacunae of science," wrote J.B.S. Haldane in 1934. "The scientist plasters up these cracks in our knowledge; the more militant rationalist swats the bugs in the open." But enough religious affirmation went on in scientific circles during the early thirties to prompt a letter to the *New York Times* deploring the "tendency of modern scientists to drift into the morasses of mysticism." Perhaps the tide of Professor Handy's "religious depression" was already turning. Robert A. Millikan, holder of a Nobel Prize in physics, claimed in 1932 that the younger scientists of his own acquaintance were joining the churches, and then as now the future presumably belonged to the young. Were the thirties, that decade of immense political energies and vast social hopes, *more* congenial to the religious mind than the twenties had been? It is a view that few recent interpreters of the thirties would accept, but perhaps the possibility should be entertained and explored.

As the statistical and societal decline of the churches bottomed out and their fortunes began to rally (at least in America), and as the public image of organized religion became more favorable, modernist religious apologists understandably listened to the Millikans and Eddingtons, ignored the Haldanes and Bertrand Russells, and interpreted Einstein to suit themselves. Moreover, there are always some discussants of this question who seek to evade its rigor by dividing up the territories respectively allotted to science and to religion and then insisting that so long as each sticks to its home turf there can be no conflict between them. Responsible fundamentalists raised the proper objection—for example, J. Gresham Machen (1925): "It is a poor religion that can abandon to science the whole realm of objective truth, in order to reserve for itself merely a realm of ideals." Some thoughtful modernists concurred.

In 1935 Willard Sperry, the distinguished dean of the Harvard Divinity School, rejected this temptation to take evasive action, in which one concedes to science the entire world of facts in order to reserve to religion the entire world of values, on the ground that his own Victorian and Gilded Age forefathers—he mentioned Henry Drummond and John Fiske—had made no such concession: "The Christian religion has never succeeded, or even survived for any length of time, when it has devoted its energies solely to the struggle to preserve itself in some pristine and uncontaminated purity." It must face up to, and at some points absorb, the best secular thinking of its time. Although this had anticipatory echoes of the "secular city" debate among Protestants during the 1960s, clearly Sperry did not expect such an encounter to lead inexorably to the death of God.

As new intellectual movements claim our attention we sometimes overlook the extent of their overlap with older ones. In 1963—just as the "death of God" debate was about to get under way—Charles K. Robinson, at that time assistant professor of religion at Duke University, published in the *Journal of Religion* an article entitled "Biblical Theism and Modern Science." From the abandonment of mechanistic physics, from developments in psychotherapy, and (perhaps more dubiously) from parapsychology, Robinson concluded that the universe was not, as nineteenth-century materialist determinism had assumed, "a very long-playing record whose grooves are all rigidly cut in advance"; rather, "the universe which God has in fact created is a world characterized by flexibility and variability in its orderly patterns of interrelation and interaction." This situation would admit the logical possibility even of miracle: "It is important to indicate vis-à-vis modern science that the concept of God's special agency in and through physical and biological levels of reality need not involve any 'violation' of the orderly integrity of wave-particles or vital organisms." (It was a point that had been made with greater logical precision by the Puritan Urian Oakes in 1677.) What, then, had become of the "leprosy of the miraculous" from which science in the nineteenth century had been expected to help people cleanse themselves?

It is, of course, arguable that theological writers like Charles Robinson and Dean Sperry were voices in the wilderness. From time to time a distinguished churchman has declared that twentieth-century concepts like relativity and quantum physics *ought* to become part of the intellectual furniture for any modern person, but this is often coupled with a lament that so far—and for Protestants especially—C. P. Snow has yet to be proved wrong. The German Protestant theologian Karl Heim explained this attitude largely in terms of the intellectually ubiquitous nineteenth century. "The history of Protestantism took an unhappy turn when, soon after the time of Schleiermacher [d. 1834], Protestant theology severed its connexion with philosophy in order to become an independent field," Heim wrote in 1949. "Since then it has shown more and more reluctance to undertake the difficult task of opposing the world picture of disbelief with a world picture of belief." For Protestantism, such reluctance could prove fatal:

> Amid the totally transformed environment of the modern academic disciplines, . . . if the confession of faith of the Reformers is stated at all nowadays it makes the same impression as would a last-remaining venerable fragment of wall, all that is left standing of a medieval cathedral, . . . appearing as a foreign body amidst the newly erected blocks of offices and flats of a modern city. During the last war a deep impression was made when, after an air raid on Mayence [Mainz], all that remained standing of a church dedicated to St. John the Baptist was a fragment of a doorway on which were inscribed the words: "Repent ye: for the kingdom of heaven is at hand!" But this ruin from the past could not be left standing like that permanently. Either it could be built up again into a complete church of a design which fitted in with it, or it would have to be pulled down and cleared away.

No doubt the articulation of a worldview of belief that would relate intelligibly to the secular city and universe has become extraordinarily difficult for the nonscientist in an age when scientists themselves dispute whether they need to posit *any* kind of ultimate reality, theistic or naturalistic, in order to do their work. Moreover the consumer of ideas, like the consumer of automobiles, is cursed with the problem of instant obsolescence. "Three centuries have passed since the beginning of the scientific revolution," wrote Samuel Miller in 1957, "and in that time the issues have changed kaleidoscopically from decade to decade. Probably nothing contrived to postpone a stable rapprochement [between science and religion] more than the shifting nature of the scientific advance."

The real intellectual beneficiary of this situation may have been the existentialist, whether atheist or Christian, who rejected all self-consistent systems and found competing theistic and antitheistic monisms equally spurious. Einstein's "conviction . . . of the rationality or intelligibility of the world" would not go down well with the kind of "postmodern" human for whom the universe, rationally or morally considered, is absurd. The very fact that some pattern of coherence or purpose has been discerned in the universe by prestigious members of the scientific establishment could be taken as an argument *against* the existence of a living God by those of that generation of radicals who condemned science and technology as inherently sterile and inhumane.

Did the "God is dead" movement of the sixties have an organic connection with the long positivist erosions of the last three centuries— a connection unknown to some of its adherents, who had only recently discovered that they lived in a "secular city"? Possibly for the reasons suggested by Oppenheimer, the radical theologians of the 1960s tended to draw their argument more from philosophy, linguistics and literature than directly from the natural sciences. God's death was not to be inferred from Darwinian evolution or from the second law of thermodynamics—or, to update the argument, from molecular biology or from Fred Hoyle's theory of the continuous creation of matter. Rather, the death of God was most convincingly experienced as an honest and inescapable subjective insight. But since subjective states can change as rapidly and unexpectedly as scientific hypotheses, it is difficult to see how the claim that God is dead could have been made, as it often was, with such dogmatic historical finality. Some of the claimants, with little sense of history, seem not to have known that they felt as the Psalmist, the Preacher, Thomas à Kempis, John Bunyan, and a host of others had felt before them—only to decide, when the chips were down, that they must trust in a living God.

In an article for *motive*, the excellent and much-missed magazine of the Methodist Student Movement, Fred M. Hudson in 1966 formulated four possible meanings of the "death of God." First, God may be *psychologically* dead: "Man has lost his inner awareness of God." But if that is so, then the vivid panorama of felt realities that William James captured in *The Varieties of Religious Experience* no longer spoke to anyone's condition, and we must ignore the testimony of modern-day evangelicals or mystics to the contrary. Second, God may be *sociologically* dead: "The political, economic, and educational institutions which used to convey and confirm the presence of God no longer do so." But if that is so, then neither the formal richness of the nationally televised Roman Catholic obsequies for John Kennedy nor the simple impressiveness of the great public Baptist memorial for Martin Luther King, Jr., pointed beyond themselves toward any shared collective reality. Third, God may be *ontologically* dead, in that today "we have no words or symbols which *mean* God"—notwithstanding those irrepressible American astronauts who decided to read from the first chapter of Genesis while orbiting the moon one Christmas Eve. To state such propositions in so categorical a fashion is at once dialectically to raise doubts about them.

There is also, however, the fourth proposition, namely that God is *theologically* dead, so that Christian (and perhaps also Jewish) theology has become only a somewhat novel mode of atheist humanism. It is this fourth definition of the death of God that seems to have aroused most of the clamor. No longer was it "they"—the freewheeling infidels like Bob Ingersoll and Tom Paine, or the scientific materialists like Ernst Haeckel, or the Marxists, or the Freudians, or the Psalmist's "fool," who said in their hearts (and on video) "There is no God." It was "we," members of "the blessed company of all faithful people," who had worked out the logic of the faith itself into atheism. Unitarians had faced up to this question long before, but they were and are numerically a small fraction of American churchpeople. The radical religion of the sixties seemed not only to proclaim the death of God but to call for the spiritual suicide of the entire evangelical Protestant mainstream.

Yet that Protestant stream in America has known many twists and turnings. The example of the rigorous-minded nineteenth century, which decreed the death of God but was unable to make it stick, and of the Roaring Twenties, which predicted a "twilight of Christianity" that turned into a religious revival instead, should warn us that it would have been a rash historian indeed who could have confidently extrapolated an observed downturn into a long-term trend. From the radical critical perspective of the mid-1960s, the later emerging "Jesus people"—equally as radical, after their fashion—could hardly have been foreseen.

PART THREE

*Science, Fiction, and the
Road to the Stars*

CHAPTER ELEVEN

Science and the Common Man

A man in a faded gray raincoat and a flopping black felt hat that nearly concealed the gray hair that straggled over his ears stood on the boat deck of the steamship *Rotterdam* yesterday, timidly facing a battery of cameramen. In one hand he clutched a shiny briar pipe and the other clung to a priceless violin." Thus on a spring day in 1921, with the Harding administration not yet a month old, America was introduced to Albert Einstein. Reportedly not fluent in English, the shy, shaggy-locked visitor shook hands all around but gave no verbal interview. Newspaper reporters had to content themselves with physical description: "Under a high, broad forehead are large and luminous eyes, almost childlike in their simplicity and unworldliness." After he got ashore, correspondents competent in German took down his remarks, and a story duly appeared in the next morning's *New York Times*:

An earlier form of this essay appeared in *The American Scholar* 45 (Winter 1975–76): 778–94, and later in *Another Part of the Twenties* (New York: Columbia University Press, 1977). Here, as with "The Negro and Methodist Union," the title of an article perpetuates an archaic and somewhat frowned-upon term, in this case "man" as a generic synonym for "humankind" or in the singular, "person." The expression "common man" was, however, an authentic cliché during the middle third of the twentieth century (as in the slogan "the century of the common man"). As such, I am allowing it to stand.

Einstein Sees End of Time and Space
Destruction of Material Universe
Would Be Followed By Nothing,
Says Creator of Relativity
Theory "Logically Simple"

The destruction of the material universe had no great journalistic urgency, and even in the *Times* this account was relegated to page 5. The front page was devoted to more immediate matters: "Talk in Ireland of Peace and War"; "Harding Summons Rail Men's Leaders"; "Illinois Legion Protests Against Release of Debs"; and—familiar enough reading for a Manhattan resident, then or today—"Two strangely shot in Madison Square Park; one of five bullets hits choir singer on way home from church; . . . police unable to discover who fired the shots and why." Car dealers in Greater New York reported good spring sales, and baseball fans looked forward to the new season. Yet the gentle visiting scientist was not lost in the shuffle. Thousands of New Yorkers turned out to greet the Einstein party at the pier, and some of them crowded into City Hall afterward for Mayor Hylan's reception.

Einstein himself seemed puzzled at the public interest shown in him and his theories. Relativity did have some bearing on ultimate philosophy, the savant acknowledged, puffing on his pipe, but "the practical man does not need to worry about it." For some Americans, interest in his scientific theories merged into enthusiasm for the political cause he championed. Traveling in company with Chaim Weizmann and other Zionist leaders, Einstein was in this country to enlist American support for the yet unborn state of Israel and more specifically for the establishment of the Hebrew University on the Mount of Olives in Jerusalem. The *Chicago Tribune* picked up a cable from Germany that gave the Zionists' mission an ugly urgency: Rudolph Leibus, a fanatical nationalist, had recently urged the murder of Einstein and had paid the equivalent in marks of a sixteen-dollar fine in a Berlin court for saying so. On New York's own city council, Alderman Bruce Falconer refused to vote the scientist the freedom of the city—the usual formality—and his vote prompted a shouting and fist-waving session on the council floor. But Falconer denied being moved by "racial or religious prejudice"; his private physician was a Jew and many of his friends were Jews, the lawmaker asserted. Three days later he found fresh justification for his vote on the grounds that Einstein had been born in

Germany, with which the United States—more than two years after the armistice—was still technically at war. Therefore, pacifist and internationalist though he was, the physicist "might be regarded as an enemy alien," the councilman explained.

If Einstein was ruffled by this teapot tempest, he showed no sign. A German-speaking *Times* man sought out the Einsteins in their New York hotel and found the physicist bubbling with enthusiasm about America: "I like the way you light up the windows with the signs. I like the cheerful way you arrange the electricity up and down the streets. . . . And the movies? I am enthusiastic about them. . . . In general, the pictures shown now are not so artistic, but they will get better, very much better all the time."

Midway through the conversation, Mrs. Einstein, whom the reporter described as "a charming little gray-haired lady," slipped in and sat down in a chair beside her husband. Perhaps the interviewer would like a copy of Einstein's book on relativity in an English translation, she suggested.

"No," said the professor. "Why that? He doesn't come here for relativity. He comes here to see me."

Other Americans, some of them having even less knowledge of relativity than the *Times* man, came in droves to see Einstein. They jammed the Metropolitan Opera House to the doors when Weizmann and he appeared there. They rode on the subway uptown to Columbia and to City College to hear Einstein lecture on relativity, in German and in halting textbook English. He journeyed to Princeton (later destined to afford him refuge from Hitler's tyranny) to receive an honorary D.Sc. He went to Washington for a meeting of the National Academy of Sciences. Again speaking in German—a language, we must remember, that had been banned throughout much of America only three years earlier—Einstein voiced his hope "that the field of activity of scientific men may be reunited and that the whole world will soon again be bound together by common work."

While in Washington, he visited President Harding at the White House, prompting a headline: "Einstein Idea Puzzles Harding, He Admits as Scientist Calls." The puzzlement was bipartisan. Into a windy Senate debate on April 18, the flowery-tongued, white-mustached Democratic Senator John Sharp Williams of Mississippi interpolated a comment on the theory of relativity: "I frankly confess that I do not understand Einstein; . . . and I do not believe that even the Senator from Massachusetts [Henry Cabot Lodge, with his Harvard Ph.D.] would make a very positive pretense in that direction." But such expressions of bafflement were curiously mingled with affection. The *New York World* was struck by the fact that of all the recent distinguished visitors from abroad, including the Prince of Wales and Queen Marie of Romania, the one who had inspired the most spontaneous popular demonstration had not been "a great general or statesman but a plain man of science. . . . It is something when New York turns out to honor a stranger bringing gifts of this recondite character." Nor was it all vulgar curiosity toward a celebrity, the *World* believed. The public was engaging in "a sincere tribute of admiration to the physicist who, amid the turmoil of war and the distraction of material interests, has kept his mind fixt on the star of pure science."

Certainly Einstein's personal style was different from that of his American colleagues, as portrayed four years later by the *Independent* under the title "Must Scientists Wear Whiskers?": "The fact is that in America . . . a convention of scientists, such as the American Association for the Advancement of Science annually brings together, is as clean-shaven, as youthful, and as jazzy as a foregathering of Rotarians." The creator of the Special and General theories of relativity hardly fitted that stereotype of the scientist, "fully as much a man of the world as his brother, the business man." Indeed, Einstein's unworldliness may have been part of his charismatic appeal—especially considering that few then had any inkling of where the harmless-looking equation $E = MC^2$ would lead.

"I have only two rules which I regard as principles of conduct," Einstein told an American journalist who traveled to Berlin nine years later to write him up for a popular U.S. magazine. "The first is: *Have no rules*. The second is: *Be independent of the opinion of others*." For many Americans with no idea of what he was talking about, Einstein's stubborn insistence upon going his own way had a familiar ring. In sixteen words he had summed up the self-reliance theme of Ralph Waldo Emerson. Ignoring his socialism and his mathematical rigor, the American businessman and the American bohemian could unite in admiring the man as a rugged individualist who was doing his own thing.

Perhaps also in the decade of the twenties, Albert Einstein, with his disarming simplicity and his concentration on goals transcending the corruptions of his time, filled a psychic need for some Americans in much the same way as did two other seemingly simple men, Charles Lindbergh and Calvin Coolidge: the German-Swiss Jewish seer may have been another kind of Puritan in Babylon. Einstein's own obvious enjoyment of America was surely not unwelcome news for Americans, and his Zionism itself may have appealed through its kinship with Puritan and pioneer traditions in the American past, however much America's own intellectuals in the twenties condemned both Puritanism and the frontier.

Not everyone loved Albert Einstein. One year after that triumphant first visit, even while American astronomers were making their way toward a desolate spot on Australia's northwest coast to observe a solar eclipse— and, they hoped, to confirm or refute Einstein's most recent theory—that theory's author was forced temporarily to flee for his life from his homeland. Members of the same extremist group that had recently murdered Walther Rathenau, Germany's foreign minister, were threatening the same fate for Einstein and other prominent German Jews, including Theodor Wolff, editor of the *Berliner Tageblatt*, and the Hamburg banker Max Warburg. Passing over the fact that the cruel ideology then surging upward in Germany rarely excused its chosen enemies for their mild behavior, the *New York Times* expressed surprise that anybody should want to assassinate Dr. Einstein. "He is gentleness personified, and it is incredible that he ever gave anybody any of the ordinary forms of offence." But perhaps the form of offense Einstein gave was not ordinary. That he was Jewish may have been less important than that he was incomprehensible.

According to another *Times* editorial, "The Declaration of Independence itself is outraged by the assertion that there is anything on earth, or in interstellar space, that can be understood only by the chosen few." Self-evident truth was what the Declaration had proclaimed, and some apparently believed that this must be the case not only in politics but also in science. "Newton's law of gravitation can be stated in a few simple sentences, and its essentials can be made clear to the average reader," complained Charles Lane Poor (himself a professor of celestial mechanics) in 1924. "The theory of Einstein . . . is, on the contrary, complicated in the extreme; it cannot be expressed in words. It is impossible to read the works of Einstein and his followers and from their words and phrases to know what they really mean." The implication was obvious: if a theory cannot be made clear to the general reader, it is probably invalid. In a democratic age, common sense was felt to be the property of common people.

Also, from the time of Francis Bacon to the time of Thomas Huxley, scientists themselves, whether aristocrats or democrats, had drummed into the mind of Western man the idea that science is organized common sense. As a weapon against doctrines judged to be contrary to common sense— such as those of the Church—that slogan had at times been highly effective, and advocates of science were understandably reluctant to give it up. Therefore, to some conventional minds the abstruse higher mathematics in which the new physics was phrased became the modern equivalent of religious mumbo jumbo. One *Times* reader in 1922 expected a "battle royal to be waged between men of science, of which one class will fight with the brilliant and dazzling arms of mathematical formulae and the other with the dull yet solid weapon of applied common sense." In 1923 Captain T.J.J. See, an astronomer in the employ of the United States Navy, cried: "The Einstein doctrine that the ether does not exist, and that gravity is not a force, but a property of space, can only be described as a crazy vagary, a disgrace to our age!" It did not matter that the notion of the "ether"—an impalpable medium pervading all space, which transmitted light, electricity, and gravitation but whose own existence was absolutely incapable of measurement—is on the face of it as wildly improbable an idea as anything dreamed up by Einstein. The wild idea of yesterday becomes the entrenched dogma of today. For the scientist as for anyone else, Einstein himself once observed, common sense can be defined as a deposit of prejudices laid down in the mind prior to the age of eighteen.

But Einstein, as a physicist, also believed that even the wildest mathematical idea must have some verifiable relationship, however shadowy, with the world of common sense. "For our purpose it is necessary to associate the fundamental concepts of geometry with natural objects," he told his Princeton hosts in 1921. One such natural object was the planet Mercury, whose eccentric orbit was predictable from Einstein's assumptions but unaccountable from Newton's. Another was the image of a star whose emitted rays had passed near the sun en route to earth and which was photographed during a solar eclipse. According to Einstein, the star would be displaced from its normal position in the sky because its light would be bent by the sun's mass. In September 1922, to check out this strange idea, Americans from the Lick Observatory in California tramped through the prickly desert scrub near Wallal Downs, a telegraph station in far western Australia, to put up their tents and temporary observatory in preparation for a total eclipse of the sun. On September 21 the appointed moment of darkness came. Behind the black circle of the moon, the sun's corona or halo appeared, displaying one streamer 2,225,000 miles long. The flickering bonfires of the solar prominences sprang into view. Five photographic plates were exposed before the moon passed by. A similar British venture in 1919, netting only seven star images, had been judged inconclusive, but when the Americans developed their plates after the 1922 eclipse, they found they had bagged more than threescore stars. Measured by other astronomers who could not know the results beforehand, the pinpoint images averaged out to a mean displacement of 1.74 seconds of arc, almost exactly as the Einstein equations predicted.

Lick Observatory director W. W. Campbell, the expedition's leader, declared he was satisfied; the Lick Observatory would make no further efforts to verify Einstein. But that did not end the argument. Two months after those observations in Australia—and a few days after Einstein had been awarded the Nobel Prize—a special meeting of the Communist party of the Soviet Union condemned Einstein's theory as "the product of the bourgeois class in decomposition . . . reactionary of nature, furnishing support for counter-revolutionary ideas." Some Americans, bourgeois or otherwise, concurred in this condemnation, if not in its Marxist rationale.

The theory of relativity became a staple item in collegiate and other public debates during the twenties. "Is Einstein Wrong?" asked the editors of the *Forum* in one typical symposium in 1924. Yes, argued Charles Poor; those "transformations" by which Einstein proposed to account for the slight kink in Mercury's orbit are what we used to call approximations, no more. No, replied Archibald Henderson, "there are no errors of Einstein." It was not necessary that the hypotheses upon which relativity rested be "in accord with 'common sense' so-called, but simply that they fit the facts— that the relativistic calculations accord with observation and experiment." But they do not, Professor Poor insisted; the alleged refractions of starlight measured by the Lick Observatory expedition could be accounted for by distortions in the sun's corona or the earth's atmosphere. Mystified by this disagreement, Professor Irving Fisher of Yale—whose own discipline was economics, in those pre-Crash years a field hardly less arcane—concluded with resignation: "Astronomers and physicists must fight it out and the rest of us must wait."

Among the many who could not follow the mathematical pros and cons, some were not willing to wait. Far from resting contented with the conclusions of common sense, imaginative listeners to such debates may have found in the strangeness of Einstein's theory precisely its appeal. "In place of gravitation, in place of the attraction of one body for another," wrote Professor Poor in what he intended as a rebuttal,

> Einstein substitutes a transcendental conception of warped space and of geodesic lines along which a body freely rolls. The sun does not attract the earth, it crumples up space, twists and warps space in some mystic fourth and even fifth dimension, and the earth, carried by its own inertia, wends its way along the easiest path amid the bumps and hollows of crushed and crumpled space. And in this four-dimensional space the ordinary laws of geometry do not apply.

None of this had much to do with stocks and bonds, or with any of the other supposed preoccupations of the twenties. And yet from time to time throughout its history pragmatic America has been hospitable to transcendental conceptions. The descendants of those who yielded to the "Divine and Supernatural Light" with Edwards, or who affirmed with Emerson "the identity of the law of gravitation with purity of heart," may have found in Einstein their guide to the new century's *mysterium tremendum*.

Albert Einstein was not the only bearer of strange new tidings about the universe. Max Planck's quantum theory, wrote Edwin Slosson in 1922, was "quite as important and even more disconcerting to ordinary ideas than the relativity theory, but the public has not yet heard so much about it— perhaps because Planck is not so picturesque as Einstein." True, the prestige of science in some quarters might be at an all-time high—too high, in the opinion of some. A disapproving *Nation* editorial in 1928 lamented, "A sentence which begins with 'Science says' will generally be found to settle any argument in a social gathering, or sell any article from tooth-paste to refrigerator." But in these higher reaches it was by no means clear *what* science was saying. In the previous century, literary folk had responded to what "science said" by writing Darwinist stories, poems, and essays; but as Frederick Hoffman noted in his study *The Twenties*, despite a modish adoption of *relativity* as a catchword by the literary avant-garde, nobody attempted to write an "Einsteinian" novel. Both the opponents and the defenders of Darwin assumed, not always correctly, that they understood him. In contrast, as *Harper's* said in 1929 of the Einstein theory, "We see an extraordinarily animated public interest in an alleged discovery which hardly anyone understands."

But events like the Scopes "monkey trial" showed that even the more "commonsense" variety of scientific endeavor in the twenties was imperfectly reported and still more imperfectly understood. "Science, of late, has been good news," H. L. Mencken remarked in 1927. The newspapers, he went on, "discuss it copiously, and with a fine enthusiasm. But . . . they seldom discuss it with any intelligence." Antidemocratic conclusions could be drawn from such a judgment, and the Sage of Baltimore often drew them. But it is noteworthy that Albert Einstein, remote though he seemed from the common man, never did. "It is of great importance that the general public be given an opportunity to experience—consciously and intelligently—the efforts and results of scientific research," the physicist would write in 1948, after the atomic bomb had made the importance of that effort more painfully obvious. But who was to give the public that opportunity? The scientist—again Einstein himself is an honorable exception—hardly qualified. "In the scientific world," Sir Richard Gregory told the British Association for the Advancement of Science in 1921, "the way to distinction is discovery, and not exposition, and rarely are the two faculties combined."

"How is scientific knowledge to be democratized?" the American historian James Harvey Robinson asked in a little book, *The Humanizing of Knowledge*, published in 1923:

> Scholars and men of science almost always write more or less unconsciously for one another. This is a natural outcome of their training. They must prove their preparation to deal with the subject at hand. . . . The specter haunts them, not of a puzzled and frustrated reader, but of a tart reviewer, likely to accuse them of superficiality or inaccuracy. There is a heavy prejudice in learned circles against the popularizer.

As a result, Robinson argued, "Scientifically and philosophically trained writers apparently have no idea how hard their books and articles are for the general reader," and he proceeded to quote some horrible examples. Much of the difficulty was sheer pedantry, Robinson contended. "A considerable and beneficent revolution" could be wrought if only the college instructor and the textbook writer would "confine himself, at least in addressing beginners or laymen, to telling only such facts as play so important a part in his own everyday thinking that he could recall them without looking them up!" Robinson was also aware of the infectiousness of enthusiasm: "It is a good rule for a writer to assume that nothing in his favorite subject that fails to interest *him* vividly and persistently is likely to interest the outsider who reads his book."

This is not an instance of the humanistic scholar condemning the scientist as a cultural barbarian; we are not listening in on the feud between C. P. Snow's Two Cultures. Quite the contrary; Robinson's polemic grew out of a session at the 1922 meeting of the American Association for the Advancement of Science. By that time, in part moved politically by the popular antiscience sentiment manifest in the statutes that outlawed the teaching of evolution, America's scientific establishment had taken steps to put its own house in more comprehensible order. In 1921 Science Service was founded in Washington, D.C., as a scientific news syndicate on the model of the Associated Press. A circular of instructions to writers of articles for Science Service made it clear that advice like Robinson's had fallen on receptive ears:

> The first consideration . . . is to tell or interpret a scientific event. But the news stories must be so well written that large national newspapers will use them without rewriting or revision, either in form or language. Write your story so that those who know nothing about science will understand and want to read it. Weave in the scientific background that the man in the street does not have. Use simple words. Make your story as graphic as if you were talking about it.

Yet the writer must not achieve his simplification by distortion: " 'By Science Service' must stand for accuracy of content and implication." It was an exacting assignment the science news bureau set for its writers, and in the case of news made by the likes of Einstein and Planck, a staggering one.

Nevertheless, the first director of Science Service tackled his job with relish. Blond, broad-featured Edwin Emery Slosson, a native of Kansas, had long had a foot firmly planted in each of Snow's Two Cultures. A Ph.D. magna cum laude from the University of Chicago in its exciting early days, he had taught chemistry at the universities of Kansas and Wyoming. But he had also served as literary editor for the *Independent*, an esteemed journal of general opinion, for which he wrote vigorous and provocative editorials between 1903 and 1921. He had conducted a course in physical science for journalists at Columbia University's School of Journalism, and in 1920 he had undertaken to write on the scarcely easy theme *Easy Lessons in Einstein.* "He was able to interest anyone," asserts the *Dictionary of American Biography,* "not only in the accomplishments of science, but in science itself, without offending the purest of the scientists." Tirelessly he poured out articles, lectures, and publicity until his death in Washington on October 15, 1929, just nine days before the Great Crash. Standard accounts of the twenties never mention him, but of all the host of journalist intellectuals who committed their thoughts to print during that decade, he may ultimately have been one of the most influential.

Science Service evidently met a felt need. Fifty newspapers in the United States and several in Canada promptly subscribed. By 1927 the agency had also ventured into radio broadcasting, with a "Science News of the Week" program carried over seventeen stations. At the end of that year, the annual meeting of the AAAS held a symposium, "Science and the Newspapers." Such a session would not have been possible twenty years earlier, said David Dietz, science editor of the Scripps-Howard chain. The scientists would not have considered the subject dignified or proper or even ethical, and the newspapermen would have been uninterested. "Those were the days when science was synonymous with ten-syllable inunderstandable words, to be treated appropriately by the staff humorist and the cartoonist." H. L. Mencken's jibes, accordingly, had come to be out of date and unjustified. Indeed, two researchers studying "biology in the public press" concluded from their statistical analysis of 4,000 articles (some 26,000 column inches) in fourteen prominent dailies that "newspapers appear to be more up-to-date in things biological than are college and high-school texts in the subject." They recommended, therefore, that teachers make use of newspaper articles in preference to those ponderously assembled textbooks whose ink was hardly dry before they were obsolete.

Books as well as newspapers carried the popular scientific message. By 1927 an *Outline of Science* had sold more than 100,000 copies; George A. Dorsey's *Why We Behave Like Human Beings* had been a best-seller for three years; and the titles in the Library of Modern Sciences—such as *Stories in Stone, Animals of Land and Sea,* and *The Earth and the Stars*—were reportedly doing well. And the next generation's attention was being engaged; thousands of children were writing entries for a national essay contest in chemistry. The commercial potential here was great, and so was the temptation to increase sales by sensational or overly simple writing at the expense of accuracy. One book publisher's secretary-treasurer, Robert S. Gill of Williams & Wilkins, warned against the latter tendency: "If the gospel is really to be spread, it must have a multitude of patrons, not a multitude of the patronized."

But how was the gospel to be spread to the kind of busy citizens who believed, in those booming twenties, that they literally could not afford to take time out to read anything in a newspaper beyond the financial page, let alone a whole book? Harrison E. Howe, the editor of *Industrial and Engineering Chemistry*, told the AAAS's symposium on science and the press that it was futile to begin with fundamental research if one were to arouse interest among such Americans. "The businessman, indeed the professional man, prefers to have you begin with something with which he is familiar—the milk bottle, a cake of soap, a mirror, his automobile." But was this assertion really true? To take so prosy an approach was to overlook the perennial lure of whatever is different and far off—a lure to which educators were (and are) largely immune. But Edwin Slosson told the American Association for Adult Education in 1928 that "archeology and astronomy—essentially remote and unpractical—head the list of the sciences in order of popular interest, and that the essentially practical sciences are low on the list." Slosson ascribed this preference "to the same cause as that operating in the selection of, say, 'futuristic art' as a subject of study in a women's club rather than 'domestic economy.' " Well might a liberated woman who had had quite enough of domestic economy, thank you, have cried, "Right on!" And perhaps her spouse also might crave more from science than counsel for managing his investments.

To insist relentlessly upon the practical was also to overlook one of science's appeals to its own practitioners. The "man in the street" conceivably might admire the scientist's self-sacrificing dedication or appreciate the contributions of science to human welfare, but he rarely suspected that the scientist was also enjoying himself. "Enthusiasm and fun charge the atmosphere at Leiden, Cambridge, Cornell, and Johns Hopkins," wrote one contributor to the AAAS's austere *Scientific Monthly* in 1928. The scientist might express his own enthusiasm and joy "on a Saturday afternoon working in a laboratory, perhaps malodorous and dark," while others were displaying theirs "standing in the rain and getting sore throats yelling 'Block that kick!' " But if the latter saw "no fun in looking through a microscope or scrutinizing test tubes or listening to radio signals coming from half way round the world, nothing is proved. It all depends on what kind of fun one likes best." If the problem was one of "humanizing" the scientist for the layman, this might have been one of the most effective solutions. The twenties, an era of Babbitt busyness, were also a time of energetic hedonism.

Moreover, to dwell upon the milk bottle, the cake of soap, the mirror, the automobile, was to leave the job of science education half-done. It was, in effect, to substitute technology for science. "The scientists have gone off all by themselves and made a magic that even they didn't foresee," wrote Robert L. Duffus in *Collier's* for January 12, 1924. "This magic is transportation and great cities and wars and Ford factories and much else. . . . [But] these are the mere by-products of science, the symbol and prophecy of its coming power for good or evil." The "common man" had taken these gifts of science but otherwise had gone on in his accustomed unscientific way, "thinking with his spinal column, his liver, his adrenal glands—with anything but his brain." And the "common man," in his capacity as a citizen, could not afford thus to let others do all the thinking about science for him. "Science, represented not by a few specialists in laboratories, but by all of us, must make possible a planned civilization. The present one is haphazard rather than planned, and—well, take a good look at it yourself."

George Horace Lorimer, the doggedly reactionary editor of the *Saturday Evening Post*, who later became an ardent foe of the New Deal, would have bristled at the idea of a "planned civilization." But he shared in this worry that basic, theoretical science was being hustled offstage by its more glamorous sibling. "The Science sisters, Pure and Applied, are a strange pair," Lorimer wrote in a 1926 *Post* editorial:

> Applied is the starry-eyed goddess, the wonder worker, who gets on the first page of newspapers and captivates the imagination of men. She speaks the language of the people, gives them what they want, and every year perfects new gifts to make life easier or longer or more amusing. . . . She is her own press agent and the sun never sets on the advertising she gets. . . .
>
> Pure Science is the wallflower, the elder sister who lives secluded and remote, unknown and unpraised. She does not advertise her astounding feats, and could not if she would, for the only language she knows is a jumble of Latin, Greek, calculus, and mathematical formulas. Only a few professors can understand what she is driving at.

For basic theoretical science, the previous thirty years had been the most fruitful in the world's history. In due course, the *Post* editor predicted, technology would harvest those findings and get the credit, while Pure Science continued to starve in her usual obscurity.

Charles E. Wilson, president of General Motors in the late forties and afterward Dwight Eisenhower's secretary of defense, once said he opposed spending good, hard money on basic research, explaining that he didn't care what made potatoes turn brown when they were fried. Some of his Establishment forebears in the twenties seem to have been more enlightened, on this point at least. In 1923, in the belief that "the funds now available for the support of research in pure science in the United States are far below what our population, education, and material resources demand," leaders in science, business, and politics created a National Research Endowment to support fundamental scientific investigation. Among them were A. A. Michelson, the measurer of the speed of light; Robert Millikan, the first American physicist to have won a Nobel Prize; George Ellery Hale, director of the mighty Mount Wilson Observatory; John J. Carty, vice-president of American Telephone and Telegraph; Owen D. Young, board chairman of General Electric; treasury secretary and financial entrepreneur Andrew Mellon; former presidential candidates Charles Evans Hughes and John W. Davis; and elder statesmen Elihu Root and Colonel E. M. House.

"It is true that money cannot buy genius, but many a genius in science has defaulted because he has had to eat," declared Herbert Hoover, who logically and inevitably became chairman of the National Research Endowment's board. America did not lack competent scientific researchers, he affirmed, but "with the comfort of their families at heart, such men reluctantly accept well-paid industrial positions instead of poorly paid academic posts." National Research Endowment support would, he hoped, give able investigators the "comfort in life, freedom of action, and opportunity for constructive thought that industrial and administrative officers in this country, certainly of no larger calibre, habitually enjoy."

The profit angle was, of course, present: the pure science of today nourishes the technology of tomorrow, which produces the dividends of the day after. Even the rarefied field of astrophysics, AT&T's John J. Carty testified, had useful applications. Still, it is interesting that Hoover—so often typecast as the Great Engineer, with an engineer's limited intellectual and social vision—should have considered "the discovery of a law of nature" to be "a far greater advance" than a study in an industrial laboratory which led to the improvement of some process or machine. "We must add to knowledge," Hoover concluded, "both for the intellectual and spiritual satisfaction that comes from widening the range of human understanding, and for the direct practical utilization of these fundamental discoveries." "The pure scientists," Carty cried, "are the advance guard of civilization."

"A new idea comes first in the mind of one man. That means that the new idea starts out in the world with a majority of 1,600,000,000 against it," wrote Edwin Slosson in 1926. "This instinctive mass reaction against new ideas . . . is essentially the same as the common aversion to a foreigner: 'E's a stranger. 'Eave 'arf a brick at 'im.'" Although the director of Science Service was careful to point out that scientists themselves were no more immune to this tendency to "neophobia" than were other kinds of men, to some extent such an argument nonetheless smacks of elitism. In the country of the blind, the one-eyed man is king, and at least the scientist has the one eye. "Newton's law would never have passed if it depended upon a popular vote," Slosson believed, and even today, in a plebiscite of the entire planet "the Copernican theory would be repealed by an immense majority." Copernican and Newtonian, not to mention Einsteinian, theories are not something the masses will discover if left to themselves.

With this leader-follower point of view pervading the writings of the science publicists, it is small wonder that in some quarters their outpourings were taken not as enlightening instruction but as arrogant propaganda. This backlash was especially apparent in the evolution controversy, as the transcript of the Darrow-Bryan clash at Dayton, Tennessee, in 1925 made painfully clear:

> Mr. Bryan: Your Honor, it isn't proper to bring experts in here to try to defeat the purpose of the people of this state. . . .
> Mr. Darrow: You insult every man of science and learning in the world because he does not believe in your fool religion!

It should be remembered that the trial judge made both men apologize.

Despite the attempts at a cease-fire between science and religion that were current in the twenties, the need to combat what they considered "fool religion" was implicit in many of the science publicists' writings. At that 1927 AAAS symposium "Science and the Newspapers," for example, William E. Ritter spoke of "the necessity of displacing the legendary, mythical, and merely authoritarian knowledge which has constituted [man's] theology by his verified and verifiable experiential knowledge of himself and the world." But perhaps all that this showed was that science educators themselves were as much in need of updating their worldview as were those whom they hoped to educate. Terms like *verified* and *verifiable* had become a good deal more slippery than they had seemed to Thomas Huxley, and some (but by no means all) scientists who breathed the new relativistic atmosphere were deciding that science was, after all, reconcilable with theism. In a sense, science was suffering through a generation gap. In 1928 James Truslow Adams argued that the scientific assumption of a previous generation—namely, mechanistic materialism—had hardened into a popular dogma whose blind advocates were as bigoted as anybody living in Dayton, Tennessee: "Were the citizens of our cities and graduates of our high schools really so much more intelligent than the shirt-sleeve mountaineers? Do they really know so much more about the universe?"

The new explainers of science raised politically troubling questions too. When a writer for Science Service's *Science News Letter* in 1927 described the mulattoes of North America as combining "something of a white man's intelligence and ambition with an insufficient intelligence to realize that ambition," such a statement could be taken merely as a reflection of the incompleteness of scientific knowledge itself; in the twenties, scientists' opinions on race were very much in a state of flux. But specific changes in scientific knowledge could not overcome a certain conservative, even antipolitical streak that ran through the popularizers' writings, Edwin Slosson's in particular. "It is an old saying in political history that 'revolutions never go backward,'" Slosson wrote in 1922 to introduce a series of articles for the news monthly *World's Work* entitled "Science Remaking the World." "Perhaps they never do, but sometimes it seems that they don't go forward either. . . . The political revolution is too much like the automobile motor when the gear is disengaged. It makes a lot of noise and some explosions and throws out a lot of hot air, but it does not move the car of progress." What, then, did move that car? Slosson's answer was explicit: "The extension of democracy which the politician promises is being widely accomplished by the scientist who, by placing the exclusive luxuries of former ages within the lives of all, raises the humblest to a higher plane. The democracy of science is a leveling-up process while the democracy of the communist is a leveling-down process."

Warren G. Harding himself might have said Amen. This was the same social conservatism that had been argued years earlier by William Graham Sumner, the laissez-faire champion, in his essay, "The Absurd Effort to Make the World Over." Later in the series "Science Remaking the World" Slosson illustrated his point in a way that cried down not only revolution but even ordinary political persuasion. When Roentgen discovered the X ray, according to Slosson, he had not had to found an "International Society for the Conversion of the World to the Idea of the X-Rays":

> He did not have to raise an endowment fund and hire a salaried staff, organize a corps of local organizers, and publish a weekly organ. No, he simply announced his discovery in a modest paper that you can read in ten minutes . . . but in a few months every laboratory in the world was taking X-ray photographs. Yet the X-ray has really accomplished more in the world than many a reform movement that makes a great noise and requires tremendous effort.

Slosson did concede in this article that "science provides the motive power, but not the motive for the use of power." Yet that is a most important hedge; to motivate that use, noise and effort and conceivably even revolution—and organization for those purposes—might, after all, have a place in the scientific scheme of things.

Edwin Slosson might have done better if he had taken a hint from one of the scientists he so successfully popularized. Albert Einstein's civic passions—Zionism, pacifism, socialism, world government—were as much a part of the man as the equations with which he attempted to unlock the riddles of the universe. Nor were they something he merely indulged in as a private or nonscientific person after he had closed the door of his laboratory. Many Americans know by now that Albert Einstein in 1939 wrote a letter to Franklin Roosevelt, as a result of which that obscure formula $E = MC^2$ was translated into the most terrifying kind of everyday reality. Not so many are aware that he was afterward instrumental in founding the Federation of Atomic Scientists, a group of men and women who responsibly labored in the arena of public and political persuasion for the purpose of bringing the jinn they had let out of the bottle back under control.

At the 1927 meeting of the British Association for the Advancement of Science, the bishop of Ripon suggested that the scientists take a ten-year holiday during which their laboratories would all be closed "and the patient and resourceful energy displayed in them transferred to recovering the lost art of getting together." "Science has been leading us rather a giddy chase for the last two or three decades," said the *Chicago Evening Post*, and as a result the good bishop's feeling was shared by multitudes. But such a proposal was quixotic. "It is not possible to call a halt," Sir Oliver Lodge replied. "If we stopt, the world would go to pieces." To hold the pieces in place it would indeed be necessary to recover—or discover—the art of getting together, but closing the laboratory doors was not the way to achieve it. One of the ways people had to get together was precisely in their respective capacities as scientist and citizen.

Sixty years later, both the bishop's proposal and the physicist's reply would have their ardent partisans. Neither politically nor intellectually have we worked our way out of this problem. To contend that science should remake the world without check or interference from the politicians (or the people) may have been irresponsible, a surrender on Slosson's part to the self-satisfied complacency that was also part of the spirit of the twenties. But to have anticipated Snow's Two Cultures argument and interpreted it to mean that the layman must abandon *any* attempt to understand and socially apply the insights of science because the scientist and the nonscientist cannot speak to each other at all would have been more irresponsible still.

CHAPTER TWELVE

Extravagant Fiction Today—Cold Fact Tomorrow

*S*cience fiction has in some quarters acquired an air of respectability. The prestigious *International Encyclopedia of the Social Sciences*, published in 1963, contained an eight-page article on "Social Science Fiction"; *Time* admitted the subject to its book review section; and science fiction titles appear regularly in the *Standard Catalog Series*, the librarian's guide to books deemed proper for general library acquisition. Science fiction writers—Ray Bradbury, Arthur C. Clarke, Robert Heinlein—were interviewed the morning after the landing of *Apollo 11* and were heard with the same respect accorded by CBS that same day to Henry Steele Commager, Norman Mailer, and sundry scientists and theologians. But it has not always been so. In 1940 Heinlein, in his third published story, "Requiem"—a touching account of an old man thwarted in a lifelong dream of personally flying to the moon who manages a modest triumph at the story's end by contriving to go and die there—made his hero at one point endure a conversational admonition which Heinlein surely had not had to invent: "The trouble with you is, you read too many of those trashy magazines. Now, I caught my boy reading one of 'em just

An earlier form of this essay appeared in the *Journal of Popular Culture* 5 (Spring 1972): 842–57, and later in Paul A. Carter, *The Creation of Tomorrow: Fifty Years of Magazine Science Fiction* Copyright c. 1977 Columbia University Press, New York. Used by permission.

last week and dressed him down proper. Your folks should have done you the same favor."

The redoubtable Hugo Gernsback, who founded the first periodical in America devoted solely to science fiction and who was thus the progenitor of all those trashy magazines, compared such hostility in all seriousness to the superstitious bigotry of the Middle Ages. "It is most unwise in this age to declare anything impossible," Gernsback defiantly affirmed in 1926, "because you may never be sure but that even while you are talking it has already become a reality . . . If only five hundred years ago (or little more than ten generations), which is not a long time as human progress goes," Gernsback wrote, "anyone had come along with a story wherein radio telephone, steamships, airplanes, electricity, painless surgery, the phonograph, and a few other modern marvels were described, he would probably have been promptly flung into a dungeon. . . . There are few things written by our scientifiction writers, frankly impossible today, that may not become a reality tomorrow."

The theme of prophecy disguised as fiction was stated in the maiden editorial for *Amazing Stories* in April 1926, and it was a *leitmotiv* to which the crusading editor was to return again and again. From the magazine's first issue onward, Gernsback's editorials, strategically visible to the reader on an odd-numbered page facing the table of contents, proudly carried the slogan "Extravagant Fiction Today—Cold Fact Tomorrow." The founder of *Amazing Stories* never lost this faith. For the magazine's thirty-fifth anniversary issue, in 1961, Gernsback contributed a guest editorial which began with the categorical assertion: "As we look back over the vista of modern science fiction, we are struck by the fact that the outstanding stories in the field—the ones that endure—are those that almost invariably have as their wonder ingredient true or prophetic science."

Not only was science fiction perfectly legitimate as extrapolation, Gernsback suggested in his 1926 manifesto, it might even become a positive incentive to discovery, inspiring some engineer or inventor to develop in the laboratory an idea he had first read about in one of the stories. Moreover, the stories were a comparatively painless way of imparting today's scientific and technical lore: "They supply knowledge that we might not otherwise obtain—and they supply it in a very palatable form." Although his editorial style at times irritatingly blended the note of Chautauqua uplift with that of the hard sell, Hugo Gernsback does seem quite sincerely to have conceived of his mission as a species of popular education, in an age when a college degree was not yet the expected goal of young Americans.

Gernsback's readers and writers quickly picked up the editor's thesis that science fiction was also a means for learning science. "Print all scientific facts as related in the stories, in italics," one eager reader of *Amazing Stories* suggested. The magazine's compositors did not take that advice literally, but many an author did provide brief cram courses in the requisite science or engineering, sometimes more than the story really required, and artist Frank R. Paul filled the generously large pages of *Amazing Stories* (and its companions, *Amazing Stories Quarterly* and the short-lived *Amazing Stories Annual*) with imaginative and at the same time faithfully literal pen-and-ink renderings of their fictional technology. Early in 1929 Gernsback lost control of the new magazines he had founded in an merciless publishing war with Bernarr Macfadden, but Thomas O'Conor Sloane, his managing editor—a chemistry Ph.D. and the son-in-law of Thomas A. Edison—stayed on under the new owners (Teck Publications) and continued very much in the founder's didactic tradition.

"Readers may complain of the wild visions exploited in some science stories, where the authors seem to deal in absurdities," Sloane wrote in a 1930 editorial. "Such people should read Eddington's latest paper"—referring to a forecast that well-known physicist had made about a power station operated by the energy contained in a teacup of water—"and see if the wildest imaginings of romancers go much beyond it." Ten years after the birth of *Amazing Stories*, under Sloane's editorship, some of the characters in the stories were still lecturing each other as if they were in school classrooms. Gathered around a campfire after traveling four days by canoe into the wilds of northern Quebec, in Edmond Hamilton's somewhat crude but chillingly effective story "Devolution" (1936), two of the campers sit digesting their hotcakes and bacon while a third, having finished his evening pipe, fills them in on the theory of evolutionary mutation: "The germ-cell of every living thing on earth contains in it a certain number of small, rod-like things which are called chromosomes. These chromosomes are made up of strings of tiny particles which we call genes . . ."

The literary damage which could be done to a work of fiction in this fashion was obvious, and science fiction writers have become very much aware of the problem: "One of the special delights of writing science fiction," Isaac Asimov once wrote, "is mastering the art of weaving science and fiction; in keeping the science accurate and comprehensive without unduly stalling the plot." "This is by no means easy to do, and it is as easy to ruin everything by loving science too much as by understanding it too little." From the standpoint of belles lettres, it is probably just as well that editors Gernsback and Sloane often broke their own rules. As early as July 1926, *Amazing Stories* reprinted H. G. Wells's "The Man Who Could Work Miracles," a delightful little yarn but one which is classifiable as science fiction only by stretching the term a good deal. In that same issue of the magazine, in a letter to the editor, the young science fiction writer G. Peyton Wertenbaker warned: "The danger that may lie before *Amazing Stories* is that of becoming too scientific and not sufficiently literary." Having in mind other kinds of fiction that were being published in 1926 (*The Sun Also Rises*, for example), some outside readers may have considered that Wertenbaker's definition of *literary* did not quite fill the bill either, for science fiction, Wertenbaker wrote, "is designed to reach those qualities of the mind which are aroused only by things vast, things cataclysmic, and things unfathomably strange."

In September 1927 *Amazing Stories* printed "The Colour Out of Space," by H. P. Lovecraft, a writer whose work indeed dealt with things vast, cataclysmic, and unfathomably strange. Yet Lovecraft, a serious literary craftsman, anchored many of his own tales in a specific, usually New England setting for verisimilitude. "The Colour Out of Space," for example, was set in the Central Massachusetts region then in the process of being flooded for the Quabbin Reservoir. In a letter written within a few days of that story's acceptance, Lovecraft argued that even in far-out interplanetary epics, "the human scenes and human characters must be handled with unsparing realism." Conversely, he warned, the interests of realism would not be served in such stories by inventing Martians or Jovians who fit all the conventional terrestrial stereotypes, even as to nomenclature, "with an Indo-Germanic '——*a*' name for the Princess, and something disagreeable and Semitic for the villain."

The shaft was aimed at *Weird Tales*, in which most of Lovecraft's fiction was being published, but it could have been fired at Hugo Gernsback as well. Some months previously, *Amazing Stories* had begun publishing Edgar Rice Burroughs (best known to nonreaders of science fiction as the author of *Tarzan of the Apes*), and the *Amazing Stories Annual* for 1927 printed his novel *The Master Mind of Mars*. Burroughs's Mars was less immediately verifiable than his Africa, but even before the Mariner probes it was obvious that he had created a Mars that never was: a planet whose male inhabitants employed rockets and atomic energy but who usually settled their personal differences with swords and whose egg-laying but otherwise pleasantly human females married earthmen and lived happily ever after.

H. G. Wells's Martians, those shuddersome "intelligences, vast and cool and unsympathetic," who assaulted humankind in *The War of the Worlds*, had not been like that at all. H. G. Wells's human scenes and human characters, on the other hand, were down-to-earth, both figuratively and literally. The effectiveness of many of his novels rests in part on their being rooted in a concrete British milieu of hedgerows and crooked streets. Even when the action moves off this planet, as in *The First Men in the Moon*, Wells's fabulous visions are filtered through the eyes of Mr. Bedford, an archetypically commonplace lower-middle-class Englishman.

Similarly, Jules Verne's main theme was man. *From the Earth to the Moon* is memorable not only for the accuracy of some of its predictions (for example, that the lunar spacecraft would be fired from Florida, in fact only about a hundred miles from the actual Apollo launch site), but also for the characters in his imagined Gun Club of America who decided upon the moon shot and carried it out, a refreshing collection of eccentrics by comparison with the prim bureaucracy of NASA. Novels by both Verne and Wells were reprinted in the early years of *Amazing Stories*, and although the new generation of science fiction writers tended to take from the masters their cosmic inventiveness more than their perceptions of human nature, there were exceptions.

One was David H. Keller, a physician from backcountry Pennsylvania with an almost Thoreau-like aversion to a society based on machine technology. One of Keller's early science fiction stories, "The Revolt of the Pedestrians," made the Lamarckian forecast that as people continued to use the automobile, their legs would atrophy to the point of complete uselessness and that technology would close the gap by providing all citizens with individual-sized "autocars." (Babies, in this world of the future, went through a phase for a few months of trying to use their legs, but it was something they were expected to get over, like thumb-sucking.) The magazine's heading for this story was determinedly Gernsbackian: "There is excellent science in this story, and if you do not believe that too much riding in cars is bad for you, just speak to your doctor." But that comment grossly misinterpreted the author's intention. The exact technology of a wholly motorized population—How, for example, did they manage school attendance, common meals, or hospital care?—*could* have been validly made into science fiction, but what intrigued Dr. Keller was the evolution of society itself under such conditions, and the opportunity this afforded for satire.

But cautionary tales like "The Revolt of the Pedestrians" stood in the early days of magazine science fiction as something of a dissenting opinion or minority report, in counterpoint to the prevailing scientism of Hugo Gernsback's editorials. As for the Burroughs type of adventure stories, Gernsback may have run them as a hedge against his basic bet, attracting readers to the magazine who would not have cared for his more technically oriented tales. In any event, his technical and scientific commitment never wavered, and he was not deterred from his quest by the demise of one family of magazines. Within weeks after the forced sale of *Amazing Stories*, the garish primary colors that characterized cover paintings by Frank R. Paul were adorning a brace of new publications, *Science Wonder Stories* and *Air Wonder Stories*.

Volume 1 of the former was inaugurated with a typical Gernsback editorial: "It is the policy of *Science Wonder Stories* to publish only such stories that [*sic*] have their basis in scientific laws as we know them, or in the logical deduction of new laws from what we know." This time the magazine's founder buttressed his claim to scientific respectability by enlisting a panel of experts "to pass upon the scientific correctness of such stories"—and an impressive panel it was. As listed in the third issue of *Science Wonder Stories*, it included two astronomers, an astrophysicist, three botanists, a chemist, an entomologist, three mathematicians, a medical doctor, a psychologist, and a zoologist. Further, they were affiliated with reputable institutions: Wellesley, Dartmouth, the Armour Institute. One, Clyde Fisher, was curator of the American Museum of Natural History. Listed under "Physics and Radio" was Lee De Forest, inventor of the triode, the audio oscillator, the phonofilm method of sound recording, and much else. The consultant astrophysicist was Donald H. Menzel of the Lick Observatory, whose subsequent publications included *Selected Papers on Physical Processes in Ionized Plasma*, *Fundamental Formulas of Physics*, *Principles of Atomic Spectra*, and, significantly, some memorable debunking of UFOs.

The hopes Gernsback expressed for his new venture in its inaugural editorial were high indeed. As with *Amazing Stories*, he seems to have aimed at a special-interest audience, not so much the general pulp-magazine reader as the zealous amateur chemist, astronomer, or radio experimenter, who might also be reading *Popular Mechanics* or *Scientific American*. Perhaps especially he appealed to the bright but introverted high schooler destined for Cal Tech or MIT, lost in one corner of a world of prestige dominated by athletes, cheerleaders, fancy dressers, and good dancers, who in his loneliness would welcome the colorful appearance each month of *Wonder Stories* as he would welcome the coming of a friend: "Science fiction, as published in *Science Wonder Stories*, is a tremendous new force in America. They are the stories that are discussed by inventors, by scientists, and in the classroom. Teachers insist that pupils read them, because they widen the young man's horizon, as nothing else can." Young men who had been dressed down for reading "those trashy magazines" might well have wistfully queried whether the existence of such teachers and classrooms was anything more than another science wonder story. But in that golden year 1929 some of their elders were believing in equally extravagant fictions of another sort. The philistine character in Heinlein's story "Requiem" who chastised the hero for reading those magazines and longing for the moon, for example, ended by advising him to "stick to your discounts and commissions; that's where the money is."

The Depression seems to have dampened even Hugo Gernsback's exuberance. Magazine circulations dwindled. *Amazing Stories* had had no difficulty in drawing a readership of more than 100,000 in the twenties, but by 1936 Gernsback doubted that that figure could be met by the combined circulation of all the science fiction magazines together. *Air Wonder Stories* discontinued after a run of eleven issues (July 1929–May 1930). Its companion bobtailed its title simply to *Wonder Stories*, reduced its princely bulk and page size to more menial dimensions, reverted to a poorer grade of pulp paper, went bimonthly, and—frowsiest touch of all—ceased trimming its edges. (*Amazing*, under its post-Gernsback management with Dr. Sloane as editor, went through the same process of physical deterioration). In a last desperate attempt to keep his magazine afloat, Gernsback proposed to take it off the newsstands and sell it by subscription only. The gambit failed. Purchased by a pulp adventure-magazine chain, *Wonder Stories* became *Thrilling Wonder Stories* in August 1936. Its first editorial paid lip service, at least, to Gernsback's canons of scientific plausibility: the magazine pledged that "the fundamentals of good science fiction will be scrupulously remembered," and first among these fundamentals was the principle of "never ignoring scientific truth." But a new slogan run in red letters across the bottom of the cover painting suggested that the new management had quite a different perception of their audience: "STRANGER THAN TRUTH."

The depth of the Depression also saw the launching of the third of the pioneering science fiction magazines. Surviving to our own day under the name *Analog*, this one has acquired a certain dowager gentility. But sixty years ago it called itself, with less restraint, *Astounding Stories of Super-Science*. The contrast in tone with Gernsback's *Wonder Stories* and Sloane's *Amazing Stories* was marked. In *Amazing*'s more affluent days (about 1927), a strip of type at the bottom of the front cover had listed its companion magazines: *Radio News, Science and Invention, Radio Listener's Guide, Radio Internacional*, and—typically, for the period—*Spare-Time Money Making*. By way of contrast, *Astounding*'s first contents page listed among its fellow travelers in the Clayton magazine chain such titles as *Ace-High, Ranch Romances, Cowboy Stories, Clues, All Star Detective Stories, Flyers, Forest and Stream*, and *Miss 1930*. Nevertheless, in a kind of pulp parody of Gernsback, editor Harry Bates made the same kind of predictive claim. There had been a time, he said, when the idea of circumnavigating the earth, or of wireless telegraphy, aircraft, sixty-story buildings, radio, and so on would have seemed fantastic, and "That is the only real difference between the astounding and the commonplace—Time." Ordinarily, however, Bates did not even write editorials. He started a letter column, which was *de rigueur* with science fiction readers by that time, but otherwise he let the raw pulp action-adventures brawl on.

In 1933 the Clayton chain (which had won the esteem of the pulp writers themselves by paying 3 cents a word, princely wages for those times) failed. *Astounding Stories* skipped seven months and then reappeared under the imprint of Street and Smith, another chain publisher. The new editor, F. Orlin Tremaine, promptly began to upgrade the magazine's contents, both scientific and literary. There were, no doubt, compromises with the Gernsback ideal, of the same kind that Gernsback and Sloane had sometimes committed. Tremaine is accused, for example, of having rejected at least one story, Eric Frank Russell's "Eternal Re-diffusion," as being "too difficult for the reader to grasp." On the other hand, the new editor introduced what he called the "thought-variant" story, opening the way to bold, if sometimes shaky, philosophical speculations and, more cautiously, to the breaking of a few magazine taboos.

Taking a cue from his competitor Dr. Sloane, Tremaine also commenced running factual articles, which by 1937 had become quite solid expository essays. Willy Ley, formerly vice-president of the Verein für

Raumschiffahrt and a member of the numerous German refugee class of '33, wrote for Tremaine's *Astounding* an article entitled "The Dawn of the Conquest of Space," a sober discussion of the advantages of liquid-fueled over solid-fueled rockets, and R. D. Swisher contributed "What Are Positrons?" which was an admirable explanation in lay language of the Dirac theory. Tremaine also encouraged his readers to address themselves to technical questions. "I have been pleased to see serious discussions of scientific data creeping into Brass Tacks" (the magazine's name for its letter column), Tremaine noted, and in the November 1936 issue, partly on the ground that by their treatment of stories and artwork in terms of superficial likes and dislikes, the letters to the editor were becoming monotonous, he announced that he was converting the Brass Tacks department into Science Discussions.

Tremaine described this change with an enthusiasm that out-Gernsbacked Gernsback: "There is no reason why *Astounding* should not serve as an exponent of scientific advancement." Out of the readers' bull sessions in Science Discussions, the editor predicted, could come major scientific breakthroughs: "We must so plan that twenty years hence it will be said that *Astounding Stories* has served as the cradle of modern science." Somehow it did not work out that way. Within the limits of their own scientific competence, some readers sought to comply, submitting letters on spectroscopy, rocket engineering, mathematical puzzles, the effect of liquid air on magnetism, and in one case a hypothesis to account for the retrograde motion of Jupiter IX. But they also took up great amounts of space riding such hobbyhorses as the Atlantis hypothesis and the question of whether achieving escape velocity was really necessary for interplanetary flight. Tremaine's successor as *Astounding*'s editor, John W. Campbell, Jr.—whose scientific credentials were rather more impressive than Tremaine's—quietly reversed the priorities, changing the name of the column to Brass Tacks and Science Discussions.

If Science Discussions never quite raised *Astounding* into a vest-pocket version of the proceedings of the Royal Society, nevertheless the scientific criticism in these letters from readers did serve to discipline the science served up in the stories. In the *Amazing Stories* Discussions column under Sloane and in the Reader Speaks department in *Wonder Stories* under Gernsback, vigilant readers had frequently spanked authors for factual errors in their fiction (providing the moon with an atmosphere, for example), and they continued to do so in *Astounding*'s Brass Tacks under

Campbell. For example, when Alexander M. Phillips contributed to *Astounding* in 1940 a story titled "A Chapter from the Beginning," detailing an adventure of a shambling primordial hominid named Nwug, one alert reader deduced that the story was to have taken place in North America during the Miocene epoch and that the life-forms Phillips described as existing then were, from the standpoint of paleontology, anachronisms; moreover, the reader suggested that a being so relatively advanced as Nwug would definitely not have walked on its knuckles.

The scientific interest of many readers ran ahead of their actual expertise, but enough readers who had advanced degrees in science or engineering read the magazines and wrote the editors to give these criticisms some show of authority. There were other limitations, of course, as to how effective this sort of discipline could be. Some of the writers, who had themselves started out as science fiction fans, turning out amateur fiction and literary criticism in their mimeographed fan magazines prior to turning professional, eagerly accepted the Gernsback-Sloane-Tremaine-Campbell guidelines. Others, however, were impatient at the necessity for interrupting their story line in order to get the science straightened out—they were, after all, writing for cash for magazines published as men's adventure pulps, in which fast action was the sine qua non, and were not being paid anything extra for doing encyclopedia research. These writers found ways of finessing the science fiction editors' and readers' requirements. As a letter to *Astounding Stories* pointed out in 1934, a great many writers were able to create superscientific marvels by the simple expedient of coining words: "subatomic condensers, geodynes, neutronic pistols, and such." But, this skeptical reader cautioned, "a tale wherein the hero dissolves the villain with a protonic blast cannot claim to be science fiction if the science part of it consists only of the name of the weapon."

Many readers eventually developed an indulgent affection for this kind of foolishness, in which, as one of them wrote in a letter to *Astounding* in 1939, "Buck Rogers chases Killer Kane through Martian skies with a flying belt and Jack Williamson uses his famous geo——s (supply your own endings, they all sound good) to send the villain to perdition in the vastness of inter-universal space." Moreover, the editors themselves, even ones as conscientious as John W. Campbell and T. O'Conor Sloane, occasionally sabotaged the effort at scientific exactness in the interest of telling a good story. Sloane, for example, did not personally believe in interplanetary travel as a practicable possibility, but he justified publishing stories on that theme nevertheless, "since our readers like inter-planetary stories; since they unceasingly ask for them in letters to us, and since there is any amount of science . . . to be gleaned therefrom." Similarly, Campbell, when chided by several readers for having accepted and published a story based on an astronomical impossibility, replied that the basic idea was "interesting enough to make the flaw forgivable."

Years afterward, in 1968, Campbell made this policy quite explicit: "Minor goofs in science—provided they're not crucial to the theme of the story—can be forgiven." Nevertheless, he warned prospective writers for his magazine that the manuscripts most frequently rejected were those written by "people who don't know the difference between science fiction and fantasy"—a difference succinctly stated by Robert Heinlein, who defined the former genre as "speculative fictions in which the author takes as his first postulate the real world as we know it, including all established facts and natural laws. The result can be extremely fantastic in content, but it is not fantasy." More loosely, F. Orlin Tremaine declared in 1934 that "*Astounding Stories* is, perforce, a medium of logical fantasy." Outside experts—particularly formal literary critics—in dealing with the medium have tended to dwell upon the fantasy and overlook the logic.

But the effort to safeguard the integrity of the science in science fiction seems, in the better magazines at least, to have been quite sincere, and nothing infuriated regular readers of science fiction more than to have an "outsider" patronize their field by asserting, as Phil Stong did in 1941, that "the first requirement of a good fantastic story—and half the magazines who specialize on these things neglect the fact—is that it should not be even remotely possible." "No self-respecting editor (even of a fantasy magazine) or writer goes on such a basis," the science fiction fan, author, and editor Donald A. Wollheim indignantly replied. But misconceptions such as Stong's continued to recur. Thus a book review in 1968, noting that science fiction seemed to be achieving a wider audience—"What was once a radio technician's pastime is slowly becoming the literature of this half-century"—nevertheless considered it a conscious manifestation of the absurd, ignoring its basic seriousness.

There was, of course, the embarrassing possibility that even when the science in the stories was accurate, as far as anyone could tell at the time they were written, the scientists themselves might one day change their minds. Moreover—and this is crucial—there are other kinds of implausibilities besides the purely scientific. "You haven't a single author on your payroll who displays any real social insight," complained one British reader of *Astounding*, J. E. Enever, early in 1940. "Briefly, you can do with some H. G. Wellses or Olaf Stapledons to supplement your army of Vernes." The charge was not quite fair. Throughout the 1930s there had been an occasional Nathan Schachner, David H. Keller, or Miles J. Breuer who had engaged, sometimes clumsily, in social criticism. But on the whole it was just, and it is a criticism of science fiction which quite rightly continued to be made. But the situation was changing. Ironically, on the page just previous to Enever's letter were printed the concluding paragraphs of a two-part serial which attempted to apply its predictions to the insights of the social as well as the natural sciences, Robert Heinlein's "If This Goes On—," and the following issue of *Astounding* saw the first installment of L. Ron Hubbard's "Final Blackout," a somber forecast—with no technological gimmickry—of one possible outcome of the then-raging World War II.

Even on this score, the magazines in a sense had the last word. The October 1939 number of *Amazing Stories*, appearing on the newsstands in the month of August, carried a grim tale of a renewed outbreak of war in Europe. Entitled "Judson's Annihilator," the story was based on the major premise that "the scientists' brains have built the twentieth century; their morals will blow it to bits." In the story, an aerial invasion of England is thwarted when the fleet of enemy warplanes is warped into another era by a time machine, but this is no conventional evil-Nazis-versus-pure-Englishmen epic. The English hero enters that future time only to discover—as have the German fliers who preceded him—that regardless of which side "wins" the present war, the world will become a savage ruin. "When I began to plan this story," John Beynon Harris, its British author, explained, "I found that there was no need to use that hoary old standby the mad scientist . . . when the reputedly sane scientists are quite efficiently getting on with the job of world destruction before our eyes." Further, the brief essay describing the magazine's back cover for that month (a painting of an atomic power plant) noted that atomic energy could also be employed in war, releasing "power so terrible that entire cities might be blasted away."

On August 6, 1945, over a crowded city in Japan, the extravagant fiction of a few years before became cold fact. It threw the science fiction community into a moral dilemma that Hugo Gernsback probably never anticipated, and on behalf of his colleagues the science fiction and popular science writer Isaac Asimov made what amounted to an act of contrition. "Well, the atomic bomb came, and it finally made science fiction 'respectable,'" Asimov wrote in 1969.

> For the first time, science fiction writers appeared to the world in general to be something more than a bunch of nuts; we were suddenly Cassandras whom the world ought to have believed. But I tell you, I would far rather have lived and died a nut in the eyes of all the world than to have been salvaged into respectability at the price of nuclear war hanging like a sword of Damocles over the world forever.

If the recoil from the extravagant fact of today could be so strong, how deeply rooted had been the Gernsbackian commitment to cold reality in the fiction of tomorrow? Had most science fiction readers experienced merely a *frisson* from the stories, of the kind a hard-headed skeptic might get from a ghost story well enough told to convince him or her momentarily that "this could be true"? The question is not entirely rhetorical; early in 1939 Campbell launched a companion magazine to *Astounding Science Fiction*, called *Unknown*. Although the new publication dealt not in rocket ships and ray guns but in elves and witches and vampires, it was quickly apparent that the two magazines had heavily overlapping constituencies. The paradox was not lost on alert readers (and writers): "The Jekyll-science-fictionist stands for experimental truth, for logic, for *proof*. The Hyde-nocturnal-seeker," concluded Seymour Kapetansky, "exists in frank fear of the dark, in the world of dreams, . . . of witches'-brew, of curses, of Kismet. . . . Fantasy fiction has bred the most illogical double-track mind in history," able to enjoy both the brisk technocratic forecasts of *Astounding* and the sinister revenants in *Unknown*.

Of course, the paradox may be more apparent than real. The fact of today may have become so extravagant that no mere fiction can cope with it. In 1927, back in Gernsback's heyday, Clarence E. Ayers compared the findings of modern science with the messages of ancient Israel's prophets and found them equally fabulous:

> These men tell tales of the creation of all living things from primordial ooze, of the origin of the earth from spouts of incandescent gas from the sun, of rays that penetrate the solidest-seeming stuff. . . . They sing of matter which is not matter but energy . . . which changes places from moment to moment, and of different moments which are simultaneous in different loca-

tions. These are the real marvels of the age of science. We must not dismiss them lightly because we believe that they are true. . . .

To be sure, science does not represent itself as folklore. . . . Folklore never does. We must not imagine Moses coming down from Mount Sinai and urging Joshua and Aaron to bear in mind that his various narratives are folklore. It was enough that they were marvelous. . . . But it should also be a mistake to suppose that the Israelites were as surprised as they would have been to hear him say that he had been borne through the clouds at 120 miles to the hour and accompanied by the sound of an awful roaring. Sufficient unto the day is the folklore thereof.

A fiction which celebrated a "fact" so numinous as this would inevitably, *malgré lui*, break down the logical-classificatory barriers between science fiction and fantasy, rigorously defended though that barrier consciously was. Even a casual thumbing of the crumbling pulp-paper pages of these old magazines turns up stories, putatively science fiction by Gernsback's (or Robert Heinlein's) definition, which at deeper evocative levels have quite a different meaning. Perhaps the antithetical critical judgments of the "outside" literary critic, who is neglectful if not hostile toward the disciplinary role of science in the stories, and the "inside" science fiction partisan and missionary, who is often insensitive to broader historical and cultural concerns, may here one day be fused.

CHAPTER THIRTEEN

Space Voyages, 1591–1920: An Introduction

Something hidden. Go and find it. Go
and look beyond the Ranges—
Something lost behind the Ranges. Lost
and waiting for you. Go!

RUDYARD KIPLING, *The Explorer*

*T*he youngster who escapes his mother's vigilant eye for the first time and toddles up to the corner is doing exactly what his ancestors have always done," one newspaper declared when Richard E. Byrd sailed to Antarctica to try for the South Pole. "So long as there is one spot of this old world of ours which holds a secret, just so long will there be explorers." And when this old world ceased to hold secrets, there would always be outer space. Science fiction builds on an abundant literature, stretching far back in time—Sinbad and the *Odyssey*, for example, must be included—that spells out this perennial human urge to toddle up to the corner and look beyond the Ranges.

Like science fiction, this exploration literature ranges from the thoroughly plausible to the entirely outrageous. Alongside the factual narratives of judicious Jesuit missionaries and the commonsensical journals of Captain Cook are more fanciful accounts, such as the *Travels of Sir John Mandeville* or descriptions of the mythical Central Asian Christian kingdom of Prester John. Particularly in the period of the discovery and exploration of the New World, writers produced a large travel literature of fantastic

An earlier form of this essay appeared in *Space Voyages, 1591–1920: A Bibliography*, compiled by Lynn S. Smith (Riverside: Library of the University of California, 1979), [5–8].

voyages to problematical places—where one might encounter creatures as otherworldly as any imagined by Stanley G. Weinbaum—or human societies, some of them wondrously utopian and others afflicted with problems which, though subject to satiric exaggeration, were not unlike one's own. "The Atlantic," Howard Mumford Jones has written, "hid in its misty vastness many wonderful islands," whose literary images were "compounded of wonder, terror, wealth, religious perfection, communism, utopianism, or political power"—in short, a literature that has much of the heft and ring of 1930s- or '40s-style pulp science fiction.

What were they really looking for, those perennial romantics who went wandering off beyond the Ranges? Gold and glory; the spread of the religion of the Cross; the might of empire—but also the sheer wonder of a world dramatically different from their own, and the utopia one could not find at home. Shakespeare's play *The Tempest*, presciently written just as the spirit of this quest was permeating the European mind, captured the mood and set the tone. All its elements—the grandiose old scientist-magician; his dumb, beautiful daughter; his sinister servant-monster Caliban—echo and re-echo throughout the history of science fiction. The film *Forbidden Planet*, for example, faithfully follows the Shakespearean story line, even down to such homely details as the drunk scene.

They came to America, those sixteenth-century European vagabonds—who were in some ways the last of the crusaders, in others the first of the entrepreneurs—in search of El Dorado, the Fountain of Youth, the City of the Sun. Even *Terra Australis Incognita*, the great hypothetical southern continent which long adorned early-modern world maps (it had to be there, for symmetry's sake, to balance the great landmass to the north), was believed to be a warm, wealthy land with inhabitants who would be eager, given the opportunity, for the blessings of European trade. Natives of Africa, Asia, and America had to listen patiently to these white men with their wild tales. The Indians of Arizona and New Mexico in the path of the conquistadores quickly learned to humor them, and encourage them to go on questing into the unknown for the Seven Cities of Cíbola—which had the advantage of at least temporarily luring the intruders away from their own hitherto untroubled villages.

That was the trouble with these vision quests, once one took the trouble to act them out: the pleasure principle, as Freud would say, gave place to the reality principle. Those seven great cities hard by the Grand

Canyon turned out to be rather modest and dusty pueblos. Antarctica's burgeoning millions turned out to be scavenging skuas, pathetically vulnerable seals, and dignified emperor penguins. When Captain Cook made his furthest lunge to the south and stopped, baffled by the barrier ice, his shipmate George Forster gave the back of his hand to El Dorado: "The ice, the fogs, the storms and ruffled surface of the sea formed a disagreeable scene, which was seldom cheered by the reviving beams of the sun; the climate was rigorous and our food detestable." It is the beauty of science fiction, however, that in the face of such disillusionment it is capable of orderly strategic withdrawal.

Jonathan Swift, Cook's equally hardheaded eighteenth-century contemporary, may have sensed the changing geographic situation when he wrote *Gulliver's Travels*. Although for verisimilitude he carefully oriented his imagined Lilliput and Brobdingnag to recently discovered real places like Van Diemen's Land or to long-known but politically inaccessible states like Japan, in Book Three of *Gulliver* Swift placed one satirized society's homeland on an island in the sky, powered by what we would now term antigravity. The elite corps of mad, or at least pixilated, scientists who work there have, in the story, recently discovered the two satellites of Mars—then unknown to actual astronomers—and a still luckier shot, they place them at the proper distances in diameters outward from the planet. It was a sign of what was coming. Stimulated by the new astronomy of the seventeenth century and the balloon ascensions of the late eighteenth, as Marjorie Nicolson has shown, the mysterious islands ascended to the heavens, and the long sea voyages to reach them were transmuted into journeys through space. You could move your Prospero's island, your lost Atlantis, your Lilliput out where Lucian of Samosata had suggested they were as early as the second century, when he composed a sequel to the *Odyssey* in which the Greek adventurers travel to the moon.

Meanwhile another influence upon science fiction unfolded: the nineteenth-century sea story. James Fenimore Cooper, for example, wrote more fiction with a maritime setting than he did tales of the Leatherstocking variety. To someone who lived on the Atlantic seaboard of North America in the first half of the nineteenth century, the frontier was not so much the ever-receding horizon to the west as it was the equally elusive margin of the ocean. And there—realistically, as in Dana's *Two Years Before the Mast*, or fantastically, as in Poe's *Narrative of A. Gordon Pym of Nantucket*—

another context was provided for space fiction. When non-science fiction readers complain of the technical astronautical or astronomical details in the stories, they should remember that people living in far inland towns used to read with pleasure many novels in which an equally technical vocabulary was integral to the story. The stream of orders the bosun on a square-rigger snapped out to his crew to take in sail is, for most modern readers, quite as impenetrable as the laconic words that pass between a party of astronauts and Mission Control. As for encounters with balefully intelligent monsters among the stars, few such creatures have been able to match one of Melville's whales. Combine the satiric consciousness of Swift (or alternatively, the humane vision of Thomas More) with the dark power of the best of these sea stories, and transplant the combination to another world, and we are ready for the distinctive vision of modern science fiction.

It follows, incidentally, that the kinds of questions science fiction writers have been successively asked with each twentieth-century scientific breakthrough—atomic energy, radar, the Apollo flights—namely, "What are you going to write about now that the 'real' world has robbed you of your ideas?" betrays an impoverishment of imagination that is a ground almost for despair. The writers of the older works of science fiction solved that problem triumphantly. Some of their solutions were clever, some foolish; some of their writing is still enjoyable, some unreadable. Whether well or badly, however, they *solved* it, and the same has to be said of present-day science fiction. From a South American El Dorado used by Voltaire and from Melville's whaling grounds the science fictional imagination moved on to the moon, to Mars, to the rest of our solar system, and as the Viking and Pioneer probes chased Bradbury's Martians and Poul Anderson's Jovians forever beyond our horizon, the science fiction writer cheerfully turned to the ever-new world of quasars and translight Doppler shifts and black holes. It was well, moreover, that he or she was able to do so. Another commentator and participant on the polar exploration of a half-century ago and more, Laurence M. Gould, has suggested that such mental outreach may be essential to the psychic well-being of humankind: "To be dauntless and to be everlastingly inquisitive—these are two traits in us that will not die out. So long as they last"—so long as people go, in reality and in imagination, in quest of "knowledge about a land that the race can never use—we can have hope."

"Writers are magpies," as Damon Knight once put it. Many a thematic element or plot twist that could be treated freshly in a present-day science fiction anthology or magazine turns out to have a very long historical pedigree. But, if Toynbee's "Archaism and Futurism" holds true in science fiction, as I believe it does, that is only what one ought to expect. In voyaging high and far, we re-embody the caveman floating across the lake on a log or the Celt in his wicker coracle. In leaping into the future, we regenerate our primal beginnings.

CHAPTER FOURTEEN

Rockets to the Moon, 1919-1944

A Debate Between Reality and Fiction

*I*f science fiction is a literary extrapolation from the known into the unknown, then the *Odyssey* of Homer is science fiction. After all, until somebody came back from the western Mediterranean with an accurate map, people did not *know* that the straits of Messina weren't guarded on one side by a whirlpool and on the other by a many-headed monster! Centuries after Homer's time, around A.D. 160, the satirist Lucian of Samosata composed a "true history" (*Vera Historia*) to supply an adventure, purportedly missing from the *Odyssey*, in which the voyagers are caught up in a waterspout and are transported to the moon. Out of Lucian grew a long tradition of literary trips to Luna, nourished especially by the astronomy of the seventeenth-century savants and by the aeronautics of the later eighteenth-century balloonists, until the genre took its modern form in the writings of Verne and Wells.

An earlier form of this essay appeared as "Rockets to the Moon, 1919–1944: A Dialogue Between Fiction and Reality," by Paul A. Carter, *American Studies* (*Midcontinent American Studies Journal*) 15 (Spring 1974):31–46, © 1974 Mid-America American Studies Association. Used with permission. It was also later included in Paul A. Carter, *The Creation of Tomorrow: Fifty Years of Magazine Science Fiction* Copyright c. 1977 Columbia University Press, New York. Used by permission.

Science fiction enthusiasts have always contended that the imaginative foreshadowings in their favorite stories paved the way toward public acceptance of concepts such as space travel and thereby helped the prophecies come true. But science fiction may sometimes have had the reverse effect: public acceptance of what scientists and engineers soberly proposed to do in reality may have been delayed because such proposals had been treated for centuries as fantastic fiction. The delay may have been greater in some national cultures than in others. The Russian seer Konstantin Tsiolkovski, who wrote in 1903 that "the earth is the cradle of humanity, but man will not stay in the cradle forever," remained a prophet with honor in his own country. The Soviet regime reprinted his prerevolutionary writings (including a science fiction novel), and a vast crater on the far side of the moon now bears his name. But when the American experimenter Robert H. Goddard proposed, in a modest Smithsonian monograph published in 1919, the use of rocket propulsion as a method of reaching extreme altitudes, he was spanked by the heavy hand of the *New York Times*.

In calling Goddard's proposition "A Severe Strain on Credulity," the newspaper committed a scientific blunder of a kind which dogged the rocket experimenter from the beginning. It stated that in the vacuum beyond earth's atmosphere a rocket could not function because it would have nothing "against which to react." So little had the elementary axioms of modern science penetrated even the educated lay consciousness in the two centuries since Newton! But the newspaper insisted that it was Goddard, not the *Times*'s editorial writer, who "seem[ed] to lack the knowledge ladled out daily in high schools." And, of course, the professor really knew better: "There are such things as intentional mistakes or oversights," forgivable as poetic license in the writings of a Jules Verne or an H. G. Wells, but "not so easily explained when made by a savant who isn't writing a novel of adventure." The Smithsonian, the *Times* hinted darkly, was being defrauded.

By taking the trouble to fire a revolver in a vacuum, and showing that the weapon recoiled even though the exhaust gases had nothing to "push against," Goddard claimed to have proved his theoretical point. But his troubles were not yet over. In the summer of 1929 the explosion of one of his experimental rockets some ninety feet above Auburn, Massachusetts, "sent Worcester ambulance and police hunting for tragedy," and public indignation forced Goddard to move his work to New Mexico, "that state whose empty stretches, so much like the surface of the moon, seem to attract the rocket men."

Urban crowding was not the only reason he was driven away, for similar accidents happened in 1931 and 1932 on the Raketenflügplatz in suburban Berlin, where German rocket enthusiasts regularly launched their liquid-fueled cylinders. Yet the Society for Space Travel (Verein für Raumschiffahrt) and the municipal authorities were able somehow to compose their differences. To be sure, the historical context was entirely different. In 1932 the VfR lost the services of its most prominent member, a brilliant nineteen-year-old named Wernher von Braun, to the secret Army Weapons Department, which was interested in rocket research for thoroughly mundane reasons. Many years later, Willy Ley, the VfR's vice-president, reported a conversation he had had in 1929 with Hermann Oberth, who ranks with Tsiolkovski and Goddard among the parents of space travel. "Do you think, Herr Professor, that there will be a need for rockets carrying a load of mail over five hundred kilometers?" Ley asked. "Oberth looked at me with the smile which old-fashioned pedagogues reserve for people whom they call 'my dear young friend' and said after a while: 'There will be need for rockets which carry a thousand pounds of dynamite over five hundred kilometers.' "

Lacking such obviously utilitarian motives, private American rocket investigators were easily victimized by public opinion. Robert Goddard "early discovered what most rocket experimenters find out sooner or later— that next to an injurious explosion publicity is the worst possible disaster," wrote his fellow experimenter G. Edwards Pendray. Understandably bitter at the press, which had "branded him 'Moon Man' and hinted he was a crackpot after the Worcester interlude," Goddard kept reporters two hundred yards off while he squired Harry Guggenheim and Charles Lindbergh around the premises of his New Mexico retreat in 1935. According to *Time* for March 2, 1936, "Dr. Goddard hates to stir up gaudy talks of moon flights"—and small wonder. Occasionally a leading magazine in the interwar years would publish an article on a topic such as "Can We Go To Mars?" and editorially conclude that "the plan is theoretically sound," but the answering voices of negation were vigorous and dogmatic.

The mass-circulation *American Magazine* interviewed one prominent American astronomer in 1927 and reported to its readers: "Professor [William H.] Pickering is of the opinion that the only feasible method of getting to the moon is visually through the eyepiece of a good telescope." For a more specialized audience—the readers of the *Catholic World*—R. L. Simons discoursed in 1934 on "Space Ship Hokum." And Science Service, a strong voice for the scientific establishment itself, sought to allay the panic aroused by Orson Welles's "invasion from Mars" broadcast in 1938 by showing that interplanetary travel is impossible: reaching escape velocity, even from the lighter gravity of Mars, would require more fuel than a rocket could theoretically carry. By then, however, Major General Walter Dornberger and Wernher von Braun were hard at work on that very problem in a region of "dunes and marshland overgrown with ancient oaks and pines, nestling in untroubled solitude" only four hours by train north of Berlin: a place with the Wagnerian-sounding name of Peenemünde. It was not quite so ideal for the purpose as Goddard's New Mexico, but it would do.

According to the British Interplanetary Society's Arthur C. Clarke, "All Goddard's initial pioneering work was financed by a grant of some $11,000, but the German War Department sank £35,000,000 into the building of Peenemünde. . . . The parallel with the history of nuclear physics is as striking as it is depressing." Even at Peenemünde, however, more than sheer militarism was involved. "Our aim from the beginning was to reach infinite space," General Dornberger later wrote. Indeed, von Braun himself seems to have been denounced to the Gestapo during the war, and briefly arrested, for dreaming about orbiting spaceships, flights to the moon, and atomic energy for voyages to the stars when he was supposed to be concentrating on the immediate necessities of the Third Reich.

Whether performed on a shoestring by the amateurs of the VfR or carried out with the backing of the mighty Wehrmacht, rocket investigation in Germany was hampered—and on several occasions all but destroyed—by skeptics within the Nazi government. But skepticism in America, as in pre-Hitler Germany, was less efficiently organized. If rocket experimenters faced the opposition of sensation-hungry newsmen, they received the occasional endorsement of periodicals like *Popular Mechanics* and *Scientific American*. They could also count on one staunch but perhaps less helpful ally in the newly founded science fiction magazines, for these also catered to a readership that dreamed of orbiting spaceships, flights to the moon, and atomic energy for voyages to the stars.

Hermann Oberth himself, who would live long enough to be feted at one *Apollo 11* prelaunch party as the man who started it all, served in 1929 as the scientific adviser to Fritz Lang's science fiction motion picture *Frau im Mond*. The plan was that the UFA Film Company would finance the building of one of Oberth's rockets, which in turn would be launched in time to serve as publicity for the picture's premiere. (Ironically, Oberth's preferred location for this public relations action was a spot on the Baltic coast not far from Peenemünde.) Max Valier, a young German popular science writer and lecturer who had spent much of the twenties in fruitless efforts to develop a rocket-powered automobile for the German motor tycoon Fritz von Opel, was killed by the explosion of an oxygen tank during a rocket experiment in 1930. A year later, the American science fiction magazine *Wonder Stories*, in a biographical sketch accompanying the English translation of Valier's short story "A Daring Trip to Mars," editorially hailed him as "the first man to give his life to rocketry."

In the thirties, the overlap between the factual and the fanciful in astronautic experimentation became even more substantial. The founding of the VfR in Germany in 1927 had been soon followed by the establishment of the American Interplanetary Society in 1930 (rechristened the American Rocket Society in 1934), the British Interplanetary Society in 1933, and similar Soviet, French, and Austrian organizations. An article in the *New Outlook* for October 1934, consisting of brief biographical accounts of the leading "Men of Space," listed—alongside figures as internationally known as Oberth, Goddard, the stratosphere balloonist Auguste Piccard, and Tsiolkovski's junior colleague Nikolai Rynin—no fewer than five other authors who both held office in these national rocket societies and also wrote science fiction for the American pulp magazines.

Willy Ley, for example, as a German refugee in America after 1934, published not only articles on rocketry and zoology—the latter in such eminently reputable outlets as *Natural History* and *La Nature*—but also, under the pseudonym Robert Willey, a number of carefully researched science fiction stories. To be sure, his characters face and solve variations on the customary pulp story problems of adventure and intrigue: they escape from a Soviet colony on Mars ("Novaya Respublika," complete with a Five Year Plan and cities having names like "Planetogorsk"), or they thwart a Japanese bid for the conquest of space. But they also wrestle, in highly convincing fashion, with such purely technical difficulties as mass-ratios, refueling in space, and, for traveling between the planets, the choice of the proper "Hohmann orbits," named after the city architect of Essen-on-the-Ruhr, Walter Hohmann, who during the 1920s had actually calculated just such trajectories.

Several of Ley's British and American equivalents led the same kind of literary double life. G. Edwards Pendray, science editor of the *Literary Digest*, president of the American Rocket Society, and designer of the first liquid-fueled rocket engine used in his society's experiments, wrote three longish science fiction yarns for *Wonder Stories* under the pseudonym Gawain Edwards. P. E. Cleator, president of the British Interplanetary Society, ordinarily wrote factual rather than fictional predictions of spaceflight, such as his book *Rockets Through Space* (1936), but he also committed to paper for *Wonder Stories* the tale "Martian Madness." Laurence Manning, a founder of the American Rocket Society, editor of its journal *Astronautics*, and co-designer of one of its rockets, wrote a dozen stories that appeared in *Wonder*, including his jaunty satire "Seeds from Space," and two others with Fletcher Pratt's collaboration. Nathan Schachner, another founder and former president of the American Rocket Society, who suffered injury in an early rocket engine experiment, wrote his first science fiction "on a bet," as he afterward testified, "and much to my surprise it was accepted." In the next two decades he published more than fifty such stories, using the informal nom de plume Nat Schachner. He reserved "Nathan" for more conventional writings, such as a history of the medieval universities and biographies of Jefferson, Hamilton, and Aaron Burr. (Along with all these activities he also found the time to practice law!)

Stories by men like Ley, Pendray, Cleator, Manning, and Schachner were far from being literary masterpieces, usually; but they did provide a kind of yardstick by which the engineering plausibility of other fictional trips to the moon could be measured. Max Valier, in his story "A Daring Trip to Mars," took time out from the narrative to discuss the errors committed by "previous novelists," most notably their descriptions of the phenomenon of weightlessness. (The occupants of the spaceship would not "feel lighter and lighter from hour to hour" as they moved further away from the earth, Valier correctly pointed out; rather, they would experience weightlessness "at that moment, a slight distance above the earth, when the rocket is shut off.") Otto Willi Gail's "The Shot Into Infinity," which appeared in *Wonder Stories Quarterly* in 1929 following prior book publication in Germany, contains too much schmaltz and Teutonic nationalism for today's reader, but Gail's moonship *Geryon* was a well-thought-out three-stage rocket, whose ascent compares—roughly but plausibly—to that of *Apollo 11*: ninety-eight seconds to burnout of the first stage, as against three minutes for *Apollo*; five minutes into the flight for ejection of the second stage at an elevation of 700 kilometers (426 miles), as compared with 9 minutes and 12 seconds, downrange 883 miles at an altitude of 100 miles for *Apollo*. Once the *Geryon* is well under way, its occupants engage in a space walk: "The sunlit helmets and suits gleamed in the absolute darkness with an unearthly phosphorescence," the novelist wrote. "Day and night had joined in a seemingly impossible union"—language not unfamiliar to any reader of *Life* or *National Geographic* during the decade preceding *Apollo*.

Shots as close to the mark as that one were accompanied, however, by other stories which make one understand why the science fiction magazines were so often dismissed with the epithet *pseudo-science* (a term that used to infuriate the science fiction fans). A prime example is Harl Vincent's "The Explorers of Callisto," published in *Amazing Stories* for February 1930. Unlike the monstrous tower of a Saturn-Apollo stack, the rocket ship in this tale is only forty feet long; in fact, it is a rebuilt airplane, lacking only struts and guy wires. In addition to rocket-firing cylinders, it has conventional landing gear and tail structure, a fifteen-cylinder 600-horsepower radial engine for getting through earth's atmosphere, and a propeller. After the proud inventor, Ray Parsons, has first shown his handiwork to his friends Gary Walton and Eddie Dowling, one of them asks, "When do we go?" and the hero replies, "Can you make it the day after tomorrow?" It is conceivable that a spaceship built by a civilization less cumbersome than ours might have successfully taken off without its inmates being first subjected to NASA's relentless simulation exercises, but this author seems to have gone to the opposite extreme.

After takeoff—barely clearing a board fence and the tops of some trees, in the fashion not of a rocket but of a heavily laden small airplane of the period—the good ship *Meteor* duly proceeds to the moon. The flight itself is somewhat more plausibly presented, although the dialogue is pure Batman-and-Robin. On the moon's far side, the three adventurers encounter space-suited soldiers pursuing a fugitive across the lunar surface. Rescuing their intended victim, our hero looks through the space suit's face plate: " 'Christopher!' he exclaimed. 'It's a girl! And a peach!' " Her name is Lola, and she turns out to be the daughter of the king and queen of Callisto, fifth of the Jovian satellites. With scarcely another look at earth's moon, the action moves forthwith out to one of Jupiter's. Perhaps it is no cause for wonder that while T. O'Conor Sloane, editor of *Amazing Stories* in the early thirties, published many stories of interplanetary travel, he personally and editorially pooh-poohed the whole idea.

Sloane's skepticism, however, was based not upon the *New York Times*'s fatuous reasoning but upon the more plausible ground that the acceleration necessary to attain escape velocity would crush the pilot—a question which was in fact not resolved until the high-altitude test-piloting and centrifuge experiments of the late 1950s. Science fiction writers sometimes sought to meet this objection by positing "acceleration compensators" or—a less question-begging response—by assuming that the astronaut would black out during liftoff: "Within the compact control room at the heart of the great space-ship, its solitary occupant lay unconscious in the straps and paddings of his seat, as the vast cylinder roared skyward" in one *Wonder Stories* serial of 1934.

Not all of Sloane's readers agreed with his negative verdict on space travel, and the skepticism of Dr. Sloane was more than matched by the enthusiasm of Hugo Gernsback, his predecessor as editor of *Amazing Stories* and his competitor as editor of *Wonder*. Hailing Robert Goddard for having routed his critics on the question of rocket flight in a vacuum, Gernsback in an editorial for *Amazing* in 1927 commented that "just as the heavier-than-air machine was pooh-poohed by scientists of repute, space flying is being pooh-poohed today by the same class of scientists." The harassed American rocket experimenter was also singled out for specific vindication in one story published under the regime of the more mistrustful Sloane: "Now that the Goddard rocket has at last made a fair hit on the moon," says one character in a story published in 1929 but presumably taking place a few years in the future, it behooves would-be space walkers to work out the technical details of a practicable space suit. Therefore, in a fictional world far more cozy than that of the V-2 and *Apollo 11*, "a little social club of amateur astronomers, . . . mostly engineers or manufacturers from New York or Boston," builds the suits while (in poetic justice to Goddard) the Smithsonian Institution on a readily granted government appropriation builds the rocket. In this instance, the implausibilities were not technical but social.

Like Hugo Gernsback, F. Orlin Tremaine, who became editor of *Astounding Stories* in 1933, disputed the skepticism of their competitor Sloane. In an editorial prompted by the publication in 1936 of P. E. Cleator's *Rockets Through Space*, with its prediction that "a trip to the moon is actually possible to-day," Tremaine declared: "Perhaps we dream—but we do so logically, and science follows in the footsteps of our dreams." But at least a few of the science fiction writers already had matured enough to know that dreams which come true sometimes yield only disenchantment.

In "Magician of Dream Valley," published in *Astounding Science Fiction* in 1938, Raymond Z. Gallun pictured Imbrium City, the first human colony on the moon, as a place of "vast slag heaps," lighted by "the greenly phosphorescent pall of radioactive waste-vapors ejected from the chimneys of the plant." Man is building not a lunar utopia but an industrial wasteland to match the moon's own natural bleakness:

> Sweeping around the ugly and eternally threatening squatness of the rocket fuel plant . . . were the gray plains of a "sea" which, on the quick-cooling Moon, had never contained water in any appreciable quantity. The aspect of those gently undulating expanses of billion-year-old lava was too awesome now, under the grimly factual stars, for any preconceived idea of romance in connection with them to overbalance their depressing suggestion of eternal death.

The only redeeming feature in this dreadful landscape consists of winking, mysterious "Hexagon Lights" which turn out to be sentient creatures of pure energy—and the radioactive waste-vapors from the fuel plant are killing them. In a desperate effort at self-preservation, the Lights seek to destroy the factory. The hero, as he usually does in such tales, thwarts them. But at the very end, like the paleface Americans after their subjugation of the Indian, he is caught up in sympathy and regret for this beautiful life-form that has fallen victim to technological pollution.

Many critics of science fiction have discerned in the genre a positivistic and optimistic bias, which indeed it had. But even in the preatomic 1930s, minority reports like Gallun's continued to offer a more somber theme. It was foreseen in the pulps, for example, that the conquest of space could have an appalling cost in human life. Manly Wade Wellman's "Men Against the Stars," also published in 1938, is told from the viewpoint of John Tallentyre, a vexed executive at a spaceport on the moon who sends men out on missions further into space with the knowledge that almost all the ships carrying them will explode. "Five days out in space, Mars-bound," we are shown the crew of Ship Number Fifty-Nine grousing at their moon-bound superiors, whom the ship's engineer regards as "straw-stuffed uniforms [who] sit back there with their feet on desks, while we're gunnin' out here, out where the danger and the work is." A spacehand comes to the executives' defense, arguing that "they've probably got worries of their own."

> "Worries of their own?" echoed the engineer. "On that buttonpusher's work? Say, if either of them worried a day of his life, I hope this ship blows apart right no——"
>
> Number Fifty-Nine was rose-red flame and sparklets of incandescent metal in that instant.
>
> Number Fifty-Nine was one of Tallentyre's worries.

Tallentyre has previously been shown gunning down a would-be mutineer. For the man in command of this imagined NASA the job is worth doing, at whatever cost.

For some fictional heroes, however, it was not. The protagonist in Edmond Hamilton's "What's It Like Out There?"—written in 1933 but, significantly, not published until 1952—receives an astronaut's welcome from his hometown and tactfully makes the kind of modest little speech that has been expected of this kind of hero ever since Lindbergh. Afterward, however,

> I wanted to go on and add, "And it wasn't worth it! It wasn't worth all those guys, all the hell we went through, just to get cheap atomic power so you people can run more electric washers and television sets and toasters!"
>
> But how are you going to stand up and say things like that to people you know, people who like you? And who was I to decide?

Or, conceivably, "what's it like out there" may be neither romantically dangerous nor realistically lethal but merely dull. A character in one story published in 1939 is portrayed as putting in his time on the moon only as the necessary prerequisite to a better-paying earthside post. He has a rousing adventure with an invisible rock-eating monster just landed from a meteorite, but he decides not to report the episode lest he be deemed mentally unbalanced and lose his job. After all, he and the bureaucracy of the "Spaceways Corporation" know well that "Nothing Happens on the Moon."

In the real world, meanwhile, at places like Peenemünde, a great deal was happening. American science fiction writers did not know what von Braun and Dornberger were doing, but many of them understandably took a dim view of the prospect of spaceflight being achieved in Hitler's Germany. In the fading peacetime months of 1939, Robert Moore Williams published in *Amazing Stories* the tale "Lundstret's Invention," in which a dying refugee scientist shoots his rocket uselessly into space to keep it from falling into Nazi hands. In his last words, Lundstret admonishes the young American scientist Martin Langley to carry out his work: "Perhaps—by that time— science will be ruling the world—instead of the hoodlums . . ." Few science fiction enthusiasts yet realized that after Hiroshima many would find such a forecast merely a choice between two equally intolerable futures.

Occasionally they recognized, however, that "it may not be mechanical faults that stop men from reaching the skies—it may be human trends." Those words editorially introduced one of Isaac Asimov's first published stories, "Trends," set in a "Neo-Victorian Age" wherein a massive religious revival puts a halt to all attempts to reach the moon, judging them to be impious defiance of the Almighty. A disastrous rocket explosion, deliberately set off by a convert to give such ventures a bad image, triggers the passage of an Act of Congress in 1973 that outlaws all research on space travel and sets up a Federal Scientific Research Investigatory Bureau to pass upon the legality of all scientific experimentation. (The Supreme Court upholds this Stonely-Carter Act by a 5–4 decision in *Westly* v. *Simmons*.) With such substitution of political for engineering verisimilitude, magazine science fiction had begun to enter upon a new phase.

The politics of the period subtly colored science fiction's technological forecasts in other ways too. Even though in science fiction rockets had long been used in sanguinary wars, both on earth and in interplanetary (and interstellar) space, sometimes in the late thirties they figured in a defense of American isolationism that verged occasionally on outright pacifism. In "Fugitives From Earth," by Nelson S. Bond (*Amazing Stories*, December 1939), World War II has been raging for three years. American rocket experimenters under the leadership of Frazier Wrenn, hiding out in the Arizona desert from government bombing planes and from "ruthless, sweeping 'drafts' which have bled the country of its finest young manhood," are building a spaceship in which to escape this war-torn world. German rocket experimenters led by Erik von Adlund are doing likewise, hoodwinking their government, which believes Adlund "is creating a new weapon with which to carry on the war." (Impudently, they use the Raketenflügplatz, where the VfR in peacetime innocence had launched its actual missiles, in the very shadow of their nation's capital.) Americans and Germans share their engineering secrets, trading America's "permalloy" for Germany's "sur-atomic power." As Frazier Wrenn explains to his associates, "There is one thing we must leave behind when we make attempt to escape our doomed earth in this rocket-ship. That thing is—national pride." At the appointed time, with a success which, at least in this one instance, convicts both the Gestapo and the FBI of monumental inefficiency, the spaceships *Goddard* and *Oberth* lift off.

As war came closer to America, this kind of opposition to national pride went by the board. A cover by H. W. Wesso for *Thrilling Wonder Stories* in June 1941 showed two spacesuited men battling horned and fanged beasts, with the planet Saturn in the background—and behind them an American flag containing at least fifty-four stars. Rockets reappeared in American newspaper headlines and general magazine stories, no longer as the insane creations of "moon men" but as sober instruments for the massive support of infantry. "From the frozen steppe of Russia to Libya's burning sands," declared one science fiction pulp in 1943, "the weapon of the future is already exacting its terrible toll."

Of course, more was to come. On October 3, 1942, a tense countdown of the kind the world would later come to know at Cape Kennedy took place at Peenemünde, with scientists, military men, and anonymous employees anxiously watching their handiwork on a TV monitor provided by the Siemens electrical corporation. The tension of those long-drawn-out "Peenemünde minutes," as they called them, broke as the "slender perfect body of the rocket, lacquered black and white," rose out of the evergreen forest into the sky to a height of sixty miles, breaking the altitude records set in World War I by Big Bertha. "We have invaded space with our rocket," General Dornberger exultingly told his co-workers, "and . . . have proved rocket propulsion practicable for space travel." Meanwhile, however, he acknowledged that there was a war to be won. The Allies concurred: in August 1943 the RAF blasted Peenemünde with a massive thousand-plane raid.

Yet there remained islands of calm even in the hurricane years of war. Late in 1942 one cover painting for *Astounding Science Fiction*, in serene contrast to the bug-eyed monsters and screaming maidens that were staple fare on magazine covers at that time, depicted in subdued hues the now classic image of a rocket standing on the silent lunar surface, while the earth glows out of a dark sky. The cover story, Lester Del Rey's "Lunar Landing," showed the mastery of plausible detail which was becoming increasingly common in the better science fiction magazines:

> With the loose easiness of motion necessary here, he reached up and unfastened the zipper above him, then wriggled out of his sleeping sack, and pulled himself down to the floor by means of the ropes that were laced along the walls for hand-holds. . . . Grey took the coffee gratefully, drinking slowly through one straw; cups would have been worse than useless out here, since liquids refused to pour, but chose to coalesce into rounded blobs, held in shape by surface tension.

The author's emphasis was no longer, as in many earlier stories, primarily upon the plausibility of his gadgets. Grey turns out to be an eighty-pound, four-foot-ten-inch midget, and much of the story probes the psychology of his relationship with a normal-sized female member of the crew. The technological reasons for this plot situation are perfectly sound: the solution of the old mass-ratio problem dictates that rocket ships carry the lightest payloads possible, and one logical inference could be that the ships' crews should consist of women and/or small men. In practice it did not work out that way; or rather, this supposedly technical and engineering question was initially answered in a nonscientific—some might say unscientific—way. In 1963 the USSR's Valentina Tereshkova orbited the earth aboard *Vostok 6*. From the standpoint of women's liberation in the West, the shame of the U.S. program was not so much that a woman pilot did not duplicate the feat as that our society, in the pre-shuttle years, did not feel that such a step was even imaginable. This kind of specific social eventuality the magazine science fiction of the thirties and forties had difficulty in foreseeing.

On September 8, 1944, the first V-2s fell on London. Both the British Interplanetary Society's Arthur C. Clarke and the German refugee rocket experimenter Willy Ley were torn between their hostility to the foundering Nazi regime and a sense of the vindication of their own previous work. Soon after the war's end, humanity reached out and for the first time lightly touched the moon, by means of a radar pulse bounced off the lunar surface from the U.S. Army Signal Corps' laboratory in Belmar, New Jersey—and at once, in the view of at least one distinguished American scholar, all the charming fantasy and fun that had gone with lunar voyaging since the time of Lucian was gone. "In our modern imaginary journeys to the planets men sail in great spaceships constructed upon sound technological principles," Marjorie Nicolson wrote in 1948. "They have gained verisimilitude, but they have lost the excitement of breathless discovery. The poetry of true belief is mute."

To this aesthetic disenchantment there was later added a political disillusionment: "I once dreamed of men touching the moon," declared one child of the sixties in 1969. "Now I saw it. And I didn't care." "We walk safely among the craters of the moon but not in the parks of New York or Chicago or Los Angeles," mused one of his contemporaries. And Nicolson's remark that the poetry of true belief is mute has been borne out by many an astronaut or cosmonaut, notoriously tongue-tied in their efforts to describe for fellow earthpeople "what it's like out there." But it would be a bit unfair to the men (and one woman) of the first generation in space to say that they had lost the excitement of breathless discovery. On the contrary, their responses to space ranged from deeply felt religious acts to exuberant expressions of physical joy. "They said it was *pretty*," said the veteran newscaster Eric Sevareid on CBS the morning after *Apollo 11*'s moon walk. That crew members could seriously employ such a word to describe the moon's ultimate desolation may have come as a surprise to some of their fellows, but any long-term reader of science fiction would have understood at once what was meant.

More surprising, after centuries during which lunar exploration was portrayed as a fantastic adventure, was the actual denouement of the Apollo program: the later abandonment of the moon, for the time being, apparently out of sheer boredom. Two decades into the Space Age, wrote Melvin Maddocks in the *Saturday Review* in 1973, "we are all, in one way or another, trying to evade that overwhelming fact"; instead, "with do-it-yourself diagrams and layman's explanations, we turn each Apollo rocket into a kind of nationally shared erector set." But the overwhelming fact was a fact in spite of television's untiring effort to cut it down to suitably trivial size. The proper metaphoric comparison of Armstrong's long step down upon the gritty lunar soils is not with Columbus's crew setting foot on San Salvador. Rather, it must be compared with the supreme effort of that anonymous lungfish which first flopped up on the beach to stay. Science fictionists, at least, knew this, and they were understandably bitter about the post-*Apollo 17* situation. "It's been a lonely business, mine, to speak for space travel the past 35 years," Ray Bradbury regretfully wrote in 1972. "I felt little or no company when I was 17, in my last year at high school, writing my first stories about landing on the moon. I don't feel much more company surrounding me today." But as Isaac Asimov's early short story "Trends" still reminds us, historical trends can and do change. The Russians, the Japanese, the French, even the Chinese evidently do not share our own still-fashionable rejection of the space frontier. One day, reflecting upon America's own past, we may also change our minds, and in that event the garish pulp magazines of fifty years ago may be accorded a place of honor. Prophets in their own time have often been somewhat unkempt characters.

CHAPTER FIFTEEN

The Constitutional Origins of Westly v. Simmons

A new author presents a new type of obstacle that may face the first rocketship's inventor—the minds of men did not always run as they do now." That story blurb introduced "Trends," by Isaac Asimov, in the July 1939 issue of *Astounding Science Fiction*. As every schoolchild knows, or ought to know, this was the story that really launched its author—not then possessed of a graduate degree and therefore not yet known as the Good Doctor—upon his meteoric career. (I don't know why careers should be referred to as meteoric; meteors after they ignite do not commonly continue to glow for five decades, as the Good Doctor has. But let that pass.)

"Trends" begins in 1973—but in a very different kind of 1973 from the year we know by that name on our own time track. Instead of the swinging yet anxious moral anarchy of our own seventies, these seventies are at the opposite extreme—a stuffy, conformist "second Victorian Age." And instead of having a national space program that is winding down, or at any rate taking a breather, after a spectacular series of landings on the moon, the 1973 of "Trends" has a space program that is just getting started; that

An earlier form of this essay first appeared in ANALOG *Science Fiction/Science Fact* 105 (October 1985): 86–96. Copyright © 1985 by Davis Publications, Inc.

is privately funded (in mere millions, not billions); and that is badgered by revivalists who charge that landing on the moon would be contrary to the will of God: "It is not given to man to go wheresoever ambition and desire lead him. There are things forever denied him, and aspiring to the stars is one of these."

The "trend" of the story's title is religious fundamentalism, and in the story the fundamentalists win the first several rounds. The story illustration (by Paul Orban, one of *Astounding*'s best pen-and-ink people) shows the hero's first moon rocket blowing up on the launchpad, not because of mechanical failure or designer error, as sometimes happened on our own time track, but as a result of sabotage by a fanatical disciple of Otis Eldredge, the revivalist leader. Public indignation leads to passage by Congress—unanimously—of the Zittman Antirocketry Bill, and the next congressional elections—those of 1974—give Eldredge and his Twentieth Century Evangelical Society control of the U.S. House of Representatives and the balance of power in the Senate. (Does this begin to sound just somewhat familiar?)

"At the first session of the ninety-third Congress, the famous Stonely-Carter bill was passed," historian Asimov continues. "It established the Federal Scientific Research Investigatory Bureau—the FSRIB—which was given full power to pass on the legality of all research in the country" and to "ban absolutely all such as it disapproved of." Because Americans have always tended to turn political and social questions into legal ones—as in the famous Dred Scott decision on slavery—the constitutionality of the Stonely-Carter Act is promptly challenged before the Supreme Court. The Court, by a 5–4 margin, upholds the right of the federal government to suppress and outlaw scientific research, in a decision that goes into the law books as *Westly* v. *Simmons*. On the "Trends" time track, the formal citation might be *"Westly* v. *Simmons*, 420 U.S. 1(1974)"—which for the benefit of us nonlawyers can be translated as: decision of the Supreme Court as between the plaintiff on appeal, whom the Good Doctor identifies as Joseph Westly of Stanford, defending his constitutional right "to continue his investigation on atomic power," and the defendant, Simmons, whom Asimov does not identify but who we presume is a federal administrator, as found in volume 420, page 1, of *United States Reports*, the official record of all the decisions handed down by the Supreme Court.

Volume 420 on our time track covers the October term of 1974 (which extends into 1975; Supreme Court cases are normally argued in the fall and decided during the following winter and spring). Asimov states that Westly made his appeal on November 9—a mere two or three days after that disastrous congressional mandate—and that it took two months for the case to be decided. Two months from November 9 puts us shortly after New Year's in 1975. Since Congress (by the Twentieth Amendment to the Constitution, adopted—on both time tracks—in 1933) normally convenes at noon on January 3, the new Congress, with its Otis Eldredge–controlled Moral Majority bias, has just met and organized. We may therefore presume an intense evangelical atmosphere in and around the splendid Greek-pillared Supreme Court building itself, and prayers and hymns on the lawn and steps outside, very likely, although in the Court's own chambers the historic sense of decorum—especially in a "second Victorian age"—would probably prevent any interruption of the reading of the formal opinion in *Westly* v. *Simmons* by unseemly shouts of "Praise the Lord!" Nonetheless, as American political folk wisdom has it, "The Supreme Court follows the election returns."

Now, there is no way—*no way*—that the Supreme Court which was sitting from November 1974 through January 1975 on *our* time track could have rendered any such judgment as *Westly* v. *Simmons*.

Consider who they were: William O. Douglas, that venerable champion of civil liberties all through the dark McCarthy era: Chief Justice Warren Burger, who voted against the president who appointed him (Nixon) on the question of the Pentagon Papers, which also involved a constitutional right to engage in private investigation and publicize one's findings; Thurgood Marshall, that doughty champion of civil rights, whose legal work for the NAACP had paved the way for the desegregation of schools; Harry A. Blackmun, who wrote the Court's landmark decision on abortion, *Roe* v. *Wade* (on our time track at 410 U.S. 113, 1972)—a decision that would hardly have pleased Otis Eldredge and his moral majoritarians; and William Brennan, who struck many blows from the bench against literary censorship. That gives you a majority of five right there, and if you add Potter Stewart, who on our time track wrote a second concurring opinion in the Roe case, and Byron White, a Kennedy appointee who would have retained something of the pro-science spirit of the New Frontier, the majority becomes unbeatable. Even if you count the other two Nixon appointees (Lewis Powell and William Rehnquist) as voting on the other side, Joseph Westly would have won his case 7–2 and presumably would have gone on experimenting with atomic power.

The time track on which "Trends" takes place must logically have diverged from the *Apollo 11* time track in 1939 when John Campbell first published the story in *Astounding*. The problem, then, is how to account for the naming of a Supreme Court which would have gone against Mr. Westly in the series of presidential elections—and opportunities for naming Supreme Court justices—between 1940 and 1972. How was that majority against the freedom of science politically put together?

Do we have to go back as far as 1939 for the divergence of the "Trends" time track from our own? Yes, I think we do. There is a clue pointing to that conclusion in Asimov's description of how the case came to trial. "Joseph Westly of Stanford upheld his right to continue his investigations on atomic power." That's quite a large subject for one scientist to be investigating all by himself, without benefit of corporate finance, foundation grants, or hosts of hardworking graduate student assistants. Atomic power, in the 1974 of "Trends," thus seems to be a field whose investigation is still in its infancy—a stage at which individual investigators are still able to do important pioneering work. Otis Eldredge can, and does, urge his minions to mob a spaceship before it takes off, but apparently the ungodly scientific menaces of his time do not include nuclear power plants, ICBMs, or radio-cobalt for treating cancer.

Whatever became of the Manhattan Project? On our time track the building of the first atomic bomb goes back to a letter which Albert Einstein wrote to President Franklin Roosevelt in August of that same fateful year 1939. On October 11 it reached the President's desk. In the meantime, World War II had begun. It was a moment when FDR had a great deal on his mind besides some theoretical scientist's speculations about the practical consequences of the recent successful fissioning of uranium isotope 235. According to science journalist Robert Jungk, Roosevelt came very near giving the whole idea the brushoff, and he was only brought around when Alexander Sachs, the financier and New Deal adviser who actually handed him Einstein's letter, reminded the president that Napoleon had blown a great chance to beat the English when he turned down American inventor Robert Fulton's offer of a fleet of steamships for a cross-channel invasion.

All we need to do here is change one tiny historical detail: Alexander Sachs comes down with the flu. He doesn't get to see Roosevelt when the Einstein letter arrives.

FDR—notoriously a person with a short attention span—reads the letter, finds it interesting (like all those science fictional notions one found in 1939 in the more sensational Sunday newspapers), and writes Einstein a typically Rooseveltian reply—amiable, respectful of the distinguished scholar's stature in the world, and absolutely noncommittal.

So there is no Manhattan Project!

Now, hold on. Wouldn't Leo Szilard and the other atomic scientists have continued to badger the president about the bomb? Certainly, but if the well-known (and popular, in his wispy-haired, absentminded way) Albert Einstein, the very image of "Mr. Scientist," couldn't get through the presidential preoccupations, could they have expected to fare any better?

Well, all right, but weren't the Germans also working on the Bomb? Of course they were; their V-2 rocket (the ancestor of Apollo-Saturn) was the first IRBM, and with a nuclear warhead it would have been a fearsome weapon indeed. But on our time track, for various reasons—including an idiotic debate over whether Einstein's equations could be trusted, since they were an example of "Jewish Physics"—the Nazi equivalent of the Manhattan Project never quite came off. We may assume the same outcome on the "Trends" world-line.

But after the war wouldn't the Russians have developed the bomb? They had at least one of the world's top nuclear physicists, up in the Einstein-Fermi-Bohr-Oppenheimer class, in the person of Pyotr Kapitsa, and physics—unlike some of the other sciences (notably Western-style genetic biology)—flourished in Stalin's Russia. What they did *not* have, on the "Trends" time track, was an incentive. Nobody in the West had the drop on them with a proven, tested atomic weapon, and they had a whole Nazi-devastated country to rebuild.

What about Hiroshima and Nagasaki, which Harry Truman to the end of his days believed had been necessary to shorten the war and save, over the long run, hundreds of thousands of American and Japanese lives? The only catch in Truman's reasoning is that we now know that the government formed in Tokyo immediately after the fall of Okinawa (April 1945) had a clear mandate to negotiate an end to the war. It was a question not of *whether* but of *when*.

Therefore—Assumption Number One—World War II ends with no nuclear bomb, ends in approximately the same way with the same messy aftermath, including a cold war, economic dislocation in Europe necessitating a Marshall Plan, and the Communization of Eastern Europe and China. But no fearsome atomic doom hovers over the planet. The "second Victorian age" in which "Trends" takes place is thus a relatively peaceful era—as indeed the *first* Victorian age had been, with no major war involving all the Great Powers at the same time for the ninety-nine years between Napoleon's fall in 1815 and the outbreak of World War I in 1914.

The time of "Trends" is an age which looks back upon no Hiroshima, no Nagasaki. But it does look back upon other scientific contributions to slaughter: saturation bombing, flamethrowers, phosphorus, proximity fuses, computers, radar. So Asimov's summary of Otis Eldredge's argument still holds: "that it was science that brought about the horrors of the Second World War. Science outstripped culture, they will say, technology outstripped sociology, and it was that imbalance that came so near to destroying the world."

It is an attractive argument, and in the absence of a perceived *scientific* threat from the Russians, it wins support for Eldredge's Evangelical Society from all sorts of people who otherwise never would have bought its theology.

The first step toward *Westly* v. *Simmons* has been taken, and one justice who will sit for that decision is already on the bench. William O. Douglas, still active on the Supreme Court in *our* 1974, was already a member of that court in 1939 when *Astounding* published "Trends." Given Bill Douglas's valiant stands for freedom of thought on our world-line, I think we may count him among the four justices in the *Westly* case who would have dissented.

But who were his eight colleagues? Harry Truman probably succeeded FDR in the world of "Trends" as in ours. There is no reason why the absence of a Manhattan Project would have affected the outcome of the Democratic National Convention of 1944. Mr. Truman in the course of his presidency (on our time track) made four Supreme Court appointments. None of them, however, were still on the bench in our 1974, and the Harry of "Trends" therefore bears no direct responsibility for *Westly* v. *Simmons*.

The next crucial divergence between our world-line and that of "Trends" comes with the election of 1952.

The Republican National Convention of that year was a rerun of the one the GOP had gone through in 1912: Old Guardsmen, led in both cases by a man named Taft (William Howard in 1912; his son Robert in '52) who controlled the party machinery and challenged the right to seats in the convention of insurgents, committed in '12 to Theodore Roosevelt, in '52 to Dwight D. Eisenhower.

Ike, campaigning on our world-line in 1952, told a crowd at Soldier's Field in Chicago that "isolationism in America is dead as a political issue." But would it have been so dead in the absence of the omnipresent Bomb? Might not the conservative, respected "Mr. Republican" from the isolationist Midwest, Bob Taft, have held the line at the convention and become the Republican nominee?

Our 1952's Democratic choice came from that same midwestern heartland: Adlai E. Stevenson. A landslide victor for governor of Illinois in 1948 (running far ahead of Truman), eloquent, brilliant, and with the devoted support of the Chicago party machine, he is easy to see as the Democratic candidate in the "Trends" world also. In the alternative world—ours—war hero Eisenhower beat him decisively. Nevertheless, even in defeat Stevenson held onto those traditional New Deal elements in the Democratic coalition—labor, southerners, ethnics, Catholics—whom Walter Mondale would not be able to command in 1984. Therefore—Assumption Number Two—Adlai Stevenson is elected President of the United States in 1952.

At once, two of the Supreme Court justices from the 1974 of our own time line—William Brennan and Potter Stewart—vanish from the bench, because they were Eisenhower appointees.

Now Adlai, with his high standards of governance, might have made —*would* have made—distinguished Supreme Court appointments—better, in a couple of instances at least, than Ike's. But they would not have included Republican Earl Warren, and Justice Warren's fifteen-year tenure on our time track decisively changed the Supreme Court and changed America. We speak of that decade and a half as the Warren Court in the same respectful way that we refer to the thirty-five-year Marshall Court (1801–1835) under the great John Marshall. In the absence of Warren's dynamism, a drift toward *Westly* v. *Simmons* becomes far more plausible.

President Stevenson makes three Supreme Court appointments, corresponding to the three in Eisenhower's first term. I propose that they be counted as pro-science and pro-freedom of thought. In due course they will join Mr. Justice Douglas in dissent on *Westly* v. *Simmons* but only if they live long enough. One of Ike's first-term appointees (Brennan) lasted until

1974; the other two (Warren and Harlan) did not. Let's give our hypothetical President Stevenson that same box score; that gives us one Stevenson appointee (perhaps that dogged, articulate liberal Hubert Humphrey) in dissent in the *Westly* case, plus Douglas. So far, the Otis Eldredges of this other America seem, if anything, to be losing ground.

Since President Stevenson, like President Eisenhower, would have had a chief justiceship to fill in 1953 (owing to the death in 1953 of Fred Vinson, appointed by Truman), he plays that card as powerfully as he can—and not necessarily by naming a new member; associate justices can also be promoted to the top position, as FDR did with Harlan F. Stone. And it would be a grand gesture indeed to name as chief justice another Roosevelt appointee, equally as renowned as Douglas for championing constitutional liberties, namely Hugo L. Black. That would also be no consolation to Otis Eldredge et al., for Black had always been a rigorous advocate of the separation of church and state; more so, indeed, than Douglas (see, on our time track, Black's dissenting opinion against "released time" for religious instruction for New York school children, in *Zorach* v. *Clauson*, 343 U.S. 306, 1952).

President Stevenson would have had the same agenda of unfinished business in his world-line as did President Eisenhower in ours. The most notably unfinished item on the list was the Korean War, and here I make Assumption Number Three: the Korean War does not end in 1953. It drags on, and on, and on.

Ike in our universe went to Korea after the election. Stevenson had made plans, if elected, to do the same, but with characteristic modesty chose not to publicize the fact during the campaign. One can visualize him, as president-elect and as president, vigorously pursuing the same mixture of push and persuasion which on our time track brought a cease-fire seven months after the inauguration. However, we must bear in mind that one wild card in Eisenhower's hand, because of Assumption One, is not there for President Stevenson to play: the A-bomb. (Ike in his memoirs stated that he let the Chinese know that if they didn't cooperate he was prepared to play it.)

Even with that card in hand, Eisenhower secured only a *compromise* settlement in Korea—and made it stick with the hotheads in Congress, who were still echoing General MacArthur's "In war there is no substitute for victory." President Stevenson, or indeed *any* civilian president, would have been vulnerable to the same "wimp" ploy that was used so effectively against Mondale in 1984 on our time line, a charge from which General Eisenhower was exempt. So, in the "Trends" universe, the hawks in Congress won't stand for a compromise in Korea; the war goes on for another year, and another, and another.

And an antiwar movement starts, ten years earlier than on our time line.

And Joe McCarthy dies in 1956 without having ever been censured by the Senate.

Chief Justice Black hands down a sweeping civil rights decision but without the unanimity in the Court secured by Earl Warren in *Brown* v. *Board of Education*. The civil rights movement awakened by that decision coalesces with the movement against the war.

The equivalent of our sixties arrives a decade early!

Stevenson faces other foreign challenges successfully. One of them he handles far better than Ike in our universe. He names as his secretary of state former UN delegate Eleanor Roosevelt—a brilliant appointment, marred only by the persistence of those awful old Eleanor jokes that went all the way back to the New Deal years. (The women's movement, triggered by this example, also jumps forward a decade as compared with our time line.) Secretary Roosevelt, unlike Ike's Secretary Dulles, has the wit to help Egypt build its High Dam at Aswan; Egypt's leader, Nasser, then has no political need immediately to nationalize the Suez Canal, so the Suez Crisis of 1956—and following from it the Lebanon crisis of 1958—do not take place. But all such successes are swallowed up in the frustration of the ongoing war in Korea, much as Jimmy Carter's diplomatic triumph at Camp David was obscured by his four hundred and forty days of trouble with Iran.

The political backlash against Stevenson proves too great to overcome. A reluctant Democratic convention renominates him in 1956, but even with Mrs. Roosevelt on the ticket as his running mate he is fated to lose the election. The Republicans, never having faced and broken the McCarthy spell, turn to the politician who once (on both time tracks) scurrilously described Adlai as "a graduate of Dean Acheson's Cowardly College of Communist Containment," and the next President of the United States turns out to be Richard Milhous Nixon.

President Nixon's 1957–1961 term coincides with what on our time track was Eisenhower's second term. That gives him, other things being equal, an opportunity to make two Supreme Court appointments. Both of them, if they live long enough, are possible participants in *Westly* v. *Simmons*, although on our time line only one of them—Potter Stewart—lasted that long.

Now *our* Nixon also became president, albeit not until another twelve years had gone by. And our Nixon also had chances to make appointments to the Supreme Court. Two proposals he made were so bad that the Senate turned them down. But the demoralized Senate of the "Trends" world—a Senate which had never censured Joe McCarthy—is more docile. So the conservative Clement Haynesworth and the hapless G. Harrold Carswell are elevated to the highest court in the land. Both are segregationists, and *that* doesn't help the cause of racial justice in America, nor the cause of civil and political tranquility. Later on, it is reasonable to assume, these judges will also become two votes for the suppression of science in *Westly* v. *Simmons*.

Nixon is a shoo-in for renomination by the Republicans. He runs in 1960 against John F. Kennedy—the logical Democratic choice—not as Eisenhower's vice-president, as on our time line, but as a sitting president, which makes a considerable difference.

The 1960 campaign is, in the main, a shrill series of "I'm even more anti-Communist than you are" speeches. Insurgent youths, blacks, and antiwar protesters find the election utterly frustrating. There are riots at *both* the Republican and Democratic national conventions. In the midst of all this uproar, one of Adlai Stevenson's Supreme Court appointees, the distinguished black jurist William H. Hastie (who had earlier been unsuccessfully recommended to Truman for the high court), unexpectedly dies in office. Anticipating by eight years the "southern strategy" which on our time track we associate with 1968, Nixon nominates for the Hastie vacancy none other than Strom Thurmond.

This not only gives Nixon in the "Trends" 1960 the southern states that Barry Goldwater would carry in 1964; it also reignites old fires in the South which had been pretty well banked since the days of Al Smith. John Kennedy's encounter with the Protestant ministers of Houston in 1960 is a far more rowdy affair in the "Trends" world than it was in ours. Fundamentalist religion, which had always heavily emphasized anti-Catholicism, becomes a major political force, counterbalancing the other kinds of protest and dissent. Otis Eldredge, displacing the good-natured and gentlemanly Billy Graham as America's leading evangelical spokesman, becomes a power in the land.

And the forces of repression moving toward the showdown of *Westly* v. *Simmons* are now tied with their opponents, 3–3.

Many liberals and radicals, in disgust and disillusion, boycott the election. Had they not done so, there might still have been a New Frontier. As it is, Nixon narrowly but decisively ekes out a second term. Then, in 1962, just as he did on our time line under JFK, Justice Frankfurter resigns, which gives President Nixon another Supreme Court vacancy. Anticipating a challenge to his own control over the GOP from the man who had been the sentimental favorite, although not the nominee, at the 1960 Republican convention (on both time tracks)—and who on the bench will be a reliable conservative—Nixon sends the Senate the name of Barry Goldwater.

From the science suppressors' point of view, that turns out to have been a mistake. The Barry Goldwater we knew on our time track notoriously did not like the Moral Majority and had some pungent things to say about its leader. There is no reason to assume he would have looked any more kindly upon Otis Eldredge. The *Westly* v. *Simmons* forces are now outvoted, 3–4.

But then another of President Stevenson's appointees, Madame Justice Rita Hauser, retires from the Court, and Nixon, with an eye to coopting the opposition, chooses a well-known Democrat: William Proxmire of Wisconsin. Senator Proxmire is as scrupulous as any Republican against wasting the taxpayer's money, and in the "Trends" world—as in ours—he usually defines waste as "any expenditure by the government for the purpose of basic scientific research." It's penny wise and pound foolish; but it gives the champions of a Federal Scientific Research Investigatory Bureau a 4–4 tie.

Suddenly, with one of those spectacular 180-degree turns for which he was famous in our universe as well, the president negotiates an end to the war in Korea (and the one in Vietnam, and the one in the Formosa Strait, and the one in Cuba, and the one in Africa). Quietly cursing the Twenty-second Amendment to the Constitution (for which he voted in 1947 as a Congressman), which will not allow him to seek a third term in 1964, Richard Nixon hands the reins of office over to Spiro Agnew. The Democrats try again with John Kennedy (who was not assassinated in 1963, of course, because he was not president), but presidential candidates, once beaten, are like the old adage about heavyweight boxers—"they never come back." Spiro (Spiro Who?) is duly elected.

His standards of political greed being no better in the "Trends" world than they proved to be in ours, President Agnew is impeached. Given the intense neo-Victorian moralism which is beginning to rise as a backlash from the insurgency of the Stevenson years, Agnew is removed from office to shouts of general satisfaction, but not before he has filled Justice Tom Clark's seat, which became vacant in 1967, with an obscure federal district judge, Jeffries Hathorne, unknown on our time line, but recommended— and pushed—for the job by none other than Otis Eldredge himself.

By this time, bending before the neo-Victorian tide, the makeup of Congress has considerably changed. Ulrich Stonely, an ultraconservative Republican from South Dakota, holds the Senate seat which on our time line belonged to George McGovern. "Ace" Carter, a born-again Baptist from Georgia, chairs a special House Committee on Science and Technology. Together they will draft the famous Stonely-Carter Act. And Howard Zittman, campaigning on the theme "Just because I come from New York City doesn't mean I have to be a liberal," captures a Manhattan congressional district and begins to line up votes for the Zittman Anti-Rocketry Bill.

But history has continuities as well as changes. Faces familiar to us continue to appear in the world of *Westly* v. *Simmons*.

Gerald Ford, stepping up from the House speakership, serves briefly as president to fill out Agnew's term until 1968. There is no Twenty-fifth Amendment, specifying the conditions of presidential succession, in the "Trends" world; and neither, in the gathering atmosphere of patriarchal neo-Victorianism, is any nonsense added to the Constitution to give eighteen-year-olds the right to vote. Nor does the District of Columbia achieve suffrage. The only constitutional amendments under serious discussion in Congress—a decade and a half early—have to do with abortion and prayer.

After two terms of Nixon and a partial one of Agnew, with no Kennedy-Johnson regimes for relief, the Democrats just about *have* to win the next election. And they do. They find a spellbinding speaker and some compelling national issues, and he pulls enough blue-collar and southern votes away from the GOP to carry the Electoral College.

His name is George Corley Wallace.

For Chief Justice Black, that is the last straw. On our time track, Mr. Justice Black retired in 1971. On the "Trends" time track, he grimly hangs on, as people will do when they have urgent unfinished work, even in the face of death itself. And so, by sheer moral determination, the venerable New Deal statesman and southern liberal survives to cast his vote in dissent in *Westly* v. *Simmons*.

In the meantime, in the absence of any federal commitment to go to the moon, private entrepreneurs have begun to probe at outer space. One of them is John Harmon, the intrepid hero of "Trends." Those of us who have read the story know that it will have a happy ending. Harmon comes back from his lunar orbit with words every bit as memorable as Neil Armstrong's—"I've reached the moon, and you can't hang *that*"—and the historical pendulum swings back again.

Yet the decision in *Westly* v. *Simmons* stands there in the austere pages of *U.S. Reports*: "Mr. Justice Thurmond delivered the opinion of the Court. . . . Mr. Justice Proxmire, together with Mr. Justice Carswell, Mr. Justice Haynesworth, and Mr. Justice Hathorne, concur in this opinion. . . . Mr. Chief Justice Black, with whom Mr. Justice Douglas, Mr. Justice Humphrey, and Mr. Justice Goldwater join, dissent." It is 5–4 against the freedom of science, and it will take years of litigation to undo.

George Wallace—an unreformed, segregationist Wallace—is in his second presidential term and will be presiding in 1976 over our Revolutionary bicentennial.

The universe of "Trends," already behind ours in its timetable for reaching the moon, has a lot of catching up to do in other areas as well.

On second thought, maybe we shouldn't so cheerfully congratulate ourselves. That repressive, racist, censorious other universe at least does not have the nuclear terror hanging over its head. Not yet.

The one common conclusion we can reach concerning both universes is that it was very, very important that humanity go to the moon. And that the line between collective folly and political good sense is very thin.

About the Author

Paul A. Carter has taught at a dozen American colleges and universities, including Smith, Amherst, the University of California at Berkeley, the University of Montana, and Northern Illinois University. He is currently a professor of history at the University of Arizona. He is the author of many books on cultural and intellectual history, among them *Another Part of the Twenties*, *Another Part of the Fifties*, and most recently *Revolt Against Destiny: An Intellectual History of the United States*. His wide-ranging interests include science and science fiction, and he has published numerous stories, essays, and articles in these areas. Professor Carter's wife, Julie Raffety Carter, is a graduate of the University of Montana and Northern Illinois University. Their four children have all attended the University of Arizona.